THE ANALOGY OF BEAUTY

THE ANALOGY OF BEAUTY

The Theology of
Hans Urs von Balthasar

Edited by
John Riches

T. & T. Clark Ltd.,
59 George Street, Edinburgh

Copyright © T. & T. Clark Ltd., 1986

Typeset by John Swain & Son (Glasgow) Ltd.,
printed by Redwood Burn Ltd., Wiltshire,

for
T. & T. CLARK LTD.,
EDINBURGH

First Printed in the U.K. 1986

British Library Cataloguing in Publication Data

The Analogy of Beauty: essays for Hans Urs von Balthasar at eighty.
 1. Balthasar, Hans Urs von.
 I. Riches, John   II. Balthasar, Hans Urs von
 209'.2'4   BX4705.B163

 ISBN 0-567-09351-4

CONTENTS

ACKNOWLEDGEMENTS

We are grateful to *Communio: International Catholic Review* for permission to reprint 'In Retrospect', originally published there, Vol. II, 1975, pp. 197–220; to Jaca Books, Milan for permission to translate 'Aucora un decennio 1975', from *Il Filo di Arianna,* Milan, 1980, pp. 47–62, here as 'Another Ten Years'; and to *The Irish Theological Quarterly* for permission to reprint Noel O'Donaghue's review of *The Glory of the Lord*, Vol. 1.

J.R.

FOREWORD

Hans Urs von Balthasar's contribution to theology, both in his major works and in his editing, translation and more popular writings, has been immense and yet far too little known. Now that the first volumes of his *magnum opus* have appeared in English, the time has come to attempt a more thorough appropriation than has been hitherto possible of the great wealth of learning and insight that they contain. This volume of essays is offered with great respect and affection as a contribution to that task.

The idea for such a volume was first mooted at a meeting of the English translators of *The Glory of the Lord* at Ushaw College, Durham. We were delighted to be joined by others who had long been students of Balthasar's work and had advocated and encouraged the translation. While only too mindful of Balthasar's own strictures on the fragmentary nature of *Festschriften,* our hope is that these essays will reflect something of the central unity of his own theology and that they may initiate more detailed investigation of at least some of its many strands.

And they come with thanks and with congratulations on the completion, with the publication of the two volumes last year of *Theologik,* of his trilogy. It is a joy to be able to celebrate the culmination of such a life's work in a literary *oeuvre* of such sustained concentration, mastery and light!

John Riches.
June 1986.

A THEOLOGY OF BEAUTY

Noel O'Donaghue

The first volume of the English translation of Balthasar's *Herrlichkeit*[1] is diffuse, repetitive, oracular, and every bit as heavy as its 683 pages of relentless German-Swiss theologising would lead one to expect. Yet it is a joy to read, and at least one reader looks forward to its successors and hopes to survive to read all seven of them.

Briefly, Balthasar asks us to look at the whole of Christian theology under the sign of beauty, as showing forth a certain form whose inner radiance is beauty and whose various manifestations are most fully known as expressions or mediations of this original form of beauty and beauty of form. 'The beautiful is above all a *form*, and the light does not fall on this form from above and from outside, rather it breaks forth from the form's interior... The content (*Gehalt*) does not lie outside the form (*Gestalt*) but within it... In the luminous form of the beautiful the being of the existent becomes perceivable as nowhere else, and this is why an aesthetic element must be associated with all spiritual perception as with all spiritual striving.'[2]

For Balthasar the 'luminous form' at the centre of Christian theology is Jesus Christ, the Word of God become Flesh, and his whole book is a sustained effort at expressing the manifold beauty of this central and centring form. He uses the Alexandrian doctrine of the *corpus triforme* (the Body of Flesh, the Body of Scripture, and the

---

[1] *The Glory of the Lord. A theological aesthetics. I. Seeing the Form,* Edinburgh, 1983. This essay first appeared as a review article in the *Irish Theological Quarterly,* Vol. 50, pp. 250ff.

[2] Ibid., pp. 151, 153.

Body of the Church) to express this manifold. In one of those strik-ing inter-connections which are a feature of this work, he shows how Eucharist and Scripture belong intimately together as liturgi-cal word and sacrament,[3] so much so that he is critical of the phrase 'preparation for the Mass' as diminishing the importance of the Word in relation to the Sacrament. (This is one of several instances where Balthasar tries to strike a balance between Catholic and Protestant theology and practice.)

The Form of Christ in-forms the Christian, bringing at once judgement and salvation. 'The form which inscribes itself in the living centre of my being becomes my salvation by becoming my judgment... The metamorphosis of which Paul speaks (Rom 12.2; 2 Cor 3.18; Phil 3.21) is above all an assumption of form, the receiv-ing of Christ's form in us (Gal 4.19), the character and the impress in us of the only valid image of God. This occurs the more im-pressively, in the literal sense, the less resistance the impress of the image encounters. Mary's *Ecce Ancilla* is the supreme instance... Allowing the Word its way in me is not an action, and is not, there-fore, an accomplishment and a work; it is contemplative obedience that of its own passes over into the Passion in accordance with the law of the image which leaves its impress on it.'[4]

So it is that the transformed heart and mind reflect the beauty of the divine-human form of Jesus Christ. So it is that the author puts at the head of this first volume of his work the words of St John of the Cross which speak of the reflection and 'giving back' of 'the lamp of Beauty' to its divine source (*The Living Flame of Love* 3.14), so that the beauty of God becomes in man 'another beauty' which somehow measures up to the Divine Beauty. The choice of 'the mystical doctor' as his first authority is no accident, for we are told later that John is one of the two 'most decidedly aesthetic theo-

---

[3] Ibid., p. 529.
[4] Ibid., pp. 485f.

logians of Christian history';[5] the other is Denys the Areopagite.

It is clear from this kind of statement that Balthasar treats the Christian mystical tradition with enormous respect. Yet he is consistently anxious to anchor the apophatic in the cataphatic, to earth the vertical in the horizontal. Indeed *Herrlichkeit* is in some ways a rewriting of Barth's *Church Dogmatics*, and a lot of the excitement of the book comes from the tension between the Barthian theology of discontinuity (and the total Otherness of God in Christ) and that Platonic and Aristotelian strand in Catholic theology which sees nature and grace as somehow continuous, and so defends the basic goodness and beauty of human life. From beginning to end the book is balanced on a razor edge between these two fundamental options, sometimes defined as theology from above and theology from below. For example the passage quoted above (from p. 485) which at first sight seems to allow for human initiative, e.g., in Mary's *ecce ancilla domini* (theology from below, building on the human) shows on closer reading an undertow of the kind of theology in which man is passively receptive and does not in any real sense work out his own salvation: 'Allowing the Word its way in me is not an action.' Although Balthasar quotes the example of Mary here, the theology from above has little place for mariology, since Mary is simply a passive recipient of divine favour and of the form of Christ. Nevertheless Balthasar follows Scheeben in giving a central place to Mary's Bridal Motherhood[6] and he is deeply imbued with traditional Marian piety.

The main difficulty, as I see it, of the Luther-Kierkegaard-Barth theology of discontinuity which serves as part of the background (or horizon?) of the present work is that it expresses living processes in terms of dead processes. Thus the living process of salvation becomes the dead process of the meeting of God's grace with the

---

[5] Ibid., p. 125.
[6] Ibid., p. 109.

massa damnata of fallen nature. God's grace is indeed life itself but the *process* is purely mechanical. So, here, the form of Christ is indeed life but the process by which this form in-forms and trans-forms man articulates itself in metaphors of stamping and print-ing. Thus a key passage on the Church (as 'mediation of the form') reads: 'Whatever the Church may possess by way of "personality" and "nature" she has from Christ, whose "fullness" she is because he has poured his own fullness into her, so that the Church is noth-ing other than Christ's own fullness (Eph 1.23)', and the passage goes on to say that the Church 'can claim for herself and for the world no other figure than the figure of Christ, which leaves its stamp in her and shapes her through and through as the soul shapes the body.'[7]

In this kind of theology there is real danger that the very meaning and beauty of the Incarnation may be lost. If Jesus of Nazareth in each generation, in each human life, does not reflect in living com-munication the misery, pathos and individual countenance of the human, then surely his presence is no more than that of an ikon or tapestry reflected more or less clearly in the passing show of human history and human lives. Surely the human heart and mind have something to *say*, something to give, really to *give* as they respond to the Father's love? At this point one wants to push Balthasar back to some of his acknowledged sources such as Scheeben, Karl Adam, Romano Guardini, Erich Przywara, all of whom in different ways have emphasised or at least accepted the place of the human in the divine-human encounter; in fact Karl Adam entitled his most influential book *Christ Our Brother*.[8] Indeed this synergic theology is always there in the background of the present book, and the ten-sion between this and the Barthian 'monergic' strand certainly contributes to the excitement of the writing.

Henri de Lubac is, I think, a key figure here. It was de Lubac most of

[7] Ibid., pp. 558f.
[8] New York, 1931.

all who sought to break down the traditional dichotomy between the orders of nature and grace and tried to see the natural and the supernatural as a living unity. This at first tended towards the naturalising of the supernatural, a position that was rejected by Pius XII's encyclical *Humani Generis* in 1950. This setback did not lead to a return to the distinction between the natural and the supernatural, but rather to a thoroughgoing supernaturalism which of course found support in the Barthian restatement of Protestant theology, and could also look for support to Scheeben, who, for all his insistence on the distinction between nature and super-nature, nevertheless tended to close off the lines of aspiration by which nature tended towards grace, while allowing nature to have its say in the process of transformation. This, as I have said, remains present in Balthasar's thinking even though many of his statements seem to affirm almost total passivity in the divine-human encounter.

Now one main result of the de Lubac revolution (which Balthasar accepted and still accepts) was the devaluation and gradual disappearance of philosophy as the preparation for and in a real sense the basis of theology. This process has coincided with the reaction against the manuals whether philosophical or theological, coincided also with the breakdown of essentialist thinking (i.e., discourse by way of clear definition, distinction, and logical demonstration) and the coming of what came to be called Existentialism on the one hand and, on the other, the revival of Nominalism in the shape of Logical Positivism and Linguistic Analysis. In other words, the Platonic-Aristotelian realism of Aquinas and the 'Scholastic' tradition came to be ousted by its natural enemies and alternative options, Subjectivism and Nominalism — the one seeing the human subject (as general and common to all men) as the horizon of enquiry and truth, the other refusing to admit any horizon other than that of sense-observation and the words that sound in the ear. So it comes that courses in philosophy in Catholic

5

seminaries and universities today provide nothing like an objective natural ground for revelation but instead provide either an analysis of consciousness or an analysis of language. That mighty theology of man, natural man in his natural integrity (damaged but not destroyed by the Fall), a theology that provides an ethic which no scriptural quotation could overturn, is now in ruins and the way is open to every kind of sane and insane biblical anthropology ranging from that of the Bultmannian, who simply affirms the call to transformation, to that of the kind of born-again Christian who would slay all the enemies of the Word of God as *he* understands it.

The central drama of Balthasar's theology comes from the fact that he has accepted the disappearance of the traditional natural man and natural law philosophy in theology, but yet shows at every step that he has been formed in the old way and brings along with him, without looking at it directly, the central principle of the traditional way, the principle of the continuity of the natural and the supernatural, the principle that Karl Barth called somewhat ambiguously the analogy of being, and which in the present book becomes the principle of the analogy of beauty.

The key statement in this matter will be found on p. 607, and reads as follows:- 'The fundamental principle of a theological aesthetics, rather, is the fact that, just as this Christian revelation is absolute truth and goodness, so also is it absolute beauty; but this assertion would be meaningless if every transposition and application to revelation of human categories from the realms of logic, ethics ("pragmatics") and aesthetics, if every analogical application of these categories were simply forbidden.' And he concludes his discussion of this point with the firm assertion that in theological aesthetics 'the categories of aesthetics are not simply annihilated, but rather raised above themselves in an incomprehensibly positive way ... in order to contain something which is infinitely greater than themselves.'[9]

[9] *The Glory of the Lord*, I, p. 610.

6

There is a sense in which every experience of beauty points to infinity, as Plato saw, but I do not want to press this point here. What is clear is that our author is here in striking contradiction to both Kierkegaard and Barth for whom all experience of earthly beauty, truth and goodness, had to be put aside totally and finally in order that the new vision be born with the new Christian man. For these authors and the tradition they articulate, any analogy between revelation and our human ideas of beauty could only come from the side of revelation and then only as a kind of overcoming and destruction of all natural aesthetics. The truth is that once we make the kind of admission that Balthasar makes in the passage just cited, we are in the world of Plato and Aristotle: as Kierkegaard puts it in his *Philosophical Fragments* we have not really got beyond Socrates and the thesis that the teacher (whether this teacher be seen as Socrates or Christ) simply brings out what is already there within the pupil. For how do I judge the beauty of the form of Christ unless by way of my inner idea or sense of the beautiful? Either Christ shatters my conception of the beautiful or he fulfils it. If he shatters it, as Kierkegaard and Barth affirm, then what place is there for a theological aesthetics in Balthasar's sense? If he fulfils it, as Balthasar however guardedly seems to be saying here, then our author's theology is much more beholden to Plato and the Greeks than he himself seems prepared to admit. (Perhaps, however, the negative tone of his remarks on Plato and Platonism is strategic rather than substantive in intent, for Balthasar has been accused of Platonism and neo-Platonism.)

It is of course difficult if not impossible to keep in touch with what may be called the Great Tradition of Western Theology (which passes through Augustine, Anselm, Scotus Eriugena, Bonaventure and Aquinas) without accepting neo-Platonism explicitly or implicitly, and Balthasar tends to do so explicitly. Moreover, he accepts and assimilates the Dionysian mystical tradition that flowers in St John of the Cross, and this is of course deeply neo-Platonist and therefore deeply Platonist. It is not possible to stay within this tradition and to accept that absorption of the natural in the supernatural which has been the (largely unforeseen) result of what I have called the de Lubac revolution. In other words there is present in *Herrlichkeit* a strong *and self-sufficient* philosophical structure which allows for the integrity of the natural, and which demands some principle of distinction between the natural and supernatural orders, a *distinguir pour unir* in Maritain's sense. This in practice heralds the return of philosophy as a discipline formally and adequately distinct from theology, yet nevertheless providing its proper context as well as its essential prelude and principle of pre-understanding.

However, one must be careful not to push Balthasar too far in this direction. In the first place one of the strengths of the present work lies in its openness to Protestant theology not only as represented by Barth but also as represented by that Lutheranism that retains its contact with the devotional and even with the mystical. There is a flow of sympathy in this direction which is especially precious in an author who is so strongly rooted in Catholic tradition and in Catholic piety. Secondly, the last thing Balthasar would want is any kind of return to the world of the scholastic manuals. There is no doubt but that his master in philosophy is Plato rather than Aristotle and Plotinus rather than Plato. As in the case of St Augustine the presence of neo-Platonism shows itself as eloquence rather than analysis, as an inner glow rather than a conceptual network. Indeed his whole work might have been written to illustrate Maréchal's principle that philosophy at its highest passes over into mysticism. It is an approach that cannot be translated into terms of definition, distinction and demonstration, and it has the strengths and weaknesses that belong to this kind of approach.

. . . . . .

At the end of this first part of Balthasar's great theological enterprise the question, as the French say, imposes itself: Is it legitimate to build a complete theological system around the concept of Beauty? It may be that for the leaping imagination of the poet, beauty is truth and truth is beauty, but at a more grounded level it is possible to think of many beautiful conceptions and ideologies which have little relationship to truth. It is possible to be *splendide mendax*, it is possible to be deceived by fair appearances. At a somewhat higher level it may be argued that the Buddhist sage is more attractive than the Christian saint, that the death of Socrates outshines in beauty the death of Christ even when the Resurrection is brought within it. Surely it is in terms of ultimate *Truth* a Christian theologian professes and expounds Christian doctrine. It may indeed be said that at the highest level Beauty and Truth are one in the unity of the transcendentals, but surely even here, indeed here most of all, the *Light* of the mind is truth, and any infusion of any other principle can only obscure this light and confuse the mind of man.

However, Balthasar is not concerned primarily with the light in the mind (at its various levels) but with the fire in the heart (at its various levels). In taking this road he is still following the general itinerary of the Great Tradition, but he is as it were following the path through the forest rather than the path through the open plain. It is the path of Bonaventure, of Bernard, above all it is the path of the Mystics, especially of St John of the Cross. It is the path vividly described in John's poem 'On a Dark Night', a poem describing a journey made in deepest darkness that is without light, a journey guided entirely by 'the fire that burns in the heart'. This fire is enkindled by the encounter with the beloved *as* beloved, by the God of love *as* love. John is standing here within a long and continuing tradition, and in following him Balthasar is following in the way of this tradition. But it must be said again that the fire in the heart is the result of an *encounter*, the encounter with God in the call and enchantment of his absolute beauty. The Thomist will say at this point that this absolute beauty must be

9

known before it is loved, and neither John nor Balthasar will deny this. What they will deny is that love can advance only step by step with knowledge. This is the crucial point. It is admitted on both sides that truth comes first, light comes first. God has to be seen by faith in order to be known by love: the Divine Attribute of Truth is prior to the Divine Attribute of Beauty, prior logically, prior in time. But does this mean that a theology of Beauty does but add a certain glow and charm to a theology of Truth? The kind of theological aesthetics which is the burden of the present book and its successors goes far beyond this. It claims that at a certain point beauty takes over from truth, the fire in the heart becomes the light of the mind: the whole object of theology is the form of the beauty of God as revealed in Jesus Christ, especially in Jesus Christ crucified. One might suppose then that at this point theology passes over into poetry and praise, into liturgy in the way of Eastern Orthodoxy. But Balthasar resists this conclusion. His theological aesthetics remains theology, indeed centres the whole theological enterprise. Is this possible?

The reader has to answer this question for himself by reading the book for himself. All that this essay can hope to show is that this task, heavy as it must be admitted to be, is entirely worth while, and can prove exciting and exhilarating.

BALTHASAR AND RAHNER

Rowan Williams

The subject is an enormous one, and there is no possibility of doing it justice in a relatively brief paper. However, most people who are at all alert to the situation of Catholic theology over the last two or three decades will be aware that there is a certain tension between these two most seminal figures in that world. Cornelius Ernst notes, in 1970,[1] the rumour that Balthasar, le Guillou and others of like mind are about to start a periodical designed to counter the influence of *Concilium* – a journal very much associated with Rahner's style and approach; and to the present day, *Communio*, otherwise the *International Catholic Review*,[2] continues to represent, if not entirely an opposite pole, at the very least a significantly different set of concerns from those of *Concilium*. It is marginally more European in its focus, rather more suspicious of 'political theologies', rather more interested in spirituality and in the world of the imagination and the arts. These are only the loosest characterisations; but they probably express for many people something of the felt difference in tone between Balthasar himself and the majority of Catholic theologians associated with *Concilium*. It would be misleading to see this simply as a conservative-radical split: the solidarity of *Communio* and of Balthasar himself with ecclesiastical tradition is a highly critical one, and the characteristic stance of *Communio* contributors was at least for its first few years

---

[1] 'The *Concilium* World Congress: Impressions and Reflections', *New Blackfriars*, 1970; reprinted in C. Ernst, *Multiple Echo*, London, 1979, p. 42.

[2] *Communio* first appeared as a bi-monthly in 1972. Its first issue (Jan.-Feb. 1972) contains, in addition to a densely-written 'Programme' by Balthasar, contributions by de Lubac and Ratzinger, and – equally characteristically – a review article on Heinrich Boll's *Gruppenbild mit Dame*.

quite sharply distinct from that of favoured curial theologians (Galot, for instance). Where, then, is the heart of the conflict? And how real a collision is it? Do we have to do here with a difference of temper only, or with a more fundamental disagreement? In this essay I hope to explore the nature of these differences, linking them to some of the basic philosophical options of the writers in question, rather than attempting to plot them on a graph of contemporary Catholic politics. Of course there are pretty obvious political and institutional aspects to, and consequences of, such options; but I think it is worthwhile to step back from a definition of conflict primarily in such terms, if only to avoid journalistic banalities.[3]

The publication in 1966 of *Cordula oder der Ernstfall*[4] made it abundantly clear that Balthasar and Rahner had arrived at a serious parting of the ways. This fiercely-worded tract reproached Rahner and his school on several counts — the reduction of the love of God to mere philanthropy, the ideas of a systematic 'hiddenness' of grace, of the natural aptitude of human beings for a 'transcendental' revelation in and through the structures of their own spiritual dynamism: everything, in short, summed up in the Rahnerian picture of the 'anonymous Christian' outside the visible Church, the person who, even if a theoretical atheist, lives by faith, hope and love. A good deal of Balthasar's work in the sixties and early seventies is marked by a similar animus: even where Rahner is not named, we find a sharp polemical insistence on the *particularity* of revealed love[5] and thus on the particularity of Christian response,

---

[3] Jeffrey Kay contributes an interesting piece on 'Hans Urs von Balthasar, a Post-critical Theologian?' to a recent issue of *Concilium* (no. 141, 1981, pp. 84–89), attempting to go beyond facile characterisations in terms of 'reactionary' and 'progressive' strategies; but it is a little ironic that the issue should be one on *Neo-Conservatism: Social and Religious Phenomenon*. Editorial policy, at least, seems to be sure of where Balthasar is to be located.

[4] Einsiedeln, 1966; reprinted with additions, 1967 and 1968. E.T. *The Moment of Christian Witness*, New York, 1968.

[5] E.g., *Love Alone. The Way of Revelation*, London, 1968 (E.T. of *Glaubhaft ist nur Liebe*, Einsiedeln, 1963), pp. 48–50, 62, 66; *Who is a Christian*, London, 1968 (E.T. of *Wer ist ein Christ*, Einsiedeln, 1965), pp. 51 ff., etc.

nourished by a concrete image, characterised by specific and unique marks.[6] Balthasar is not, he assures us,[7] attempting to force theology back into a narrow ecclesiasticism, denying the existence of God's grace beyond the frontiers of the Church: 'the Christian may have the new and rather confusing experience of discovering that most of what he brings with him to the world has in some way or another already reached the world, not in its entirety of course, but only in fragments.'[8] But he is insistent that in so far as Christian action is *significant* action, action demanding interpretation and enriched and stimulated by interpretation, it requires a normative and generative focus. It is not enough to say that the Christian image or language gives shape to existing forms of action; distinctive forms of action arise in response to a fundamental event of address or call, and are constantly interwoven with speech and image in a single process of interpretation — a process which is best understood as the testimony *of* love *to* love. And to speak of Christ as 'image' is not to reduce him to a hermeneutical projection on our part, a vehicle of understanding; he is image *as* Word, the projection to us of a 'free self-expression', an absolute initiative.[9] The beauty of God incarnate can never be determined in advance by a

[6] E.g., *Love Alone*, ch. VIII; *Engagement with God*, London, 1975 (E.T. of *In Gottes Einsatz leben*, Einsiedeln, 1971), pp. 47-48, 56-60, 63 ('Christian involvement ... has always been initiated with a persistent and sometimes almost stubborn preference for places where, humanly speaking and from the point of view of this world, no further hope remains ... for the dying, for life grown old and worn out, for the incurably sick, for the mentally ill, for the handicapped'), and chs. 5 and 6 *passim*.

[7] E.g., *Engagement with God*, pp. 17-18.

[8] Ibid., pp. 97-98. L. Malevez, S.J., reviewing the French translation of *Cordula* in *Nouvelle Revue Théologique*, Vol. 89, 1967, pp. 1106-1107, picks out a similar admission in this book, and regrets that it is confined to a footnote. *Engagement with God* is obviously in part an attempt to respond to such comments by giving far more prominence to the acknowledgement of extra-ecclesial grace.

[9] E.g., *Love Alone*, pp. 66-67; also several of the essays in *Word and Revelation. Essays in Theology*, New York, 1964. (E.T. of *Verbum Caro. Skizzen zur Theologie I*, part I, Einsiedeln, 1960), especially 'The Word and History', pp. 31-55, and 'The Implications of the Word', pp. 57-86.

theological *a priori*.[10] It appears as a phenomenon whose necessity is internal to itself, and thus as a manifestation of freedom.[11] No outer condition or plastic force dictates the form of beauty: it cannot be other than it is, simply because of the logic of its own inner balance and inner adequacy, even 'comprehensiveness'.

Such a view will inevitably challenge a transcendentalism which takes as axiomatic the need to establish an epistemology primarily on the basis of *Vorgriff* — formal 'pre-understanding', determining in advance the possibility of specific (categorial) knowledge. In his immensely important early work, *Spirit in the World*,[12] Rahner develops the concept of *Vorgriff* in detail. 'Agent intellect', the power of making differentiations between perceived things, objectifying them and so rendering possible linguistic reference, is the condition for knowing any particular object *as* a particular object ('something actually intelligible'). However, this capacity can only operate if it has at its root the sense of difference between the concrete formal object, the object which is this-rather-than-that, and the unlimited existential possibility 'underlying' it. Or, in other words: to understand *contingency*, the truth that things are as they are but might have been otherwise, is in the same moment to understand the entirely open-ended potential of being itself. Nothing *need* be as it is; thus everything specific we grasp, we understand as *one* possible limitation or determination of an infinite range of possibilities.[13]

---

[10] See Jeffrey Kay, *Theological Aesthetics. The Role of Aesthetics in the Theological Method of Hans Urs von Balthasar*, Berne and Frankfurt, 1975, pp. 41–45, for a useful account of what Balthasar understands by 'apriorism' in contemporary theology.

[11] E.g., *Love Alone*, pp. 44–45; *The Glory of the Lord*, I, part III, *passim*, especially pp. 481–490 (the form of Christ is described on p. 488 as 'a mystery of the divine freedom, which, as in the work of art, coincides with supreme necessity'); and cf. vol. II, *Studies in Theological Style. Clerical Styles*, Edinburgh, 1984, p. 27.

[12] London, 1968, 2nd edition, with additional introductory material by J. B. Metz and F. P. Fiorenza, 1979 (from 2nd German edition, with introduction by Metz, Munich, 1957; the first edition appeared in 1939).

[13] Ibid., pp. 135–142.

If this is so, we can say that 'agent intellect' is a pre-apprehension, *Vorgriff*, of unlimited possibility,[14] and ultimately of being-as-such, *esse*, the very act of existing, which is the universal ground of each and every specific possibility. It is affirmed as an entirely formal and simple concept, but not in such a way as to make it empty; rather it is the ultimate and total 'overplus of meaning', 'absolute fullness in unity'. It can only be thought in and through particulars, as we grasp at once their particularity and limitedness and the unlimited possibility out of which they come; it cannot be conceived abstractly (in independence of particulars), although it is conceived in the *act* of abstraction (thinking away specific limits and determinations, to reach an ideal fullness of potential). In so far as this *esse* is presupposed (or pre-apprehended) as absolute and real, the *Vorgriff* of *esse* is a pre-apprehension of God — not as an object, but as the condition for grasping all objects.[15]

The act of abstraction, by which the transcendental condition of any and every particular is grasped, is not, Rahner insists, separable from what Aquinas called *conversio ad phantasmata*, turning to the particular in its concrete manifestation.[16] Abstraction and conversion are two aspects of a single act or process, and neither is unilaterally prior to the other. Knowledge does indeed begin in space and time, with sense data; yet, as we have seen, the knowledge of sense data as intelligible, as having form, includes and presupposes the priority of abstraction, though that abstraction would be logically unthinkable without concrete *sensibilia* to abstract *from*. So in knowing the particular as intelligible, knowing it 'spiritually', spirit becomes conscious of its own structures; and it would not become self-aware in this way without the *conversio*, the apprehension of the particular object as *object*, as *other*. And if spirit is fundamentally constituted by desire for absolute and unconditional

[14] Ibid., pp. 142–145.
[15] Ibid., pp. 169–183.
[16] Ibid., p. 226.

being, by a pull towards the infinite, it requires sense knowledge as a mediation of itself to itself — something which enables it to act in the way necessary to reach absolute being; i.e., to abstract. Thus we must see spirit as in some sense 'producing' sensibility 'as a condition of its own fulfilment'.[17]

Spirit in the World concludes with some general reflections on revelation, distinguishing 'the revelation of being-as-such which places man before God' from the revealing act of God in the particularities of history. Abstraction 'reveals' a real but unknown God; but in doing so it provides a basis for the question of whether God has acted or spoken in the world, because it points dumbly to an absolute freedom and opens itself to the possibility of encountering it and *recognising* it in wordly events. Abstraction reveals the human subject to itself as a potential 'hearer' of communication from absolute freedom; and again, in affirming the possibility of free, gratuitous self-communication, it affirms the possibility of love, which can be grasped fully only in a response of love.[18] So to be 'placed before God' in the transcendental self-awareness by which the spirit comes to itself establishes the spirit as capable of love, hope, faith; and there are all sorts of human activity in which these capacities are realised, when men and women act as authentically spiritual, self-transcending subjects, responding to the inner pressure of unconditional claims. When the possibility of love has been opened up, there is a call to love unconditionally and radically, and the refusal of such a call is the spirit's denial of its own nature.[19] And when the spirit does freely and consciously respond to its pre-conceptual grasp of a transcendent and infinite horizon

[17] Ibid., p. 284; and see pp. 280-286 *passim* on this subject.

[18] Ibid., p. 408; see also Rahner's earlier essay, 'Religionsphilosophie und Theologie', in *Die Siebenten Salzburger Hochschulwochen*, ed. G. Baumgartner, Salzburg, 1937, and the longer treatment in *Hearers of the Word*, New York, 1968. (E.T. of *Hörer des Wortes*, Munich, 1963).

[19] See, e.g., 'Reflections on the Unity of the Love of Neighbour and the Love of God', *Theological Investigations* VI, London, 1969, pp. 231-249.

not only for its knowledge but for its love and desire, it is receiving and responding to saving grace, living in obedience to a God who may not yet be named but is none the less actively present.

There is therefore a universal *praeparatio evangelica*, a tacit expectation of hearing loving self-communication, in the radical openness of the human spirit's love and searching. This means that we possess in advance a framework within which to understand Jesus Christ: a person who lives out unreservedly and wholeheartedly the response to an 'infinite' vocation to love and trust, who 'hears the Word' with no resistance or doubt, will be the complete realisation of human potential, and will thus express humanly the unconditional love of God himself, God's total commitment to the world.[20] This realisation depends upon God's initiative, God's freedom; but it is an answer to the quest for fulfilment implied *a priori* in the structures of the human spirit. We cannot 'deduce' Jesus of Nazareth from our anthropology, although we can demonstrate from the transcendental analysis of spirit that he does in fact fulfil the conditions there apprehended for a concrete manifestation of the absolute.[21] In fact, Christology illustrates precisely the unity between transcendental *Vorgriff* and particular apprehension that we have seen to be fundamental to the whole of human knowledge. Without the particular ('categorial') revelation of Jesus, we should not be able fully to articulate the range and sig-

[20] E.g., 'I Believe in Jesus Christ', *Theological Investigations* IX, London, 1972, pp. 165-168; more fully in, e.g., 'On the Theology of the Incarnation', *Theological Investigations* IV, London, 1966, pp. 105-120.

[21] Karl-Heinz Weger, in his *Karl Rahner: An Introduction to his Theology*, London, 1980, confuses the question considerably by speaking of a 'transcendentally deduced Christology' (p. 154) and a deduction of the 'idea of Christ' from human self-understanding, and then proceeding to *deny* the possibility of a deduction of the 'idea of Christ' (p. 156). Clearly, for Rahner, the deduction involved in the enterprise of Christology cannot be a prescription in advance of what the *event* of revelation will involve, yet Christology involves a deduction of the idea of an absolute fulfilment of human potential. What Weger does not make clear is the exact range of the vague expression 'idea of Christ' — despite a promise to expound this (p. 157).

nificance of the already existing transcendental apprehension of love and absolute trust;[22] without that precondition, we should not be able to recognise the event of Jesus as decisive and revelatory. We must in some degree know our own hearts before we can recognise the heart's desire which is the Incarnate God.

So, just as knowledge is one,[23] revelation is one. 'Transcendental' and 'categorial' revelation have the same content and the same purpose, God's gracious giving of himself.[24] When a human being accepts the gracious invitation to self-transcendence, he or she receives the grace of revelation, even when the mind's object in this process is purely formal and not consciously grasped in relation to the events of 'categorial revelation'. Here, though, there is something of an unclarity. Given that the transcendental *Vorgriff* cannot operate without some categorial occasion, how are we to understand the categorial element in revelation to non-Christians? Rahner himself is not all that helpful here (he has written comparatively little *explicitly* dealing with non-Christian religions, as opposed to European secularism)[25]: he suggests that, as in the Old Covenant there is a concrete institutional religious structure which both expresses God's saving will and incorporates ambivalent and even corrupt elements, so, in religions in general, the institutional form may mediate, though not in an uncriticisable way, 'the legitimate and concrete form of the divine law',[26] until the advent of a faith in which the relation of institution and moral or spiritual form of life is an intrinsic one, the institution becoming 'an element of this form itself'.[27] This is in effect to say that the

[22] See especially 'Anonymous and Explicit Faith', *Theological Investigations* XVI, London, 1979, pp. 52-59, in particular pp. 58-59.

[23] *Spirit in the World*, pp. 237-239.

[24] E.g., *Theological Investigations* IX, pp. 162-163 (in a paper on 'Atheism and Implicit Christianity'). Cf. Weger, op. cit., pp. 128-134.

[25] 'Christianity and the Non-Christian Religions', *Theological Investigations* V, London, 1966, pp. 115-134, is the main essay in this area.

[26] Ibid., p. 129.

[27] Ibid.

transcendental revelation outside the Church has an inadequate but never wholly invalid categorial form. The *conversio* of the spirit to concrete forms is not controlled by the particular categorial and historical event willed by God as the uniquely adequate and comprehensive manifestation of the human destiny. Though Rahner does not develop the argument in precisely these terms, various of his followers and pupils have done so.[28]

Thus Rahner's thesis about 'anonymous Christianity' has its roots firmly in a philosophical grounding which also determines the shape of his Christology. The foundations laid in *Spirit in the World* represent a bold attempt to interpret St Thomas's insistence on the epistemological primacy of sense experience from a post-Kantian standpoint, reckoning with the irreversible shift in philosophy towards the critical analysis of subjectivity as the starting-point for discussion. If metaphysics is to be done again after Kant, it can only begin by observing the Kantian prohibition against the speculative deduction of non-apparent states of affairs: metaphysics must be shown to be demanded precisely by and in the analysis of the knowing subject.

And it is just this philosophical starting-point which Balthasar consistently queries. His debate with Rahner goes back to the very early days of their careers, and it is a great error to represent it as merely a part of Balthasar's alleged 'conservative evaluations and negative criticism of contemporary tendencies within the Church'.[29] In discussing the later and post-conciliar Rahner, Balthasar several times[30] refers back to his review of the first edition of *Geist im Welt*.[31] Here, at the end of a very careful and sympa-

---

[28] See especially J. Heislbetz, *Theologische Gründe der Nichtchristlichen Religionen* (*Quaestiones Disputatae* 33), Freiburg, 1967.

[29] F. P. Fiorenza, in his introduction to the 1979 edition of *Spirit in the World*, p. xxxii.

[30] E.g., *Cordula* (3rd edition), p. 124, n. 5.

[31] *Zeitschrift für Katholische Theologie*, Vol. 63, 1939, pp. 371-379 (also reviewing J. Lotz, *Sein und Wert*).

thetic summary of the book (and of an earlier paper by Rahner[32]), he sets out his questions and reservations. Rahner's mentor and precursor Maréchal seems, in Balthasar's eyes, to have transformed what should be only the starting-point of metaphysica into metaphysics itself — i.e., (presumably) he has so concentrated on the analysis of subjectivity as to make the metaphysical pre-apprehension of *esse* excessively formal and abstract, and virtually empty. Rahner corrects this — to some extent: his concluding section on metaphysics and imagination[33] repeatedly stresses the necessity of the objective other, imaginatively and sensibly grasped, for any self-understanding and any openness to 'the absolute breadth of *esse*'. However, Balthasar is concerned that the experience of inter-subjectivity is not much developed in this discussion, and also that the 'agent intellect' of Rahner threatens to become more and more an inaccessible inner capacity, so abstractive in its mode of operation that it is hard to see how it can really deliver an affirmation of *esse* as *plenitude* rather than merely as a void of pure negative indeterminacy. In other words: can the *Vorgriff* of *esse* actually do a useful theological job, pointing to a source of creative freedom — quite the opposite of sheer indeterminacy, as Rahner is well aware? Might it not be preferable to begin from the basic experience of the *Gestalthaftigkeit des Wesens*, the potential orientation of being towards concrete form, rather than a pre-apprehension of limitlessness? This at least permits us to distinguish satisfactorily between negative infinitude and positive capacity.[34]

What Balthasar seems to mean is this: 'being' is apprehended primarily in the endless variety of particular forms, and it is only by attending to the fact of this *variety* that being may be grasped as gratuitously creative — and thus as concrete fullness. The formal *Vorgriff* of unlimited possibility is not enough: if we attain to the

---

[32] 'Religionsphilosophie und Theologie', see n. 18, *supra*.

[33] In the 1979 edition, pp. 387–408.

[34] *ZKTh*, 63, pp. 378–379.

affirmation of *esse* only through the rich plurality of worldly experience, that *esse* must be affirmed as containing not simply unspecified potentiality but the potentiality for existing in and as the world's particularities. Behind this is not only Balthasar's fundamental Platonism (the One is not simply *innominabile* but *omninominabile*) but also the specific Christian Platonism of a writer like Maximus the Confessor,[35] with his theory of the *logoi* of all things pre-existing in God as *particular* creative intentions, dependent upon the eternal *Logos* who is the divine ground of the possibility of all otherness, all differentiation.

Balthasar elaborates this in a densely-written conclusion to his survey of Western metaphysics.[36] Conscious experience is experience of being in a world, being part of a whole; and to experience another entity is to experience it likewise as a part of a whole. Thus the fundamental cognitive moment is the apprehension of *participation*, the participation of beings in being; and this affirmation of being is not the grasp of a formal limitlessness, since there is no possibility of expressing or thinking being without beings. Being depends upon the existence of particulars — in the Heideggerian language Balthasar employs here, *Sein* is dependent upon *Dasein* — and so is non-existent in itself. So being cannot itself be the source of beings, of concrete forms; and if (with Heidegger) we regard the *Sein-Dasein* distinction as ultimate, we risk the nihilistic and tragic conclusion that being overall, instead of offering illumination and significance to the world of *Dasein*, is an organic, impersonal and alien process of fate or necessity. But if I am genuinely aware of the world as contingent, a different consequence suggests itself. I participate in the world, but I am not a *function* of the whole; I am aware of my unique, non-necessary concrete being as distinct from

---

[35] See Balthasar's major monograph on this great Byzantine thinker, *Kosmische Liturgie: Höhe und Krise des griechischen Weltbilds bei Maximus Confessor*, Freiburg, 1941; reprinted with revisions and additions, Einsiedeln, 1961.

[36] *Herrlichkeit*, III/1, *Im Raum der Metaphysik*, Einsiedeln, 1965, pp. 943-957.

the 'necessity' of the world around. Yet *all* particular subsistents have the same characteristic of participation in the whole in a unique, non-functional manner. If this is so, it is impossible to conceive being-as-a-whole in a mechanical, supra-personal mode: it is a system of contingent and flexible interdependence, in which novelty and gratuity are possible — and in which therefore beauty is intelligible. It is not to be understood as necessity, and therefore points to a deeper ground and context which equally cannot be conceived as necessity. It is 'ultimate freedom', such as neither *Sein* nor *Dasein* can possess, a freedom which is both total concrete fullness (limitless possibility, if you like, though conceived in strictly personal, therefore non-abstract, terms) *and* utter 'poverty', since it wills to keep nothing back, but is entirely gift and love. From this freedom flows the liberty of created *esse*, capable of endless particular transformation, and 'seeking' ever greater variety because — as an image of the divine freedom — it can hold nothing back for itself. And, finally, from the freedom of *esse* flows the freedom of particular being, which is again fullness and poverty together: the fullness of having received the act of being in all its richness as a gift, the poverty of 'shepherding' it (Heidegger again) in chance and limited circumstances, and also the poverty of knowing that only in 'ekstasis', in letting go of the particular as something to be possessed, clung to, privatised or hoarded, is the fullness of the act of being realised in the world of particulars, in its own infinite poverty and 'ekstatic' self-gift.[37]

This, for Balthasar, is the abidingly valuable aspect of the notion of an *analogia entis*[38] — the *analogia libertatis*, which affirms that created

[37] On this last point, see once again Balthasar's *Kosmische Liturgie.* For the encounter of creative with created 'ekstasis', cf. the writings of the Russian theologian Vladimir Lossky. Balthasar's work on Maximus was clearly influential for Lossky, and his own researches in patristic thought were familar to Balthasar. For a discussion of Lossky's ideas, see the present writer's paper 'The *Via Negativa* and the Foundations of Theology. An Introduction to the Thought of V. N. Lossky', in *New Studies in Theology* I, ed. Stephen Sykes and Derek Holmes, London, 1980, pp. 95-117.

[38] *Herrlichkeit* III/1, p. 956.

freedom is the more fully realised the more deeply it gives itself up to uncreated freedom.[39] And this analogy depends upon that basic sense of belonging in a world, of radical contingency, which Balthasar makes his metaphysical foundation. Thus his objection to Rahner is in fact an objection not so much to one contemporary theologian (for whom, in fact, he has enormous respect[40]) as a protest against the whole tradition of European 'mainstream' philosophy between Kant and Heidegger — what he refers to in *Cordula* as 'the system' — a tradition which he sees as negating the 'sense of belonging in a world' by its obsession with subjectivity and the self-constitution of the subject. Kant himself, Balthasar is careful to point out, is very much a frontier figure, whose thought cannot simply be collapsed into the idealism that came in his wake. His ethic is anything but an individualistic eudæmonism: the experience in which I become aware of myself in the summons to *Achtung*, attention to the imperative of the Good, reveals a self called to belonging in the world, a self to which the world is prior. *I* become authentic and significant only because I have been touched and called by the demand made on me by *another* whom I recognise as an 'end in himself' and thus as possessing value and significance independently of my will and my prior consciousness. My autonomy as an ethical being depends upon my obedience, my humility.[41] Clearly, this is not far from Balthasar's formulation about created and uncreated freedom — at least from the human side. But this is the point where Kant is fatally ambiguous, since the deduction of the postulates of practical reason leaves little room for the affirmation of a free, infinite subjectivity.[42] He is poised between the *reflexio* of an earlier philosophical style, reflection establishing the possibility of knowing supra-empirical reality, and the idealist model of reflective rationality as itself constituting objective

[39] E.g., *Cordula*, p. 67.
[40] Ibid., p. 124.
[41] *Herrlichkeit* III/1, pp. 831–835.
[42] *Love Alone*, p. 29.

23

being;[43] his strong sense of the essential receptivity of consciousness prevents his taking the final step towards the latter option.

Yet, once again, the mode of deduction of the transcendental postulates illustrates a deep cleavage between the 'pure' ego which is merely 'the unity of apperception, the thinking subject, pure spontaneity', and the empirical ego which is the object of self-reflection, in its manifold experiences; the latter, the human person as *Naturwesen*, has nothing to do with metaphysics.[44] And so the ground is cleared for the separation in Kant's aesthetics between beauty and objectivity, between beauty and the realms of truth and goodness:[45] we are already on the road to Fichte, for whom the starting-point of metaphysics is solely the ego in its autonomy. The material world is, for Fichte, instrumental in the realisation of the ego, it is without significance independently of the ego; thus it is incapable of manifesting God. Spirit swallows up nature, and the non-human world is wholly subordinated to human self-fulfilment (and in this sense, says Balthasar, there is a paradoxical convergence in practical consequences between idealism and materialism).[46]

What has been disastrously lost in this metaphysical rake's progress is the possibility of *wonder*, of contemplative receptivity in the face of the world's richness, the overthrowing of a contemplative (and thus potentially God-directed) mode of knowledge by a model of *Bewältigung* — thought as mastery, domination, even exploitation, Bacon's nature on the rack.[47] This is the anthropocentric distortion to which Balthasar takes such exception; and when, in *Cordula* and elsewhere, he so sharply questions the redefinition of salvation as 'hominisation', it is not in any anti-human-

<hr>

[43] *Herrlichkeit* III/1, p. 827.
[44] Ibid., p. 831.
[45] Ibid., pp. 840–841.
[46] Ibid., pp. 883–884.
[47] E.g., *Cordula*, pp. 68–69.

ist sense. He is posing a profoundly important question about our understanding of the human *vis-à-vis* the world as a whole, echoing Heidegger's polemic against the technocratic distortion of human relations with the natural order.[48] It is a point worth pondering by those who regard Balthasar's theology as reactionary or uncritical in the socio-political as well as in the ecclesiastical sphere, or as psychologically regressive[49] (since his protest against the anthropocentric approach could be fruitfully read as a critique of the mentality of 'infantile omnipotence' in our attitudes to nature and matter).

Now it is precisely the Fichtean development of Kant's transcendentalism which Balthasar identifies in Rahner (and in Maréchal[50]). The transcendental *Vorgriff* of *esse* establishes the priority of spirit to sensibility, even though the former cannot realise itself without the latter; and, as we have seen, Rahner does speak explicitly of the 'production' of *Sinnlichkeit* by spirit, without giving any very satisfactory account of this ambiguous expression. He can also, of

[48] On which, see the essays in *Poetry, Language, Thought* (tr. A. Hofstadter), New York, 1971 (especially pp. 165-171), and in *The Question Concerning Technology* (tr. W. Lovitt), New York, 1977; see also George Steiner, *Heidegger*, London, 1978, pp. 131-132, 140-141, and H. Alderman, 'Heidegger's Critique of Science and Technology', in *Heidegger and Modern Philosophy*, ed. M. Murray, York, 1978.

[49] See, e.g., the extraordinary remarks of Jeffrey Kay, *Theological Aesthetics*, pp. 94-95: 'Balthasar's implicit rejection of this "selfish", "egotistical" stage [the 'middle stage' of human development as seen by, e.g., Erikson] and his exaltation of the innocence of past childhood and future sainthood are typical of apocalyptic religions. Christianity must come to an honest affirmation of the indispensable value of the self-centred feelings and passions that seek expression during this middle stage. It must encourage people in the straightforward expression of anger, aggression, sexual desire and pride as well as receptivity and self-sacrifice.' The scale of the misunderstandings implied here, not only of Balthasar but of neo-Freudianism as well, defies summary in a footnote.

[50] *ZKTh* 63, p. 375. Rahner reproduces Fichte's 'radikale Bindung des Geistes an die [als Material der Selbstverwirklichung, als die Ebene des Nicht-Ich, des anderen als solchen, der "materia" erfahrene] Sinnlichkeit.' On Maréchal, there are some scattered pertinent remarks in *Love Alone* (p. 34), *The Glory of the Lord* I, p. 149; *Herrlichkeit*, vol. III/1, pp. 799, 881, 884, 904, etc., and a rather longer treatment in *Karl Barth. Darstellung und Deutung seiner Theologie*, Cologne/Olten, 1951 and (with new preface) 1962, pp. 303ff.

course, stress that sense and spirit stand in a position of 'mutual' origination,[51] and even describes sensibility as 'the *receptive* origin of spirit';[52] so that there is no suggestion that there exists a real prior positive intuition on the part of spirit to which sensibility is 'later' added (Rahner is rightly dismissive of this kind of two-storey epistemology, whichever way up it is erected). Yet there is a good deal in *Spirit in the World* which lends colour to a suspicion that the concrete and historical world is in some degree seen as instrumental in furthering the fulfilment of spirit, and has no significance apart from that. The tight connection forged between *abstractio* and *conversio* is one of the most impressive intellectual achievements of Rahner's study, but it does not in itself provide a wholly satisfactory account of the experience of the *Wunder des Seins* as Balthasar understands it — the apprehension of being as a system of interdependent contingencies, the response to which can never be *abstractio*, but only the yielding of a privatised, self-enclosed perception to an 'ekstatic' participation — a self-forgetful lived involvement, both active and receptive, in the world as a whole.

This may help to explain the importance to Balthasar of the category of *drama* in explicating his theology. If knowledge is essentially participatory (not in the sense of a transcendental pre-conscious union of subject and object, but as recognition of a place within a network of relations), it is inseparable from history and *praxis*: there is 'no neutral "teachable" truth'.[53] Knowledge occurs and develops as reflection on the process of interaction between God and the world, a drama in which we are actors and not spectators.[54] Without this 'dramatic' dimension theology runs aground in various rationalistic abstractions. Paraphrasing (fairly freely) Balthasar's programme at the beginning of his second *magnum*

---

[51] *Spirit in the World*, p. 266.
[52] Ibid., p. 285 (my italics).
[53] *Theodramatik* I, *Prolegomena*, Einsiedeln, 1973, p. 16.
[54] Ibid., p. 17.

opus, Theodramatik, we might say that theology requires not only the exegesis of its foundational deposits but also their 'performance' – as if the text of Scripture were a 'libretto', says Balthasar.[55] This means a call to human subjects to enter into the dialogue of God with 'the other', which is grounded in his own Trinitarian life,[56] and enacted in the drama of Jesus and his Father, and Jesus and the human world. 'Drama' involves the active-and-receptive encounter with 'the stranger', the contingencies of relationship and reaction; it is truth manifest in dialogue, in a narratively-structured interaction which resists theoretical reduction and premature or facile resolution – in current literary terms, resists 'closure'. The drama is at one level determined by the form of revelation, which is the reflection of an eternal form, a final source of meaning, yet is also indeterminate in so far as it can only be realised and re-presented in the world of historical contingency, diversity and liberty. The form of the paschal mystery is not a theoretical programme, not a total structure of functional relations. Thus in the 'dramatic' perspective, with its inbuilt tension between rôle and plot, the creation of meaning and the imposition of meaning, Christian theology offers a deliverance from the menace of pure (structuralist) functionalism, without simply taking refuge in a static essentialist dogma or a privatised existentialism. By means of the Trinitarian doctrine and the controlling symbol of Good Friday and Easter, it enables an affirmation of both subject and structure without 'freezing' or absolutising either term.[57]

---

[55] Ibid., p. 22; I am indebted here to some reflections by Professor N. L. A. Lash in his paper, 'Performing the Scriptures – Interpretation through Living', published in *The New Testament as Personal Reading*, ed. Ronan Drury, Springfield, Ill., 1983, pp. 7-18.

[56] For the idea of the Trinitarian relation as the ultimate ground and norm for all otherness or object-relatedness, cf. *Cordula*, p. 68: 'Gott ist nicht die Welt, es herrscht deshalb zwischen beiden ein Urphänomen von *Gegenständigkeit* analog wie zwischen Ich und Du, und analog zum innergöttlichen Mysterium der Gegenständigkeit zwischen den Drei Personen, das die letzte Wurzel aller andern Gegenständigkeit ist.'

[57] *Theodramatik* I, pp. 23-46.

This is a most imperfect summary of one of Balthasar's most brilliant and condensed bits of writing, unsystematic and aphoristic in many places, but showing a remarkable range of awareness of the contemporary intellectual scene. And not the least point of interest here is the implicit community of interest between Balthasar and the whole post-Heidegger approach to philosophical hermeneutics, insisting as it does on the 'historicity of understanding', the inseparability of the knowing subject's mental history from the encompassing structures of language and culture. 'Self-reflection and autobiography — Dilthey's starting-points — are not primary and are not an adequate basis for the hermeneutical problem, because through them history is made private once more. In fact history does not belong to us, but we belong to it.' 'Understanding begins . . . when something addresses us.' These remarks, from Gadamer's classic treatment of the foundations of hermeneutics,[58] present the act of understanding as wholly bound to the sense of belonging in a world: what is 'transcendental' here is the hope or expectation of the discovery of meaning in the givenness of the past, the trust involved in any interpretative enterprise that participation in 'linguistic being', in communities and continuities of speech, is also participation in meaning, in a community of vision of how the world is. Truth is disclosed in so far as this trust proves to be sustainable.

If we follow Ricoeur[59] in widening the notion of the 'text' which interpretation encounters to include all systems of significant human action, capable of interpretation through present responses of significant action, we have a very clear convergence with Balthasar's *Dramatik*. It is curious that Balthasar so seldom refers to Ricoeur, though he is evidently familiar with at least the

---

[58] Hans-Georg Gadamer, *Truth and Method*, London, 1975, pp. 245 and 266.

[59] See his extremely important essay, 'The model of the text: meaningful action considered as text', in *Hermeneutics and the Human Sciences*, ed. and tr. J. B. Thompson, 1981, pp. 197-221.

major early essays of *Le conflit des interprétations*[60] and with *Le symbolisme du mal*;[61] but the parallels have been noted.[62] A. Moda, in his excellent discussion of Balthasar, speaks of his 'ontology of language', worked out in *Das Ganze im Fragment*,[63] but implicit elsewhere. Language, for Balthasar, is the means of opening the human subject to 'being', it is the sacrament, we might say, of the totality to which we belong; and for Ricoeur likewise, the fact of language testifies to the truth that consciousness is not self-originated, and is called to response — in the Christian case, not 'merely' linguistic (if there is such a thing) but, because of the character of the speech and symbol involved — the Cross of God's love — a language of loving action and relation.[64]

Rahner's relation to this hermeneutical development is less easy to assess. Certainly the Heidegger of *Sein und Zeit* is a considerable (if muted) presence in *Spirit in the World*; but whether the later Heidegger has left any serious impression on Rahner's mature work is dubious. In so far as Rahner remains firmly within the limits of a transcendentalist analysis of subjectivity, he belongs in that world of 'onto-theology' and Cartesian introspection on which Heideg-

---

[60] Referred to in *Theodramatik* I, p. 41, n. 7.

[61] Apparently referred to in *Theodramatik. Bd. II: Die Personen des Spiels. 2. Teil: Die Personen in Christus*, Einsiedeln, 1978, p. 430, n.10. *Theodramatik. Bd. II: Die Personen des Spiels. 1. Teil: Der Mensch in Gott*, Edinburgh, 1976, also mentions Ricoeur's *Philosophie de la volonté*, Paris, 1949, on p. 177, n. 4.

[62] L. O'Donovan, 'God's Glory in Time', *Communio* Vol. 2, 1975, p. 268; Aldo Moda, *Hans Urs von Balthasar, un' esposizione critica del suo pensiero*, Bari, 1976 (perhaps the best critical monograph on Balthasar yet written), pp. 510-514; Jeffrey Kay, art. cit. (see n. 3, supra).

[63] Einsiedeln, 1963; E.T. *Man in History*, London, 1968. See especially ch. 7, 'The Word and History'.

[64] Moda, op. cit., pp. 512-513, referring particularly to Ricoeur's 'Contribution d'une réflexion sur le langage à une théologie de la parole', in *Exégèse et herméneutique*, Paris, 1971. Compare also 'Toward a Hermeneutic of the Idea of Revelation' and 'The Hermeneutics of Testimony' in Ricoeur's *Essays on Biblical Interpretation*, ed. with an introduction by Lewis S. Mudge, London, 1981.

ger so firmly turned his back. Attempts have been made[65] to present Rahner as the author of a historical hermeneutics comparable to Gadamer's, chiefly on the ground of Rahner's repeated insistence upon the historical mediation of all consciousness; but the question remains of whether, if this historical mediation is taken with complete seriousness, the whole transcendentalist apparatus will not need radical revision, such as Rahner has not in fact chosen to undertake. L. Malevez, in an early attempt to confront Rahner with Balthasar,[66] tentatively suggested that Rahner's *Vorgriff* needed transposition into the terms of the historical pre-understanding of the hermeneutical philosophers if it was finally to avoid being elevated into a prescriptive norm against which tradition could be measured (so that elements of dogmatic development not conforming to the demands of transcendental anthropology could be jettisoned); and a more sustained critique has come from J.-P. Resweber,[67] who stresses the ambiguity and inconclusiveness of a supposed apprehension of *esse*, and demands closer attention to the question of whether the fact of language as such can provide a starting-point for speaking about God — precisely the question which, in their diverse ways, Ricoeur and Balthasar are struggling with.

We have come some distance from the deceptively straightforward problem of 'anonymous Christianity', to which the Rahner-Balthasar disagreement is so often reduced. Balthasar has granted (with slightly ill grace) that there *might* be a defensible interpretation of 'anonymous' faith — largely thanks to the conciliatory for-

---

[65] E.g., V. P. Branick, *An Ontology of Understanding. Karl Rahner's Metaphysics of Knowledge in the Context of Modern German Hermeneutics*, Saint Louis, 1974.

[66] 'Présence de la théologie à Dieu et à l'homme', *Nouvelle Revue Théologique*, 1968, pp. 785–800, especially pp. 799–800.

[67] 'La relation de l'homme à Dieu selon K. Rahner et M. Blondel', *Recherches des Sciences Religieuses,* Vol. 46, 1972, pp. 20–37, especially p. 37; also his monograph, *La théologie face au défi herméneutique*, Paris and Brussels, 1975, discussed in a review article by M. Sachot in *Recherches des Sciences Religieuses*, 50, 1976, pp. 168–173.

mulae of de Lubac, distinguishing 'anonymous Christians' from 'anonymous Christendom';[68] and so he has made it fairly clear that the disagreement runs deeper than a mere division over how best to speak of the 'natural' ground upon which faith builds. This paper has sought to show how the debate may be seen as one to do with the problem in contemporary philosophy about the status of the 'autonomous' subject or consciousness. Of course Rahner is anything but an uncritical idealist; and of course Balthasar does not ignore the discussion of 'transcendental conditions' for religious and Christian meanings. But Rahner does not engage directly with recent hermeneutical thought, and Balthasar makes little attempt at stating a sustained and coherent account of the 'ontology of language' he regularly presupposes;[69] and so it is proportionately difficult to assess whether the disagreement is comprehensive and radical. I suspect it is more so than some of Rahner's sympathisers have made out (if less so than Balthasar himself, in his more bitterly polemical moments, implies). Balthasar's challenge to the residual hints in Rahner of a 'self-constituted' consciousness remains a serious and profound question, both philosophical and theological, to any incautious uses of 'transcendental deduction' in Christian thought; and it has yet to generate a comprehensive response from the Rahnerian school.

And behind all of this lies the one decisive issue of Christology. Balthasar accuses Rahner of avoiding a *theologia crucis* in his vision of Christ as the (undialectical?) fulfilment of human potentialities.[70] Faith in Christ is not straightforwardly a recognition of the

[68] *Cordula* (3rd edition), p. 129. For a development of what such a distinction might involve, see the very interesting discussion of non-Christian faiths in *Theodramatik* II/2, pp. 376-388.

[69] Though it is *very* misleading to suggest that he is unaware of or unconcerned with the 'question of theological meaning in its last implications', as Peter Mann, O.S.B., does, in 'The Transcendental or the Political Kingdom, II', *New Blackfriars*, January 1970, pp. 4-16 (see especially pp. 15-16).

[70] *Cordula*, pp. 89-92.

satisfaction of my needs; the form of Christ is always a revelation of our untruth (and thus unreality and unloveliness) and so a demand to follow Christ into the abyss of Holy Saturday, into *silence*, before the Holy Spirit is capable of bringing forth a new language in Easter and Pentecost, the Word restored to the Father's throne, yet simultaneously given to the community of believers as their heart and their life. From first to last, Christ is *gift*. Even if a Rahnerian transcendentalist insists that it is *practically* only *a posteriori* that we can say that the form of Christ fulfils our needs, such a statement still diminishes the depth of gratuity in the paschal event, and still implies that it is abstractly possible for us to know our needs truly independently of Christ.

This is less than fair to Rahner on many counts: he is by no means insensitive to the need for a theology of the Cross,[71] though it is true that his system as a whole could not be so described. The heart of the difference here seems to be that Rahner thinks of human frustration in terms of incompletion, Balthasar in terms of tragedy. Freedom is not simply a smooth trajectory of finite towards infinite; it is, more importantly, the possibility of self-deceit, self-destruction, refusal. And the 'question' to which God's incarnation is the 'answer' (the terms are hopelessly imperfect) is of how 'God can gather back into himself the whole freedom of his creatures including all the consequences of such freedom, including, that is, rebellion and self-damnation, can gather it up and bear it up. And still remain God.'[72] The resolution of this can only be in terms of drama, dialogue, enacted in the singularities and risks of our own history, speaking to us of a God who is dialogue in his very being, who can be 'other than himself' and yet restore himself to himself, who because he can 'lose' and 'retrieve' himself can lose and

---

[71] See, e.g., the short piece on 'Self-Realisation and Taking Up One's Cross', *Theological Investigations* IX, pp. 253-257, and Rahner's various pieces on the 'theology of death'.

[72] *Elucidations*, London, 1975, pp. 50-51 (E.T. of *Klarstellungen. Zur Prüfung der Geister*, Freiburg, 1971).

retrieve the world, can lay down his life and take it again. Fulfilment alone leaves the tragic problem of self-loss untouched, and so fails, in the long run, to take freedom sufficiently seriously. And this also helps in understanding why, for Balthasar, dialogue with 'the world' is so much more complex a matter than it sometimes seems to be for Rahner; because the world is *not* a world of well-meaning agnostics but of totalitarian nightmares, of nuclear arsenals, labour camps and torture chambers. *Cordula* contains a savagely satirical little dialogue (the word is deliberately ironic) between a Christian and an — anonymously Christian? — commissar.[73] Unjust, perhaps; but Balthasar's harsh clear-sightedness is an important disturbance of any assumptions about easy 'humanist' convergences in our world.

That particular dialogue is, in effect, a trial scene. Deliberately or not, it echoes other such scenes, as a shameful parody of the *Acta* of the martyrs, and perhaps of the single great trial of Christ himself by human power. Dostoyevsky's Inquisitor claimed to know better than Christ what human needs were, and to love humanity more than he did; and George Steiner, in his brilliant essay, *Tolstoy or Dostoyevsky*,[74] hears in Tolstoy's confident and impatient humanism more than a trace of the Inquisitor's voice. 'If Christ had not existed it would have been easier for men to arrive at rational, Tolstoyan principles of conduct and thus to realise God's Kingdom. Through his humble ambiguity... Christ had made human affairs infinitely more difficult.'[75] Christ's mediation of human meaning interferes with the rational recognition of God in direct human self-understanding. But 'The Dostoyevskian position is gathered into the silence of Christ; it is realised not in language, but in a single gesture — the kiss which Christ bestows on the Inquisitor.'[76] Steiner

[73] Pp. 110-112.
[74] (2nd revised edition), London, 1967.
[75] Ibid., p. 239.
[76] Ibid., pp. 308-309.

rightly notes that this is a *dramatic* resolution which may equally be read as a philosophical evasion. Whether there is a way of stating such a resolution without evasion, whether there is — so to speak — a metaphysics of the Cross, is precisely the issue to which Balthasar's monumental *oeuvre* addresses itself. It has been said that to understand a philosopher you must understand what he is afraid of. Balthasar's dread is the Inquisitorial claim to love humanity more than its maker does — the most comprehensible and sympathetic of all blasphemies — and that is why, for him, revelation is a radical assault on what we know of love, or of liberty, or of hope. If Rahner's Christ is an answer to the human question, a faintly but distinctly Tolstoyan figure, Balthasar's Christ remains a question to all human answers, and to all attempts at metaphysical or theological closure.

Additional Notes

i) Balthasar appears never to mention Lonergan (nor Lonergan Balthasar?); but there is a further and quite interesting job to be done in comparing and contrasting Lonergan's achievement with that of both Balthasar and Rahner. For a preliminary sketch, see A. J. Kelly, S.J., 'Is Lonergan's "Method" Adequate', *The Thomist*, Vol. XXXIX, April 1975, pp. 437–470; on Balthasar, pp. 465–468. Kelly is not alone in finding Lonergan's epistemological scheme difficult to apply in aesthetics.

ii) I have to acknowledge a great debt in the composition of this paper to my student Christopher Seville of Trinity Hall, Cambridge, now researching on Balthasar's understanding of analogy and his use of Przywara. Mr Seville's exceptionally detailed knowledge of Balthasar's work has illuminated and clarified many areas for me.

BALTHASAR AND THE ANALYSIS OF FAITH

John Riches

Questions of the analysis of faith in Catholic theology have, over the last hundred years, been primarily directed towards 'the problem of the act of faith'.[1] In this Catholic theology has taken its lead from Vatican I's definition of faith[2] as a supernatural act (virtue) by which we believe those things that are revealed (*revelata*) to be true. Such an act is said to be supernatural, positively in the sense that it is assisted by the grace of God; negatively in the sense that such assent is not given because human reason can itself perceive the grounds of such propositions but rather because of the authority of the Revealer, who can neither be deceived nor deceive. Such a definition clearly raises questions *both* about the relations between human reason and will in assents given *propter auctoritatem Dei and* about the relation beteen the human act of faith and the divine grace which assists it. Thus the main stream of post-Vatican I Catholic theology has attempted to define, often with great precision, the extent to which the will's assent to God's authority is directed or prepared by rational considerations. It has also con-

---

[1] Cf. the magisterial study of the development of these themes in the post-Vatican I period by Roger Aubert, *Le Problème de l'Acte de Foi*, 3rd ed., Louvain, 1958.

[2] The definition of Vatican I runs: Hanc vero fidem, quae 'humanae salutis initium est', Ecclesia Catholica profitetur, virtutem esse supernaturalem, qua, Dei aspirante et adiuvante gratia, ab eo revelata vera esse credimus, non propter intrinsecam verum veritatem naturali rationis lumine perspectam, sed propter auctoritatem ipsius Dei revelantis, qui nec falli nec fallere potest (Dz 1789). The two related canons (Dz 1810f.), with their attacks on ideas of the autonomy of human reason, which thus cannot be imposed on by God, and on the denial of the distinction between natural religious knowledge and divine faith based on authority indicate the context of these formulations in the struggle against various forms of rationalism.

sidered the extent to which in such an act of faith the truth of what is revealed is in fact perceived. Such theological analysis is deeply concerned with the rationality of Christian faith but in seeking to uphold the faith it has often tended to construe theological truth and assents in terms borrowed from the very rationalism which it wishes to counter.

Alongside these developments in Catholic theology there were however others. At the turn of the century Maurice Blondel developed his *méthode de l'immanence*, seeking an apologetic which was more firmly grounded in anthropological analysis, while in the forties and fifties the Jesuit school at Lyons expounded a *nouvelle théologie* which renounced apologetics altogether and instead sought to ground faith more firmly in the contemplation of the central Catholic mystery. The purpose of this essay is to show how Balthasar's theology is both influenced by and transcends these two important reactions to the more dominant theology of the post-Vatican I period as well as to show how Balthasar's concern with the aesthetic dimension helps to deepen and correct these earlier developments.

Blondel represents an attempt on the part of French Catholics to counter Catholicism's increasing isolation from the main stream of French intellectual, cultural and scientific life in the nineteenth century. The account of faith as assent to the truth of revealed propositions on the basis of the authority of the revealer was offensive, not only because of the shakiness of the traditional proofs of such authority but because of the widespread rejection of heteronomy in all spheres of life. Thus Blondel concluded that it was, in view of the widespread belief in man's autonomy, necessary to argue not only for the validity of the Church's claims to possess an authoritative divine revelation but also for the 'necessity *for us* of adhering to this reality of the supernatural'.[3] Equally, Blondel had received his

---

[3] *Lettre sur les exigences de la pensée contemporaine en matière d'apologétique*, in Annales de philosophie chrétienne, vol. CXXXI, p. 345, quoted in Aubert, p. 279.

own intellectual formation from a neo-Kantianism which stressed the limits of scientific knowledge, its inability to grasp 'things in themselves', and which pointed to moral experience as the source of our faith in things eternal. Such a critique of the scope of human reason was of course strongly at odds with the rationalism of much neo-Scholastic theology with its firm commitment to a neo-Thomist metaphysic. It is thus part of Blondel's debt to the Kantian tradition that he attempts to give an account of faith which relates it not only to the rational grounds of assents, but to the whole realm of human experience in both its intellectual and moral aspects.

Thus in his *méthode de l'immanence* he argues from a prolonged analysis of human moral and intellectual experience to a double impossibility: the impossibility of not recognising the insufficiency of the whole natural order and the presence in us of an ulterior need; and the impossibility of finding anything within one's self with which to satisfy this — religious — need. And this opens up the way for seeing the *revelatum* as that which satisfies a person's deepest needs, as that which fulfils rather than as something imposed arbitrarily from without. This recognition of the possibility and desirability of the supernatural in turn raises the question whether it be real. Blondel himself was critical of proofs of the reality of the supernatural — in Christianity — from miracle, as well as believing that if such compelling proofs could be offered they would destroy the basis of faith in a *free gift*: 'In order to be believed as it wishes to be believed, revealed doctrine must itself provide its reasons for being believed and bring its own certitude as a supernatural gift.' And he adds, in his own interestingly distinctive gloss on the second Canon of chapter III of *Dei Filius*: 'If it (sc. revealed doctrine) has to be admitted then in no way in virtue of its clarity to us and of its coming from us (in any case such clarity is never entirely transparent), it can be accepted as it should be only in so far as it is communicated to us and remains fundamentally mysterious. But this raises the great and delicate problem: how can we introduce into ourselves and give life to another thought, another life than our own?'[4] For Blondel such a gift can be appropriated only in an act of the whole person; it is in the exercise of the whole interior life that the divine finds its way into man. Such action is the only receptacle that can contain it. Man must reach out in action in order to receive the gift which God offers, which will then enter his life and unfold itself. In the resultant enrichment of his life he will find the best guarantee that he is not mistaken, the certitude of the reality of the supernatural gift. Such enrichment is an '*expérimenta-tion effective*' of the supernatural life, which while it remains mysterious and therefore cannot be fully understood nevertheless brings the certainty of its reality.

Much could be said in comment: for our present purposes we may note the way in which Blondel's work suggests a number of new strategies in the understanding of theological faith after Vatican I. Balthasar has suggested that perhaps the most serious deficiency of the neo-Scholastic understanding of theological faith and knowledge was its indebtedness to the rationalism it attacked. Instead of attempting to discern the mode of knowledge which is proper to faith such theology assumes the rationalist notion of clear and distinct ideas, only qualifying this by asserting that in this life our apprehension of such — theological — truths is still impaired and that therefore assent to their truth is given on the basis of the trustworthiness of the God who reveals them.

Now it is clear that Blondel rejects outright accounts of the act of faith which see it as an assent based on a judgement that the revelation contained in the Christian Scriptures and the teaching of the Church is divine because attested by the fulfilment of prophecy and miracles. Faith for Blondel is rooted in the experience of the entering of the divine life into the life of the believer as the believer offers his whole life to God. This clearly is not an isolated act,

---

[4] *L'Action*, Paris, 1893, p. 400, quoted in Aubert, p. 280.

though Blondel can give an account of conversion in terms not unreminiscent of Pascal's wager. Rather it is in the continuing life of 'action' that the reality of the divine life which is revealed and communicated to us is recognised. Now the truth which is communicated in such experience of the divine life cannot be defined in terms of some generally applicable standards of rationality whether conceived in terms of clarity and distinctness or of certain agreed procedures for assessing a common stock of experience. The whole point about Blondel's account is that the entry of the divine life into the experience of the believer is something mysterious which breaks the normal pattern of his existence. Hence there can be no question of providing compelling proofs for faith. Not only would such proofs impugn the 'freedom' of faith; they cannot be provided precisely because of the particularity of the experience of faith. What he can argue is that this normal pattern of existence, properly understood, cries out for some such fulfilment. And such arguments are themselves based on a readiness to read moral experience in a way which itself cannot simply be justified in terms of generally agreed rational procedures. Again one is reminded of Pascal, whom Balthasar indeed sees as a forerunner of the 'method of immanence',[5] and his distinction between the spirit of geometry and the spirit of finesse. What is required is a greater attention to the way in which moral judgements are made, a greater awareness of the distinctiveness of such judgements as against judgements in the field of either mathematics or the physical sciences. In this Blondel was opening the way in theology for 'personalist' accounts of the life of faith; he was too laying the ground for the explorations of human modes of existing and knowing which were so vigorously pursued by philosophers on the Continent during the earlier decades of this century.

The issue here is crucially: in what sense can the kind of knowledge we have of others in our normal moral intercourse (and, by anal-

[5] *Herrlichkeit*, II/2 pp. 576f.

ogy, of God in faith) help us to move beyond the rationalist views of knowledge on which much of the thinking behind Vatican I relied? Classically knowledge is thought properly to be predicated only of what we learn on the basis of generally agreed procedures applied to generally available experience, but there is good reason to doubt whether such views of knowledge serve adequately to illuminate what it is to understand wide areas of moral and — we shall also suggest — aesthetic experience. Thus in personal knowing we may well incline to suppose that there are those who have a superior moral insight or predisposition which enables them to understand and interpret the ways and meanings of others' behaviour, gestures, speech with a greater clarity and accuracy than those not so endowed. Whether this is in fact a matter of greater personal endowment, of greater sensibility or sympathy, or the result of greater self-discipline and schooling oneself in attending to the details and particularities of human forms of communication, we do in fact recognise such ability in our assessment of, e.g., great novelists; but also more simply in the common-sense distinctions we make between the sensitive and the insensitive, the 'healthy-minded', the perceptive and sympathetic, etc. And we recognise too that those so endowed have in virtue of their ability to understand moral experience access to a far wider range of experience than those not so gifted. Precisely such an understanding of 'personal' knowledge may provide important analogies for the understanding of theological faith.

And Blondel's discussion may suggest further avenues of enquiry. Firstly, we need to take seriously his suggestion that our moral, personal and religious knowledge and insight is something that grows and matures as we form relations with another person or community of persons; that it is therefore not simply a matter of the detached and objective judgement of an — isolated — individual, but that such knowledge is the result of an interaction between persons. Second, that such knowledge is therefore the outcome *both* of a willingness or readiness to be drawn into such relations *and* of a person's attempts to understand the nature of such relations. Third, that the growth in moral understanding which occurs — or may occur— within such relationships is to be thought of as the apprehension of a reality which moulds or transforms the whole of a person's life. It is that which — ideally at least — may allow a person's life to achieve a wholeness and unity as the expression of such a central truth, which, that is to say, may satisfy the need which Blondel had argued for.

To turn now more briefly to another movement in French Catholic theology which provides a further piece in the complex pattern of influences and interests which contribute to Balthasar's intellectual formation: the movement centred on the Jesuit School at Lyons, known as the *nouvelle théologie*. Like Blondel the *nouveaux théologiens* were deeply concerned at the growth of secularism in French society, as were the worker priests of the same period.[6] Both the theologians and the worker priests were inspired by a desire to point to God's presence and reality within the Church, whether by bringing that reality — in silent witness — into the lives of those who had become alienated from the Church or by centring theological reflection on the perception of God's presence within the mystery of the Church, as in de Lubac's *Catholicisme*, and in urging the significance of such a mystery to the alienated world.[7] Both were concerned to present the divine presence as that which answers to the world's deepest needs. In this respect the movement has obvious links with Blondel's attempt to demonstrate the 'double impossibility' of man's finding satisfaction for his deepest

[6] Cf. M. Ward's revised version of L'Abbé Godin's book *France Pagan?* London, 1949, for an account of the French worker priests.

[7] De Lubac's work is subtitled *Les aspects sociaux du Dogme*, Paris, 1937. In an address to the Catholic University of America Balthasar emphasised the continuities between de Lubac's work and the aims of notably Latin-American theologies of liberation, 'Current Trends in Catholic Theology and the Responsibility of the Christian', *Communio. International Catholic Review*, Vol. 5, No. 1, pp. 75-85, cf. especially 83f.

needs. The difference is that the *nouvelle théologie* is addressed not to philosophical enquirers, but to the Church. Its arguments are arguments about the tradition whose purpose is to urge support for an overall view of Christian faith in the world; they are not apologetic because the only apologetic is the contemplation of the divine mystery revealed in the Church.

The nub of the argument which led to the condemnation of certain of the school's theses in Pius XII's encyclical *Humani Generis* (1950) relates precisely to Blondel's claim that the Christian revelation satisfies man's deepest needs. Put in terms of the tradition the question is: how far and in what respect is man by nature ordained to see God, how far does man possess a *desiderium naturale* for the vision of God? The question turns, that is, on the definition of nature, specifically of what is required for man to fulfil his — natural — needs. The Scholastic doctrine of man's nature taught that man had a natural and a supernatural end. As 'purely' natural[8] man's end was peace, justice, and the common good; as supernaturally elevated by the infused habits of faith, hope and love man was destined to enjoy the vision of God himself.[9] The crucial question raised by this doctrine of a double finality in man was of the nature of the relation between two. Aristotelian doctrine asserted that natural kinds could claim as a right (*debitum*) that which was necessary to the proper achievement of their duly ordained end. Thus if the end or purpose of a wing was to fly it also required air in order to achieve its end. The theological problem is that it is admitted (a) that grace is necessary for the achievement of the vision of God, (b) that grace is gratuitous, i.e., not owed to man as a *debitum*, and that it

---

[8] Cf. especially H. de Rondet, 'Le Problème de la Nature Pure et la Théologie du XVIe Siècle' in *RSR* XXXV, 1948, pp. 480-521. Balthasar's own carefully differentiated discussion of these topics is best found in *Karl Barth*, pp. 278-334.

[9] Cajetan, in *I ad Partem q.12 art. 1.n.9*, distinguishes between the vision of God himself which man desires only when he has tasted the effects of grace and desires to know their cause, and the vision of God as creator, governor, etc., as he appears in us.

therefore seems to follow that man is not naturally ordained to the vision of God as his end.

The Scholastic answer to the obvious question: In what sense is natural man (*in puris naturalibus*) ordained to see God absolutely is that he has a *potentia oboedientalis* which is further defined as an *aptitudo rei ad hoc ut in ea fiat quidquid faciendum ordinaverit Deus*:[10] it is the purely passive capability of man's being of such a kind that God may achieve his work of grace in him. There is thus no direct connection between man's knowledge of God as *causa rerum* and *secundum substantiam in se*; nor does man naturally desire the vision of God as his true end.

The subject is complex, not least because of the Scholastic insistence that the notion of man *in puris naturalibus* is a purely theoretical one, which nowhere finds its instantiation. Nowhere — so Balthasar — is there 'ein Stück purer Natur'![11] In the actual order of things man is always somehow in contact with grace. But it does nevertheless raise important theological issues: in what sense can man properly be spoken of at all as existing independently of God? Is not man's *true being* only to be found *in relation to*, in communion with God? De Lubac's studies of the Greek fathers, Balthasar's own work in that field and his deep indebtedness to the Fourth Gospel, have all underlined the sense in which for the Christian 'to be', 'to live', is to live in the Son as he lives in the Father; to be cut off from that life is to inhabit the world of the flesh, of the transitory. Man lives only as he is drawn into the personal knowledge of the Father in the Son. But then what of man's knowledge of God outside grace? Can we say, after Blondel, that man has no natural desire for God as he is in himself, even if of his own he cannot satisfy that desire? Was not Blondel's apologetic designed to show precisely the desire — and yet the impossibility of natural fulfilment of the

---

[10] Cajetan, ibid, n. 9.
[11] *Karl Barth*, p. 298.

desire? To show moreover that this desire is desire for that which people require if they are truly to find themselves. And again do not studies of Antiquity and of the great religions of the world show the deep desire for God and the real sense of God which is to be found there, neither of which seems to be done justice to by the doctrine of *natura pura*? Such questions only serve to point out the weaknesses of Scholastic anthropology and the need for a reconsideration of the issues raised.

Thus the work of de Lubac, who was of course Balthasar's own teacher, raised sharply again the question of the inadequacy of any attempt to understand the nature of faith which would abstract from the personal interchange between the believer and his God. At the same time it directed attention, in works like *Catholicisme*, to the central place in the life of faith of contemplation of the divine mystery. However much we need to be alerted to the analogies between the life of faith and personal relationships on the human level, we should not lose sight of the sense in which the presence of the Other in faith is mediated through contemplation of the central Christian mysteries in the Scriptures, the sacraments and the Church.

Our aim so far has been to show the extent to which certain issues, epistemological and ontological, were under discussion in the earlier decades of the twentieth century, in which Balthasar found his theological formation. In an important sense these issues turn on the question of human autonomy, of a person's self-sufficiency, both cognitively and ontically. If the classical idea of knowledge saw everyone as possessing fully the means for and access to knowledge, a comparable anthropology saw people as achieving a full stature in emancipation, in independence from external laws and rules, in sharp rejection of religious dependence.[12] What we have

[12] Cf. Hegel's celebrated rejection of Schleiermacher's definition of religious self-consciousness as 'total dependence' on God: then my dog would be the most religious of all beings.

seen so far have been examples of quite widespread tendencies in Catholic thought which embraced personalist models of knowing, seeing in our moral experience elements which are in sharp discord with the classical view of knowledge and finding in the *interrelation* of persons something essential to the understanding of their true nature and work.

Balthasar has recorded his debt to personalist thought on a number of occasions[13] and there can be little question but that the work of groups like those around Blondel and the *Nouvelle Théologie* acted as a powerful catalyst on post-Vatican I theology, which was in danger of being driven into a position too simply determined by its opposition to various forms of rationalism. But Balthasar's own starting-point does not lie simply here. If for him attention to the analogy between human loving and the encounter with divine grace demonstrated clearly the need to rethink older, more 'rationalist' models of faith, his studies of German literature and his love of music pointed him to other analogies, complementary to the analogy of personal encounter, which in turn suggested ways of developing and grounding more thoroughly those earlier insights.[14] What particularly exercised his mind was the way aesthetic judgements are made, e.g., about the excellence, uniqueness of a work of art, of poetry, of music. Why is it that we judge Mozart's *Idomeneo*, for all its similarities with other works of its genre, to be unique within its kind? What is it that informs such judgements? What is it in the work itself that justifies them? May answers to such questions suggest ways of answering similar ques-

[13] Cf. Balthasar's more recent address to the Catholic University of America 'Theology and Aesthetic', *Communio. International Catholic Review*, Vol. 8, No. 1, 1981, pp. 62-71. For a more critical appraisal see *Love Alone*, ch. 1. I have discussed the importance for Balthasar of aesthetic analogies in 'The Theology of Hans Urs von Balthasar' in *Theology*, 1972, pp. 562-70, 647-55.

[14] Cf. for example the opening chapters of *Love Alone* which along with its critique of the anthropological reduction suggests other ways of developing the analogy of personal love.

tions about the way in which we discern the uniqueness, the value of a particular religious tradition or figure?

It is not Balthasar's method to develop a systematic theory of aesthetics and then to proceed to apply it point by point to matters of theology. Rather the analogy with aesthetic discernment alerts him to elements in the tradition which have been sadly lost sight of in the post-Reformation period and which it is his hope to recover.[15] Hence his massive engagement with the tradition which is by no means simply traditionalist but a creative attempt to develop his own perception of the nature of faith. In what follows we shall examine his treatment of certain important themes in the tradition, showing how these serve to open up the discussion of the nature of faith in new and creative ways.

Talk of the analogy between aesthetic *discernment* and theological faith clearly raises broad questions about the relation of faith and *knowledge*, which as we have already seen become problematical in the rationalist models of faith suggested by Vatican I and by certain forms of neo-Scholasticism. For Balthasar[16] faith is not to be contrasted with knowledge, as for example one might contrast assent to testimony with knowledge of clear and distinct ideas. Rather, faith has its own kind of knowledge, a contemplative *theoria* of the divine mysteries which develops and grows within the deeply personal relationship which is established through faith by God's gracious act of revealing and drawing men to himself. The doctrine is set out clearly by the Alexandrians. Christ, for Clement, is the teacher who leads men to the Father. Faith entrusts itself to him in order to be led into the light by pure grace and yet also by men's intellectual, ascetic and loving efforts. Faith is the foundation, *gnosis* is built upon it. But each is indispensable. 'There is no *gnosis* without *pistis*, and there is no *pistis* without *gnosis*, just as there is no

---

[15] Cf. the opening section of *The Glory of the Lord*, I: 'The Elimination of Aesthetics', pp. 45-79.

[16] *The Glory of the Lord*, I, pp.131-141.

Father without the Son.' (Strom V, 1.3) 'Truly to find the Father in the Son is to open up the sphere of absolute trinitarian truth, and of the knowledge into which we grow more deeply the more we entrust ourselves to the Son in faith and allow ourselves to be drawn into his innermost disposition.'[17]

From such a basic awareness of the *gnosis* of faith a number of points follow. In the first place it is seen clearly that to attempt to isolate Christian faith from the living spiritual context of man's real encounter with God is to court disaster. Such a move inevitably leads one to contrast faith as assent to divine authority too sharply with the supernatural vision of God where the supernatural truths could be clearly and distinctly perceived (what Balthasar calls 'supernatural rationalism'). But this is to lose sight of the biblical understanding of faith — knowledge as an encounter with the personal God, the Father of Jesus Christ. The truth into which we are drawn is the glory of God which both in respect of its undeservedness (*gratuité*) and its inner quality deserves the name *gratia* — all of which suggests again the analogy between aesthetic and theological revealed reality.[18] And from this it follows again that the element of authority in faith is of a very particular kind. Divine authority in its revelation as *doxa* requires no other justification than itself; its rightness, like that of a work of art, has its own evidential force for those who see it. Appeal to such authority is of a very different kind from the appeal to the authority of the Church which proclaims it made by Scholastic theology.

Another consequence follows for Balthasar. If the analogy between aesthetic and theological, revealed reality holds good, what is perceived in both is something — albeit of a very different kind — of the mystery of being. The questions here raised are large and yet largely forgotten. What of the relation between myth, the ancient,

---

[17] *The Glory of the Lord*, I, p. 138.
[18] *The Glory of the Lord*, I, p. 140.

aesthetic form of such revelation, and philosophy, with its tendency to abstract from the particular and to seek the non-contingent necessary grounds of things? What of the relation between myth and Christian revelation? Balthasar's answers to these questions are worked out in great detail in the fourth and fifth volumes of *The Glory of the Lord*. In the simplest terms Balthasar cannot reject the whole ancient tradition of myth from Homer to the Greek tragedians, to its later mediation in German writers like Hölderlin, as void of any disclosure of being. Those who formed the myths were those who sought to penetrate the mysteries of things and what they saw and discovered found imaginative form in the great metaphysical tradition which embraces Homer and Plato, Hölderlin and Schelling. Of course we may wish to dismiss all this as so much uncontrolled speculation, at best reduce it to the brave attempt of man to provide a 'sacred canopy' for his perilously balanced societies. But Balthasar is only too well aware of the impoverishment of theology which follows in the wake of such positivism. For Christian theology takes its terms and images from the myths and their philosophical reflection: like myth and philosophy it too contemplates the mystery of being. If we deny the language of myth and philosophy any adequacy to their supposed object, then we also deny any conceptual sense to the language of Christian theology. And this is effectively what has happened in the analysis of faith offered in Vatican I. Of course there is a deep distinction to be made. What the great myths and philosophies perceive of being is one thing: awesome, *tremendum et fascinans*. Yet it is — so Balthasar — from within this vision of the Holy, of being, that there breaks forth the gracious self-disclosure of the divine that is the Christian revelation.

> In other words, the formal object of theology (and, therefore, also of the act of faith) lies at the very heart of the formal object of philosophy (along with the mythology which belongs to it). Out of those mysterious depths the formal

object of theology breaks forth as the self-revelation of the mystery of Being itself; such a revelation cannot be deduced from what the creaturely understanding can of itself read off the mystery of Being, nor, even in the manifestness of the mystery of God, can such revelation be grasped by this intellect without the divine illumination of grace. Nevertheless, the self-revelation of God, who is absolute Being, can only be the fulfilment of man's entire philosophical-mythological questioning as well. As such it is an answer to men's questions which comes to us in God's revealing Word (and becomes history and flesh) and which is, therefore, to be heard in a particular existent. But it is no less a Word from God, an intelligence concerning Being itself and thus, at the same time, philosophy. As the highest personal authority of the self-revealing God (to whom 'every creative intellect is wholly subject' as to its Lord, Vatican I Dz 1789), this intelligence challenges man essentially in his act of faith and brings philosophical knowledge, along with its *eros*, to its interior goal.[19]

All this provides the broad context within which Balthasar can then articulate more fully his own understanding of Christian faith-knowledge as it is developed within the divine encounter between God and man mediated through the 'revelation *Gestalt*' of

[19] *The Glory of the Lord*, I, pp. 145f. This insistence on the continuity, for all the even greater discontinuity, between Christian revelation and the great myths is of course of major significance for the interpretation of the New Testament Literature. The questions about the place of Christianity within the development of first-century religious traditions posed importantly, though often from a strong positivist or idealist standpoint, by the History of Religions School are only now being raised again after a long interval. One of the more interesting attempts from the point of view of New Testament scholarship to do justice to the kinds of concern voiced by Balthasar is to be found in G. Theissen, *On Having a Critical Faith*, London, 1979. There are of course deep divisions between the two writers; but it is important to realise that the questions Balthasar raises do have a very direct bearing on contemporary problems in New Testament scholarship.

Christ. What this amounts to, as he expressly says,[20] is an attempt to move beyond the *analysis fidei*, the description of the particular characteristics of faith in *isolation* from all elements of insight and knowledge, to a reintegration of faith into the personal encounter between the believers and God through which they are drawn deeper and deeper into his knowledge through his self-disclosure in Christ Jesus. This attempt embraces many elements and topics from the tradition. For our purposes we shall have to limit ourselves to consideration of his discussion of the notions of *Gestalt* and signs as applied to the events of biblical history.

The question can be set out as follows. Whereas the philosopher's understanding of being is derived from his observation and contemplation of the world of existents in general, the believer's understanding of God is directed to a particular existent among existents, the unique revelation in the saving history of Israel which culminates in Christ. What then is the nature of the relation between the historical events of the revelation and the truth, that which is revealed?

It is in the first instance, as we might expect from the above extended quotation, more analogous to the relation between myth and its revealed truth. It is the perception of beauty — of an expressive form in that which is perceived — which creates a dimension between the ground and its appearing which opens our eyes to a perception of being, to a perception of an objective reality set over against the beholder which is lovely and desirable.

> This is what Kant somewhat misleadingly calls the 'disinterestedness of the beautiful': the evidence that here an essential ground has risen up into the appearance, has appeared *to me*, and that I can neither reduce this appearing form theoretically into a mere fact or a ruling principle —

[20] *The Glory of the Lord*, I, p. 139.

and thus gain control over it — nor can I through my efforts acquire it for personal use in the luminous form of the beautiful. The Being of the existent becomes perceivable as nowhere else, and this is why an aesthetic element must be associated with all spiritual perception as with all spiritual striving. The quality of 'Being in itself' which belongs to the beautiful, the demand the beautiful itself makes to be allowed to be what it is, the demand, therefore, that we renounce our attempt to control and manipulate it, in order truly to be able to be happy by enjoying it: all of this is, in the natural realm, the foundation and foreshadowing of what in the realm of revelation and grace would be the attitude of faith.[21]

Two points may be highlighted: first the unity between the ground and its appearing in the form (*Gestalt*). What Balthasar stresses throughout his work is the relationship between the medium of expression: the *Ausdrucksgestalt* and what is expressed: its *Grund*, the reality, glory, *Herrlichkeit*, which shines through the *Gestalt*. What characterises the great work of art, of music, is precisely the fittingness of its *Gestalt* to what is expressed: its necessity, '*rightness*', such that no other theme or development would do here than that which Mozart has chosen. And second, it is precisely this fittingness — the intimacy of ground and its appearing — which means that there is no question of as it were passing 'beyond' the outward form to its inner essence. The perception of the beauty, the revealed reality, glory, is certainly not just a matter of simple viewing of the object; the casual view may well fail to perceive the deeper dimensionality of the work of art, music, myth. It is only as the eyes are opened in and by the contemplation of the object itself that the beholder learns to read and understand the proportions and rightness of the form, to see the unity of ground and appearing;

---

[21] *The Glory of the Lord*, I, pp.152f.

and it is in so doing that he is inspired to love and desire what he sees.

The application of this analogy to the facts of Christian revelation is developed by Balthasar in the course of a running debate with the neo-Scholastics on the one hand and Blondel and his followers on the other. The question may be put simply: What is the relation between the 'facts', the particular experience of sacred history and the truth which is revealed in it? For the neo-Scholastics the historical particulars were *signs*, historical, discernible signs which pointed to, established the *divine authority and authorship* of the *revelatum*. Thus the events of saving history are clearly perceived, or at least perceivable by all: that to which they point, however, is something to which assent has to be given but which is not itself perceived as a revelation of truth after the manner in which truth is perceived in the aesthetic perception of the myth: there is no perception of the unity of the ground and its appearing. The understanding of truth is positivist: experience takes us so far but does not lead us into a perception of being. The events of saving history stand in an external relation to the truth which is revealed. They could have been other without affecting the substance of the *revelatum*.

The alternative way embraced in contemporary twentieth century theology focuses attention much more sharply on the *revelatum*: on the vision of the divine life which is, if not received in full, then desired and anticipated, and which has the power to illuminate and fulfil the human spirit. In its search for the truth the spirit reaches out beyond itself to embrace being and the inwardness of being which is disclosed in God's self-revelation — and so to find its true fulfilment. Balthasar argues strongly that such a tradition is powerfully represented in classical Christian theology: both in Augustine and in Thomas. And he notes their agreement on two central points:

For both the dynamism of the cognitive spirit is determined by its innermost disposition to press on to the vision of God, so much so that God's self-revelation and the elevation and grace required for the perception of his inner mysteries appear as the final stage in the perfecting of the structure of the created mind. And, secondly, they both see God's active deed of self-revelation as the bestowal of the innermost light of Being: faith endows the mind with a new light (*lumen fidei*) which does not yet allow what is thus revealed to be seen in its own principles, but which becomes comprehensible only when it is seen as the beginning of just such a vision (*inchoatio visionis beatae*).[22]

Balthasar sees Blondel and others like him — Maréchal, Rousselot — as belonging essentially to this tradition. Its dangers can be seen in the developments in modernism where the *revelatum* becomes no more than a function of the *conatus* of the human spirit. Its strengths over against the positivist traditions of Jesuit apologetics lie in the way in which the historical, positive elements of revelation are from the outset incorporated in the process of interrelation and exchange between divine and human spirit. The dangers of extrinsicism and heteronomy are avoided; the act of faith is in its very roots both 'supernatural' (because borne up by the light of faith) and 'natural' (because it is the fulfilment of all spiritual aspirations): it is rooted both objectively in God's act of revelation and subjectively, existentially in the spirit's dynamism. In this it takes account importantly of the way in which the spirit's vision is something to be striven for, not simply something accessible to all, but won only as the eyes are opened in the action of the spirit as it reaches out to embrace the other.

[22] *The Glory of the Lord*, I, pp. 148f.; see the fuller treatment of Augustine in Vol. II, pp. 95-143.

But in all this there is — so Balthasar — a tendency to press on beyond what is given in the historical events of revelation to the mysterious life in God which lies beyond it. The danger indeed is that as the objective, given revelation is seen more and more as a means to the fulfilment of the spirit's striving, so that *conatus* may become the measure of the *revelatum* itself. In this way such an understanding of faith may fail fully to appropriate themes which are central to the Christian understanding of the life of faith: the dark night of the soul where the human understanding and will are bound, where the *authority* of the revealer imposes itself in his escape from the beloved's grasp, where the soul bewails its loss.[23]

Thus while Balthasar clearly takes a very different view of the merits of each of these two tendencies, he equally clearly points to a common defect. Both positions see the events, the positive historical elements of revelation as *signs*, pointing to or transparent to the divine truth. Such a view of the place of historical facts within the process of revelation may be acceptable within a perspective which sees the *revelatum* as *true* and which finds confirmation of its truth in the — existential — benefits, *goodness* of what is revealed: *mihi adhaerere Deo bonum est.*[24] What such theologies lack is the aesthetic dimension: there is no place for a more than external or functional relationship between sign and signified. The sign is that which points one to, a means by which one rises to that which is signified. But against this, Balthasar insists that while Jesus may indeed work signs, he himself is more than a sign. He can be known only when his *Gestalt* is seen as the divine-human *Gestalt*; when what appears of him is 'seen' or 'believed' as the 'surfacing' of the personal, divine

---

[23] Balthasar points to Garrigou-Lagrange's work on Thomas and St John of the Cross as an example of the way in which the emphasis on the subjective drive of the spirit towards the divine vision leads theologians of different kinds to anticipate too eagerly the eschatological *visio beata*, The Glory of the Lord, I, p. 150.

[24] This, with suitable substitutions, will be a criticism which Balthasar will level against R. Bultmann; see The Glory of the Lord, I, p. 534.

depth. In this way Christ can be spoken of as the formal object of faith, in that God reveals himself *in* him. Looking back to Clement we can see how essential is the Trinitarian element in Balthasar's thought. Knowledge is not without faith, just as the Son is not without the Father, but neither is faith without knowledge. It is as we believe the Son that we come to know the Father. Yet such knowledge does not mean that we pass beyond the divine-human form of the Son, but rather that we come to a continually deeper understanding, through all the darkness, of the inner-Trinitarian depths of the Son's relation to the Father.

We may now attempt to draw together some of the many strands which run through this all too brief account of the background to Balthasar's work on the nature of faith-knowledge in the first volume of *The Glory of the Lord*, attempting to see how his own fundamental insights into the aesthetic dimensions of theology promise solutions to problems already much canvassed in the decades after Vatican I.

One of the points that Balthasar has often made is that there is no neat distinction in his work between fundamental theology and material dogmatics, viz., that it is not profitable to treat matters of the nature and the grounds of faith in isolation from questions of the nature of the object of faith itself. The same point is made when, as we have seen, he protests against the *analysis fidei* conceived as an isolation of faith from the knowledge of God which is proper to faith itself. There is, that is to say, a necessary and proper circularity about his work: the understanding of the subjective, experiential aspects of faith (*die subjektive Evidenz*) illuminates and is in turn illuminated by its object which enlightens and opens the eyes of faith as it informs it with the self-disclosure of divine love (*die objektive Evidenz*). Thus his work takes the form of a series of explorations, first of traditional topics from the field of dogmatics, then of Church theologians, before turning to his studies in Vol. III of the metaphysical tradition and culminating in his biblical volumes. One may also see his studies of the lives of the saints[25] as forming part of this continuing search for a deeper understanding of faith-knowledge and its object.

All this helps to explain and indeed is clearly informed by his reading of controversies and debates about the problem of the act of faith in twentieth-century Catholic theology. If faith is understood as the acceptance of the authoritative witness of Scripture and the Church to the revealed divine truth, then, at least if the analogy with acceptance of authoritative witness in the human sphere is pressed, faith will be sharply contrasted with the knowledge of the authoritative witness/witnesses. Faith will then be understood as the acceptance on trust of truth whose grounds are not yet seen, but which, beyond death, will be clearly and distinctly known. That is to say, here the vision of God is understood by analogy with knowledge as contrasted with belief, taking things on trust in the human sphere. And it follows, once this step has been taken, that a further sharp distinction has to be made between such knowledge as is presently enjoyed of God, *natural* knowledge of God, and the ultimate, *supernatural* knowledge.

As we have at least partly seen there is a rich history of criticism of these basic positions from within Catholic theology itself. In their different ways Blondelians and *nouveaux théologiens* attempted to bridge the sharp divide which was thus created between Christian faith and supernatural knowledge of God. Blondel's criticisms were founded on his philosophical analysis of human knowing and action and represented a strong corrective to the inherent extrinsicism and heteronomy of the neo-Scholastic accounts of faith. His criticisms were clearly informed by his own neo-Kantian views. The criticisms of de Lubac and the *nouvelle théologie* of the

---

[25] Cf. esp. Balthasar's two studies *Thérèse of Lisieux*, London 1953 (E.T. of *Therese von Lisieux. Geschichte einer Sendung*, Cologne/Olten, 1950), and *Elisabeth of Dijon*, London 1956 (E.T. of *Elisabeth von Dijon und ihre geistliche Sendung*, Cologne/Olten, 1952).

understanding of faith stem rather from their reading of the Fathers with their greater openness to the metaphysical tradition and centre therefore more on the divide between natural and supernatural knowledge of God. Both schools are at one, though, in attempting to relate the knowledge of God in faith, the *inchoatio visionis Dei*, to man's freedom, to his striving and natural desire for the truth, for the vision of God. Both schools equally express dissatisfaction with what Balthasar refers to as the supernatural rationalism[26] of the neo-Scholastic, Blondel looking to a more personalist understanding of theological knowledge, the *nouveaux théologiens* attempting to restore contemplation to its proper place within theology.

But if Blondel and the *nouveaux théologiens* properly drew attention to weaknesses in the neo-Scholastic understanding of faith and its object there were dangers too in their work, not least in the way their understanding of the object of faith was formed by the emphasis they placed on man's *conatus*, on the transcendence of *Geist*, that is to say by a philosophy of *Geist* as that which — naturally — seeks to transcend the limits of its empirical knowing. Subsequent developments of Blondel's approach in modernism, but also of aspects of the *nouvelle théologie* in Rahner's theology have been sharply criticised by Balthasar[27] as effectively imposing the measure of the human spirit on the divine revelation and as failing, that is, to allow due weight to the interpersonal, aesthetic character of both natural and supernatural knowledge.

Balthasar's theology may thus be seen as deeply informed by the work of Blondel and the *nouveaux théologiens* but equally as concerned to develop and strengthen their understanding of faith by further reflections on its *objective evidence*. For him the transcend-

---

[26] *The Glory of the Lord*, I, p.139.

[27] For Balthasar's criticisms of Rahner, see *Cordula*, *passim*, and R. Williams's essay in this volume.

ence of *Geist* is to be grasped, not simply in the human spirit's reaching out beyond the limits of experience to penetrate the mysteries of being but in its learning to see in the object of its contemplation the opening up of a deeper dimension; in its learning to see, that is, the *ground* which *appears* in the *Gestalt* which it contemplates. Here 'seeing' indeed transcends 'normal' sense experience, not by virtue of passing beyond that experience, but by learning to see the form, the uniqueness and distinctive otherness of what is presented to view, which is grasped precisely as we learn to see its form, the interrelation of ground and appearance, the fittingness, rightness of the expressive form as the medium of that which it manifests.[28]

From here the way opens out to a rich field of theological and philosophical exploration. It leads Balthasar to a reappraisal of the great metaphysical tradition with its roots in ancient mythology; it leads similarly to a reappraisal of the biblical tradition as rooted in the mythological world yet transcending it in virtue of the self-disclosure of divine grace and glory which lies at its heart. It leads again to a reconsideration of classical doctrines of epistemology. If such doctrines urge us to see knowledge as something generally accessible, as based that is on generally accessible experience evaluated by generally agreed procedures, then Balthasar invites us to consider again in this context the nature of aesthetic judgements, the sense in which the eyes of faith have to be opened by the grace

[28] It would be interesting to explore from this standpoint questions raised at least tentatively by some New Testament scholars about the bearing of recent literary theory on theological understanding of the authority and truth of the Biblical *texts*. I think here first of the insistence, now almost outmoded among literary critics, but still to be heard by many Biblical scholars, that texts should be allowed to speak for themselves and not simply read as windows on to another world as in so much historical critical study; second of the more recent emphases in 'reader-response criticism'. Here the text is seen as forming part of an act of communication between author and reader in which the readers' 'horizon of expectations' is transformed by the reading of the text, but which itself has a history as the text is mediated from one generation to another within a particular literary tradition. Cf. here especially H. R. Jauss, *Literaturgeschichte als Provokation*, Frankfurt 1970.

of the object which it beholds. Of the originality and creativeness of such an approach there can be little doubt, nor indeed of the rich fruits it has already yielded in Balthasar's own gargantuan labours; what still remains an open question is whether the Church at large will listen and learn.

BALTHASAR ON GOETHE

Ulrich Simon

Theologians are well known to avoid the encounter with Goethe. In German-speaking regions, both Catholic and Protestant, there is an instinctive recoiling from the great Olympian. He threatens all Christian claims in quite a singular manner. Atheists are easier to contend with in theology than believers in God who refuse to be classified. However, Karl Barth really envisaged a theological encounter, for the whole purpose of his famous *Protestant Theology in the Nineteenth Century* had been to lead up to this decisive confrontation. But, alas, it was not to be. One may perhaps add, it could not be.

In the English-speaking world the situation is different and worse. To begin with, Goethe is hardly known at all. During centenaries there is an attempt to produce *Faust*, and a few references to *Werther* find their way into journalism. But the total Goethe has never been apprehended in England or in America. The linguistic barrier is only one of many, for despite our much-vaunted European heritage and common culture the fragmentation began soon after Goethe's death. Whereas Shakespeare really is a European possession Goethe is not. In theological circles the ignorance is astounding, considering that Schleiermacher is studied at some depth. Yet this presentation of German liberal theology occurs outside its context. Goethe, Schiller, Hölderlin and many others might never have existed: the 'cultured despisers' of the Christian faith have remained as unknown as their views.

There have, of course, been many monographs in this field, e.g., on Goethe and the Bible, Goethe and Mariology. But Balthasar goes about it differently. In almost one hundred pages he endeavours to connect Goethe and Christian theology by means of the concept or aspects of *Herrlichkeit*.[1] At first this seems almost too easy, since, as any concordance shows, Goethe uses this term and its related forms with great frequency. Clearly, splendour is found on many levels and it pervades Goethe's life and perceptions.

The richness of the concept creates a difficulty. It cannot be treated in an abstract way. Goethe apprehends the world directly and in reflection. Balthasar's approach to reality as a *concretissimum* happily agrees with this view of things and he places Goethe within the broader context of what he calls the *Mediation of Antiquity*.[2] Goethe can be seen as a fighter in the battle of reconciling the modern world with its ancient roots. Balthasar assigns this effort to transcendental Reason in aesthetic operations.

Goethe resisted the trends of his time and loathed the spiritual environment, whether the weak pietistic Protestantism, with which he had once flirted in his youth, or sectarian enthusiasm, or popery and clericalism. Later he also becomes a stranger to the life at court. His escape to Italy is the turning point, for it brings the encounter with classical form. On his return Goethe remains independent of all movements. His religion is one of reverence, unalloyed by political radicalism and moral idealism. Balthasar in a catena of citations shows how the rebel of *Prometheus*, who will not pray and submit, grows into maturity through painful crises. These are so severe that they threaten to break 'the middle ground', i.e.. the ideal of the classical form itself.[3]

To understand the ruptures in Goethe's life one needs the biographical details from childhood to old age. Balthasar can only give hints and his thumbnail sketches are necessarily confined to the

---

[1] *Herrlichkeit*, III/1, pp. 682-748.
[2] '*Antike Vermittlung*', ibid., pp. 593f.
[3] Ibid., pp. 683-687.

light they throw upon the works. The titanic period of *Sturm und Drang* was not to last long and evidently contributes nothing to real *Herrlichkeit*. Balthasar is so out of sympathy with all that early enthusiasm that he merely endorses Goethe's own verdict that his pre-Italian ventures were amateurish and that until nearly forty years of age only very little was achieved. *Tasso*[4] figures as the genuine documentation of the break, for here all the tensions inherent in poetical genius struggling in a hostile and materialistic world are worked out. The defenceless heart is wholly exposed to the 'real' world. This drama, says Balthasar summarily, is by no means the pathology of the unhappy individual but the ontology of poetical existence. And Goethe has his feet in both worlds (Werther shot himself!). But so far we are not told how all this connects with *Herrlichkeit*.

Still the problem (as manifested in *Faust*) is far more complex and for Balthasar a philosophical one. He contrasts the laws of the divine coherence, apprehended in analogy, and experienced as 'divine', with the demonic Cosmos where a Faust seeks immediate identity and consequently action. 'In the beginning was the deed . . .', and that without conscience. Balthasar senses here another deep gulf between Goethe's demonic, even existentialist and erotic desire (which culminates in the pact with Mephistopheles, magic, and murder) and the eternal contemplation, the serene classicism and even grace.[5] But still we ask, how does all this connect with *Herrlichkeit*?

Balthasar continues to peruse the major works and Goethe's vigorous attempt to create a national German literature and to make the stage the centre of the spiritual and cultural home. *Wilhelm Meister*[6] symbolises this ascent from virtually nothing to splen-

---

[4] Ibid., pp. 689-691.
[5] Ibid., pp. 691-694, especially pp. 691f.
[6] Ibid., pp. 694-699.

dour; but it is doomed to failure. After Italy and the great break Goethe seems to endorse Plato's ban on the theatre. No doubt Balthasar shares this scepticism which leads Goethe to the second part of *Wilhelm Meister*, namely, of renunciation and surrender. Unfortunately this section is kept to a laconic brevity where the outsider will not easily grasp what is at stake. On the surface there are ways of and towards *Herrlichkeit*: total detachment from the world and a share in objectivity; a vocation of some sort, as a surgeon first, then as an emigrant to America to start afresh; education (the *Paideia* of the ancient world) in which the Christian religion holds the highest place; a world citizenship; a mythical supernatural Sibyl in a mysterious astral system of cosmic entelechies; and lastly the climax of the end of *Faust* with its affirmation of Dante's monotheistic and hierarchical universe of eternal blessedness. All this is . . . splendid to be sure, but how does Balthasar judge these ingredients of splendour?

Balthasar reverts to Goethe himself and his autobiography.[7] Goethe is himself nature, reflects the macrocosmos in his microcosmos, the splendour of God in his own greatness. Every moment spells newness, every act is creative, born of Eros, and step by step Goethe ascends the scale of splendour. As every concordance confirms, *herrlich* is a constant word to describe the physical bloom, the loving quintessence of life, goodness and beauty, enjoyment and also suffering. Goethe the geologist, even during years of disenchantment, never loses his grip on this *Herrlichkeit, multum in parvo*.

But how does this 'pagan' Yes to the world, which Goethe himself distanced sharply from traditional Christianity and even more polemically from Church institutions, fare with a contemporary Christian critic? Balthasar stresses Goethe's freedom from the taint of pantheism, despite Spinoza's influence.[8] *Herrlichkeit* is the key to

[7] Ibid., pp. 699–706.
[8] Ibid., p. 706.

closed doors which, when opened, lead the non-pantheist and non-deist to further apartments, floors, and mansions of individuated splendour: from the bright sky to a spectacular view, from gentle delicacy to heroic stature, and thence to the sacred. Immanence and transcendence criss-cross without giving rise to chaos. Form (*morphe*) dominates the circles of organic and inorganic nature.[9] But still Balthasar withholds his judgement as a Christian. Or does his simple reporting from the sources imply not only approval but an acclamation of the cosmic metaphysics?

Goethe certainly dislikes a polarisation, as between ideal/idea and experience, but rather sees in the polarisation or the opposition of contraries an intimation of the structure of the universe. Therefore, as Balthasar observes, he is singularly free from a higher and lower spirituality and that moral critique which turns the universe into an anthropomorphic projection. Following Pythagoras and Plotinus and that unbroken tradition of the manifestation of the One in the Many, Goethe does not regard polarities as a disturbing factor. On the contrary, as Balthasar shows, the famous (infamous?) *Farbenlehre* owes its vehement polemics against Newton and all later mathematical physicists to the dogma of Light, objective and subjective, whose organ is the sunlit eye. Balthasar is at his best in explaining and summarising this basic classical doctrine of the elementary phenomenon of nature: intimation by analogy, like by like.[10]

Even so, if Balthasar were to rewrite his evaluation of Goethe's scientific papers now he would give them a more positive place in the scheme of *Herrlichkeit*. Balthasar is still inclined, as were his generation, to regard Goethe's anti-Newtonian stance and his aversion to a quantitative analysis of universal phenomena, as a quasi-mystical and subjective insight. The poet's privilege was

[9] Ibid., p. 709.
[10] Ibid., pp. 712-716.

then conceded, and the whole Pythagorean and Platonic system of reflecting harmonies, as in music, would be drawn upon to contain analogies of analogies. True, Goethe, as Balthasar notes, did give music the highest place in this universe, and this despite his somewhat simple tastes which prevented him from welcoming Beethoven and encouraging Schubert. Nevertheless our present climate sees Goethe's polemic in a different light. Without denying the presence of an Orphic element of world-harmony and the relevance of the *Novelle*, with its beautiful and legendary canvas of a harmony established between the boy and the wild beast where guns fail, we are now compelled to take Goethe's scientific papers, including the optics, seriously in their own right.

If this approach may now be called appropriate as a scientific method we reach the apex of our concern in a different and more organic way. Instead of turning to the problem of the relationship between the classical heritage and the modern world as a literary one, or as something pertaining to aesthetics in general, we adopt now a more objective stance. In other words, we are not content to indulge in subjective fancies but, with Goethe, require an objective foundation in factual knowledge. This is only limited by the fact that Goethe wrote before the electronic age, nuclear fission and fusion, particles, and radiation. Did he not have a prophetic intimation of all that?

However, Balthasar is well aware that the commerce between objective and subjective ideas is manifold and ambiguous. The latter, according to classical theories, may be radiated or acquired within the natural pattern.[11] But Man remains inevitably central and the artist's vocation is to imitate the Supreme Artist, for then the confused world of nature becomes a vehicle for the Beautiful. The hidden Paradise is thus released by the priestly and the prophetic dignity of the artist. We are back with Winckelmann's

[11] Ibid., pp. 716–723.

famous dictum of the 'Noble Simplicity and Still Grandeur' as the canon of Goethe's time, which Balthasar mentions marginally to be as ancient as the art it describes. Balthasar also reminds us that the popular application of this naturalism in aesthetics, as in the search for suitable subjects, did not succeed. Goethe also readily failed in a wholly unacceptable task of cataloguing and identifying materials for, and awarding prizes to, aesthetic programmes. Yet, as Balthasar shows at some length, Goethe traverses many stages in the search for the imitation of the Beautiful. Goethe is seen as a child of his time in affirming before the French Revolution the principles of the microcosmos of genius and its coextension with the macrocosmos of nature. The question which always needles the artist is the How: thinking, imagination, sensibility need to focus so that the immeasurable takes form and is actually born. But this birth leaves the magnificent and holy free, for it would lose its majestic Transcendence if it were used and abused by human hands and ambitions. This is the kind of classicism which the Epistle to the Hebrews mediates to the Christian: the principle by which the Divine is imprinted in nature and in man. Balthasar, however, dares not draw such a conclusion.

This is not surprising, for if we give Goethe's so-called humanism a Christian *imprimatur* do we not at the same time betray the Christian claim to a unique revelation? I can see that Balthasar is here in a quandary, probably made more acute for him by his friendship with Barth, who alleged in his famous terms that the *analogia entis* was comparable to the snake in Paradise. Though Balthasar is not a Barthian he knows what is at stake, and therefore the following discussion[12] — still on the place of classicism — is of absorbing interest, both for what he says, and for what he does not say. According to Balthasar Goethe's stance under the heading of *Herrlichkeit* is a reflection in the inner life and a quickening process. But

---

[12] Ibid., pp.723-748.

this inner experience bursts into the feast of classical triumphalism, such as painted by Mantegna.[13] Balthasar obviously enjoys Goethe's participation in the triumphalism of the Renaissance and the Baroque. Christian readers of this last quarter of the twentieth century may at first shudder at this 'triumphalism', as inherited from the classical past, simply because the left wing propaganda in the Church has continually eroded emotional support for what is now called 'triumphalism' in a pejorative sense. But Balthasar obviously responds lovingly to the trumpets and shawms, the processions of martial character, the abundance of cornucopia and flowers, and all sensual aspects and elementary signs of ecstatic trains of triumph, for this art transports nature into a symbolic celebration. Rightly and memorably does Balthasar hail these climacteric intimations of greatness in Goethe's total achievement, from beginning to end. Here is and remains the reflection of cosmic light and effervescence.

The uninitiated can hardly help misunderstanding Goethe's triumphalism. He will appreciate that he did not seek personal glory. Nor did he fall into the trap of identifying the supreme greatness with national aspirations. His reluctance cost him much popularity during and after Napoleon's 'triumphs'. Far more telling is the idealism of the eighteenth century which stretched out towards a unified world picture. We know how sharply Hölderlin reacted in this generation, both in the search and in the disenchantment after failure. But Goethe, despite years of black depression and many sayings of extreme despair, rose above the contradictions. For him they become even desirable. Balthasar shows how the youngster watched the busy fairground and its amusing fermentations. As in every other respect Goethe never outlives genuine observations but reflects these impressions. In a felicitous formulation Balthasar characterises Goethe's symbolical interpretation of earthly pomp,

---

[13] Ibid., p. 724.

as once witnessed in 1765 in Frankfurt: the feast has become a metaphysical experience.[14] What is again perceived to be at stake is the principle of correspondence, operating in the sphere of heavenly transcendence and earthly reflection. The individual effects his kinship to the divine in this relationship by affirming it in reverent submission and prayer. So far Goethe in his retrospect, and Balthasar utters not a word of criticism.

Goethe's court business, his share in ceremonial, even the craze of the carnival, of masks, and popular excesses, exposes him to charms which involve danger. Pleasures and disgust pertain to the madness. How does this breathless traffic along the Corso find a niche in *Herrlichkeit*?

Balthasar finds an answer to this query in Goethe's *Sankt-Rochus-Fest* of 1814.[15] This precious prosaic description, which Staiger[16] hails as a unique jewel, both unprecedented and without successor in literature, deals not only again with the spectrum of booths and stallholders, statues and standards, baldachinos and Catholic festivities, but also the specific religious problem of humanism, and the tension which concerns us throughout. Balthasar can give us only a hint, and the English-speaking reader is not likely to come across this Raphael-like canvas of a classical and yet topsy-turvy world. Goethe faced two things he now disliked and looked at from a distance with ironic eyes: political issues, and romantic Catholicism (better though than arid Protestantism!). Nevertheless, the translation of both into art serves Goethe to humanise the Christian world. He speaks of a 'Christian Mount Olympus'. This 'new religion' confesses a supreme deity, not like Zeus, but human, and he refers to the Father of the mysterious Son who represents the moral attributes of deity on earth. He greets the amazing clover leaf

---

[14] Ibid., pp. 724f.
[15] Ibid., pp. 726f.
[16] E. Staiger, *Goethe*, vol. 3, Zurich, 1959, p. 72.

which the winged innocent Dove completes. Even Virginity and Motherhood are acceptable as a legacy from the pagan antiquity. Staiger rightly comments that Goethe expresses himself with cunning; his artfulness pursues the twofold goal of alienating the all too familiar and rejecting the absurdity of the Christian confession. In this spirit Goethe writes his 'bright and inwardly pious presentation' of Catholic festivity.[17] Critics commented that he did not seem to know the difference between sacraments and ceremonies. But the humanist does not bother as long as he can appropriate harmonious ease: bread and wine, so to speak, with humour and goodwill. The spiritual becomes tangible, the material takes on a reflection from beyond. Distance remains; the ageing poet and scholar knows too much. The Rochus Feast unites abstraction with concrete images in a unity which may be called 'impressionistic'.[18]

And so on to *Faust*[19] under the heading of Half-Reality, since beauty requires a shadow over reality. Balthasar certainly feels with and like Goethe in his understanding of beauty as a channel of *Herrlichkeit.* The glory of aesthetic perfection brings rebirth and new growth from within. It is as much certain truth as an encounter with God. But a dream-like quality surrounds this glory, most perfectly articulated in Faust's marriage with Helen of Troy. And since this marriage in its unreal reality symbolises the utopian ideal of the union between Hellas and Germania we look again at, and for, *Herrlichkeit,* not directly but as longed for. What seems may also reflect reality, and the ideal, and even its failure, may still reflect the elemental truth, the glow of opposing forces. The elements which pervaded the work of the young Goethe have lost nothing of their force in the closing years of his creativity. Balthasar does not censure Goethe's expression of the Gospel of the Beautiful as it is communicated to our perception and distilled by

[17] From a letter of Feb. 1813 quoted in Staiger, op. cit., p. 73.
[18] Ibid., p. 79.
[19] *Herrlichkeit,* III/1, pp. 728-732.

our apprehension. But Balthasar ends this brief discussion on Appearance with a somewhat sober and negative estimate. Goethe had not failed to take into account the Ugliness of Paganism (e.g., the Nibelungs) and once you admit the radiation of the sordid you are recalled to earth and the deceit of appearances. Hence, concludes Balthasar, Goethe's *Herrlichkeit* suffers from an instability alien both to the antique world and even more to Christianity, since it is only a mode of reflection, not a substance in itself. Goethe, sympathises Balthasar, knew only too well that the Form of beauty as well as the Force of Eros is set in twilight. Only the moment (dawn, sunrise) allows us a fragmentary entry into the glow. No wonder Helen and Faust not only have to separate, but their child must die.

So we are forced to confront not only Goethe but also *Herrlichkeit* in a light of doubt and even disenchantment. Since, in human experience at least, nothing lasts, only the moment, the twinkling of an eye, can grant satisfaction. Indeed, as we remember, Goethe's terms of Faust's pact with Mephistopheles hinge on the 'moment': 'If I can say to the moment stay, abide, continue',[20] and thus seize its beauty then I must also surrender to the defeat of being satisfied: the soul is then ready to be caught by the devilish minions. Balthasar does not deal with this intricate problem in any detail, which is a pity; for although the terms of the pact seem to be almost forgotten for the greater part of Faust II they do re-emerge at the end and pose the greater problem of Faust's salvation. This occurs against the pact's blood-signed stipulations, for Faust ironically does ask for the lasting moment (true, in the subjunctive mood and mistaking the preparations for his own burial as colonial land reclamation by a free people), and yet is not only reprieved but rising into an undeserved bliss. He is not a repentant sinner. It would be worth asking why he is admitted to the *Herrlichkeit* which Christians in the traditional scheme of things barred to murderers.

[20] *Faust* Part 1, Faust's Study, 2nd scene.

For Balthasar Goethe's response to the fading moment, once experienced as the intimation of eternity, is to be heard throughout his work. The author of *Werther* shuns the disgust of living, nausea at the dreary repetitiveness of experience, especially love. This suicidal tendency develops as he surveys the ruins of time. Nor is the future bright: the human race is not made for wisdom or happiness. English readers must attempt to get hold of good translations of the *Elected Affinities* and *Wilhelm Meister* to appreciate Balthasar's sketching-in of Goethe's specific scepticism.

The marvellous surprise — almost in itself a piece of *Herrlichkeit* — is not only Goethe's survival, made possible by a deliberate and successful policy of keeping misery and death at bay (no funerals to be routed near his house, failure to attend his mother's funeral), but also his affirmation of life. It is a pity that *Hermann und Dorothea* is virtually unknown outside German-speaking countries and, if rumours are to be trusted, proving unteachable to their young people. Here we have classical culture lived against a background of war, refugees, exile, etc. The image of the stumbling, tripping, moving, sprightly foot — on the way from privation to a stable home and marriage — is a constant reminder of the deceitfulness of riches and the transitoriness of life. But the inward affirmation of life is not negative once you renounce false expectations. Balthasar is right in his interpretation of Goethe's unique and central call to a form of resignation. As he briefly reminds the reader the concept of resignation expresses the Stoic policy in antiquity and is caught up in the Christian term of surrender.[21] But Goethe eschews both and often relies on Spinoza as a symbol rather than as a source to portray a 'giving-up', neither Stoic nor Christian.

Balthasar comments on the 'tragic Eros', the divided selves in *Pandora*,[22] proximate to the 'tragic pathos' found in Shakespeare's Son-

---

[21] *Herrlichkeit*, III/1, pp. 734f.
[22] Ibid., pp. 735f.

nets — only even more hopeless. I like Balthasar's helpful judgement: Pandora is personified Absence of the erotic longing for wholeness, in contrast to Dante's Beatrice. But our quest cannot end there, for can *Herrlichkeit* be retrieved despite loss and resignation?

The question does not admit an easy answer. Christians generally identify resignation of some sort with sacrifice in a specific sense. Goethe seems to resist this pietism which he abandoned after his earliest years. Yet his life, and especially his highly moving loves as an old sage, not to mention loss of son and friends, move into a transcendent realm of high pathos. Balthasar rightly turns to *Elected Affinities* as the most moving metaphor which transforms fiction into truth.[23] The story is amazingly 'modern' since it envisages a freedom of sexual relationships perhaps found in eighteenth century comedies but never seriously entertained as an ethical conflict with a religious issue above it. What is marriage without love? Should marriage stand in the way of love? Is the image of new love liable to the charge of inner adultery? Again the erotic moment seems to stand over against the eternal principle of union. Goethe has created in Ottilie a '*herrliches Kind*', but this wonderful child poses the problem acutely, and she, as Balthasar stresses, does become a sacrifice precisely because she does not resign. She must go further in vowing abstinence from food and speech, consecrated to dying and death. She also converts disaster into martyrdom and the end of the novel is a stylised version of unselfish love in intercession.

Balthasar retains his reserve and does not fully acclaim Goethe's last stage as a Catholic stance, with a Madonna figure and miracles as a delicate framework. Strangely, Balthasar acclaims only the convergence of Spinoza, Christianity, Homer, and the pre-Platonic forms of thought. I suspect that the professional theo-

---

[23] Ibid., pp. 737–739.

logian and dedicated churchman and priest must distance himself from Goethe's individualism which does exclude the sacramental and corporate nature of Catholic practice.

This reserve may also explain Balthasar's curious reluctance to get involved in the salvation of Faust. Since he wrote, so much has been said on both sides, viz., that the Dantesque ending in which an unrepentant Faust is caught up in heaven by angels, innocent babes, intercessory ladies, mystical saints remains unacceptable to Christians, and moreover is not intended by Goethe to promote Christianising notions of salvation; or, in straight contrast, that Goethe is the apostle of salvation by grace extending even to modern man in his haste and energy to transform the world. Instead Balthasar is content to remind us that Goethe classified the earthly Jesus among the wise and the prophets, a 'divine Man', a true philosopher.[24] This brings him to a well-trodden field which has also been ploughed with the thoroughness appropriate to a Ph.D. thesis by many a researcher, viz., Goethe's attitude to the Bible.[25] Leaning towards a reformed or progressive Catholicism he rejects Protestant supernaturalism, or revelation and orthodox moralism. His love for the Bible remains indisputable, the basis of an ecumenical piety and goodwill and of the peculiar human longing for bliss and love. But, it must be admitted, clichés such as these cannot be said to compete with the grandeur of the tensions in Faust, where he *uses* biblical texts and episodes. Faust the criminal resembles Ahab who has Naboth murdered, and Faust is certainly never a Christ figure. He does not redeem, he is redeemed. Hence, it seems to me, Balthasar and his generation are too timid in their theological understanding of Goethe. Indeed, one could claim that the last Act brings together two strands of doctrine often held to be incompatible: the justification by faith, *sola gratia*, on the one hand, and the eligibility for salvation, through moral striving, on the other.

[24] Ibid., p. 742.
[25] Ibid., pp. 742–745.

This salvation of Faust is not an incidental matter. Out of it arises the Goethean experience of conditional immortality. In the conversations with Eckermann Goethe speaks serenely about death. It is, of course, his own death he views with a strong conviction that the deity owes him a completion of what has been begun. This is the doctrine and the assured hope of Entelechy, a philosophical concept applied both to the physical sciences and to human existence. Goethe envisages, as we have seen, an organic fulfilment which crowns the energetic striving in time. Hence he pairs the mystical salvation, as portrayed in Faust, with a naturalistic survival of the deserving. The immortality is certainly conditional inasmuch as no entelechy can be thought of in the absence of a positive germ of life. This germ is based on desire as well as an attainment of spiritual stature. At this stage it does not concern Goethe to tell us what happens to the so-called ordinary people. He is not interested in punishment and damnation, but he certainly implies a gradual upward movement through purgation.

Balthasar ignores this aspect of *Herrlichkeit*. His key to the final legacy of Goethe is not to be found in atheism nor in religion, but in cosmic being as regulated in the natural universe.[26] Yet it is an affirmative legacy which Balthasar contrasts with Hegelian and Marxist self-fulfilment and develops across many eddies of psychological and sociological novels to Heideggerian being. Countless names indicate the complex fragmentation which has some links with Goethe, if only by opposing his genius. Balthasar altogether shuns the 'new naturalism', derides Teilhard de Chardin, and regards Heidegger as the heir to the task of mediating antiquity, and thus *Herrlichkeit*, to Christian theology.[27]

This conclusion reached more than twenty years ago will not now find many subscribers. Balthasar's readers will not want to drop the

---

[26] Ibid., pp. 746-748.
[27] Ibid., pp. 769-787.

matter there. The 'miracle of Goethe' is mentioned again in his creativeness for its gift of fullness. This Grace in Nature is not anthropological as with Schiller, nor a past glory as with Hegel. The decay and disillusionment after Goethe lead, and must lead, straight to Marx and thence to our disastrous age. No wonder Balthasar invites us to lament dispassionately the vanishing of *Herrlichkeit*: the transcendent glory loses its savour in tasteless academic activity and psychoanalytical research. Decomposition prevails and aesthetics as a subject is dead. Yet the light shines and human beings are driven by, and created in, love. Balthasar sees Goethe at least in the long chain of a tradition which regards light and love not only as appearances but as radiations of reality. Can a metaphysic be constructed which will rid us of spiritual bankruptcy and a total void?

In the section 'Love protects *Herrlichkeit*'[28] Balthasar sets out a kind of programme. He distinguishes between beauty and *Herrlichkeit* and distances himself from elated feeling and a cosmology of being. He warns against the irresponsible acceptance of polarised Light and Darkness as symbols of an ontological unity, or God. He cannot tolerate a trendy theology which juggles with systems in a 'neutral' metaphysics. The concrete encounter with the Other, Man with Man, is indispensable if *Herrlichkeit* is to be apprehended and sustained. Goethe would not disagree with this. After all, one of his most famous poems begins with 'Man, be noble, helpful and good . . . ', which sounds a little trite in translation. Moreover, neither Goethe nor Balthasar could realise that the sub-human electronic age would spawn a totally amoral and non-spiritual world, whose children make blank faces at moral *Herrlichkeit*. Christa Wolff's recent writings portray the apathy (in the DDR) which greets the teacher's presentation of the ideal.

But the polarisation has remained with us and grows daily.

---

[28] Ibid., pp. 964–984.

Goethe's failed creatures evoke the liveliest response: Werther, Prometheus, Wilhelm Meister, Faust. The infidelities of *Elected Affinities* touch on the latest local gossip. This may not pertain to *Herrlichkeit*, except in a strictly dialectical manner. Our plight and our need are already powerfully stated at the end of Goethe's autobiography in the Latin tag, *Nemo contra deum nisi deus ipse*, taken over from Spinoza. This 'tremendous saying' refers to the struggle in the universe, where demonic powers of elementary force and destructive intent battle against human reason and ethical principles. Despite the citation Goethe transcends a dualism in which god fights god. The chain of being, the universe, the nature of light, the reflection of splendour, the correspondence of the lesser with the major emerge from the struggle. Balthasar has at least put Goethe on the map of theological analysis in the Christian world threatened by the total loss of *Herrlichkeit*.

IDENTITY AND ANALOGY:
BALTHASAR'S HÖLDERLIN AND HAMANN.

Martin Simon

As a literary critic, I came to 'Hölderlin' to bury, not to praise it.

Balthasar's Hölderlin is framed by the 'night' of atheism.[1] Here is
no piously naive Christianiser, making straight the little crooked-
nesses which the path of the history of the mind has sometimes
indulged in; the first pages draw a firm line between Hölderlin's
religion and Christianity. The ancient world reigns 'supreme': the
'theophanous Nature-cosmos' to whose glory Hölderlin 'transferred all the forces and motifs of Christian revelatory glory'.[2] In
these pages we find 'all Christ's prerogatives made over' to Diotima, the priestess of love, and that 'true pantheistic mediator'
Empedocles; and when Hölderlin sought to return to Christ 'no
more was left... than a tree stripped bare of leaves, an empty trea-
sure-chest'; while, in a most important footnote, Balthasar's sin-
cerity and clear-sightedness are well demonstrated by the rejection of the aspiring Christian interpreters of 'Friedensfeier'.[3]

The theological basis for Hölderlin's excommunication is also
decisively stated. 'In that he took up his definitive philosophical
standpoint beside Parmenides-Heraclitus... the basis... was identity and not analogy, which enables ... agreement with Leibniz-
Shaftesbury, Schelling-Hegel ... '[4] Later we read that 'Homer's
"analogy" (God-world) is interpreted in terms of Heraclitean-

[1] *Herrlichkeit*, III/1, pp. 644, 682.
[2] Ibid., p. 645.
[3] Ibid., p. 645, especially n. 6.
[4] Ibid., p. 645.

Parmenidean "identity"',[5] a radical statement, for it means that 'the classical difference between gods and men dissolves into the idealistic difference between . . . spirit and . . . Nature'.[6] As for Empedocles: 'Hölderlin has broached the innermost treasures of Christ, and placed them at the disposal of a messiah of identity.'[7]

On the first page of his chapter on Hamann Balthasar writes: 'Christianity is the front on which he takes up his outpost'.[8] Against whom does Hamann, the 'faithful Christian',[9] defend Christianity? Mendelssohn, Herder, Nicolai, Jacobi, Starck, Frederick II, is the list, but we, thinking of the 'night' of atheism, must say that these are not sufficiently significant opponents. Against Kant; and if against the 'Moses of our nation',[10] then Hamann must also be the 'conscience incarnate of the advancing German Idealism'.[11] 'How close he was . . . to becoming the theological mentor . . . of German Idealism.'[12]

'Analogy' is the key. 'The principle Hamann follows and to which everything he writes is related he himself called analogy.'[13] How may this principle be defined? 'In so far as God is *causa prima*, everything that happens in the world is divine; "however, everything divine is also human, since man can neither act nor suffer save after the analogy of his nature".' 'In these aesthetics beauty will be treated as a transcendental concept constituted by analogy, and analogy will claim the status of the central method, so that no objective or historical sphere of existence can be either excluded,

---

[5] Ibid., p. 665.

[6] Ibid., p. 647.

[7] Ibid., p. 674.

[8] *Herrlichkeit*, II, p. 603.

[9] Ibid., p. 642.

[10] 0. Friedrich Hölderlin, in the larger Stuttgart edition [− SE] (ed. Friedrich Beissner and Adolf Beck), VI, 305 (Letter 172).

[11] *Herrlichkeit*, II, p. 604.

[12] Ibid., p. 643.

[13] Ibid., p. 639.

or falsified through open or secret identification . . . for we are shown an all-embracing beauty . . . none other than the glory, the *schechina*, of God.'[14] 'The analogy provided by our animal house-keeping is the only ladder to the anagogic knowledge of the spiritual economy.'[15] Man must see himself, in particular as the unique user of language, in analogy to God.

But Balthasar-Hamann's definitions by no means afford a definitive barrier between Christianity and 'identity'. That the presence of God permeates the world and man, that God's glory is all-embracing beauty, these ideas lead easily to Hyperion's 'But man is a god, so soon as he is a man. And if he be a god, then he is beautiful'.[16] The introductory summary to Hamann's conception of *kenosis* — 'The God-man is the key to God and the world alike' — will stretch to comprehend Michelangelo's risen Christ, Winckelmann's divinely-human Greeks, Hyperion's hereticism and the false climax of Hegel's *Phenomenology*. The theme of Socratic ignorance belongs in the *Sturm und Drang*, itself part of the incipient Romantic movement. 'For Hamann, the jurisdiction of reason as conceived in the Enlightenment does not extend to the areas of decisive truth; as we define this thesis more closely we shall see how near and how far from Kant he is.'[17] But the 'closer definition' leaves the distance from Kant still only intuitively apparent; for neither the comment 'reason is absolutely dependent upon the senses' nor Hamann's own complaint 'to what purpose such a violent, unwarranted, wilful divorce of what Nature has joined together?'[18] amount to more than a paraphrase of Kant's own strict insistence on the absolute dependence of human thought upon the senses. If we gain an intuitive sense of Christian feeling from this

---

[14] Ibid., p. 609.
[15] Ibid., p. 613.
[16] Quoted, *Herrlichkeit*, III/1, p. 653.
[17] *Herrlichkeit*, II, p. 629.
[18] Quoted, ibid., p. 628.

chapter, we also feel the by no means easy, indeed wearingly intractable, task undertaken by Hamann in 'defending' Christianity intellectually, with that double-edged weapon, systematic and philosophical theology. Is the distinction between analogy and identity sufficient?

Balthasar laid down this distinction in the first two pages of 'Hölderlin'. Yet his description of how the classical difference between gods and men 'dissolves' — 'The glorious is equally holy and equally divine when it is *Hen* (spirit) as when it is *diapheron* (Nature), when a "god" as when "man"' — retains the premiss of analogy. By placing 'god' parallel to 'spirit' and 'man' to 'Nature' he reverses the epistemological reduction of 'spirit' to 'man', while 'equally' should be irrelevant, since it presupposes a hierarchy that no longer exists.

These adverbs of analogy ('equally', 'in so far as', 'like [unto]') often slip into what in Hölderlin were straightforward expressions of 'identity'. Hyperion the heretic says 'Oh, if a Father's daughter glorious Nature be, is not the daughter's heart his own? Her innermost being, is't not he?'; Balthasar paraphrases 'Nature is glorious in so far as she reveals God'.[19] Similarly, 'things and beings are holy in so far as they point to the presence of the eternal Spirit and intimate his infinite worth.'[20] This case presents the translator with a dilemma, since he must in English write either a small or a capital s; actually the context is so strongly affected by the word 'worth' that even 'spirit' sounds Christian; Hölderlin would never use 'worth' like this because it is too stolidly ethical. And what of the heading to the final section, 'The apocalypse of the spirit'? 'With the help of the spirit humanity will . . . come to own the gift [of revelation] from within.'[21] Hamann writes, or rather trumpets,

---

[19] *Herrlichkeit*, III/1, p. 649.
[20] Ibid., p. 651.
[21] Ibid., p. 678.

'GOd', with two initial capitals. For indeed the gap between the Holy Spirit and the human 'spirit' is wide.

So too the titanically heretical Hyperion is not criticised but disarmed. The Homeric transfiguration of the hero combined with the 'dissolving' of Homeric 'analogy',[22] a potent hubristic brew, Balthasar finds belied by Hölderlin's adoption of the 'Platonic *theion*' which then becomes the key to an 'understanding' of certain vital lines from the Diotima epigrams on the immanence of 'God' in the lovers' love. But have we not been told that Plato is interpreted in terms of 'identity'?[23]

Vagueness often results from an over-liberal use of the definite article. To this 'spirit' is inevitably susceptible. In the context of *kenosis* and *Logos*, Balthasar writes: 'His great love for Susette Gontard serves as proof positive that the descent of the spirit into the "servant-form" of defenceless need is the ultimate truth and glory of all being.'[24] Hölderlin did say something similar. But the 'spirit' involved here is his, Hölderlin's own, and thus here too is an illicit assumption — via analogy! — of identity. Listen to Hyperion: 'Then did my heart loose the reins of Fantasy, and told me, how, in the forecourt of Elysium, Hyperion's spirit with his lovely Diotima had played, e'er descending to earth . . .'.[25]

This use of the definite article where there should be a possessive adjective can amount to an actual substitution. For Hölderlin does not say that 'the heart is holy since love came to it', but 'Is not holy my heart . . . since/Love came to me?' Similarly, the question (expecting the answer 'Christ') 'when the other "intransigent genius powers" are frigid with winter, what is the single one left to a man?' and the attractive summary of Hyperion's elegiac nature 'mean-

---

[22] Ibid., p. 652.
[23] Ibid., p. 645, especially p. 643.
[24] Ibid., p. 660.
[25] *Hyperion* I/125, 3-5 (SE III).

time nothing is left to man but complete self-devotion to the departed being'[26] both beg the question: which 'man'?

For this vagueness is not so much an irritating lapse, occasional or frequent, as a methodological tool whose purpose is now amply clear: to transform the private, subjective, individual statement into public, objective, *universal* statement.

In his conclusion on the 'Fragment of *Hyperion*' Balthasar writes: 'Thus an absolute love is demanded, while at the same time the self-sufficiency of the beloved glory is feared. The fragment will, then, have achieved its ultimate goal when the hero is content to leave the beloved object of beauty as it is; when the lover is so purified as to be absolutely free from self.'[27] By means of a series of abstractions — 'love', 'the beloved glory', 'content to leave' (literally 'the leaving-be'), 'the beloved object of beauty' (German neuter gender), 'the lover' — the fictional characters, Hyperion and Melite, are eliminated (note especially the disappearance of gender) and a philosophical statement is constructed which, however, in the context of the whole chapter, carries the strong suggestion that the 'beloved glory' and 'beloved object of beauty' may constitute the search, by himself but dimly perceived, of a lover of Christ.

But the vital significance of this Christianisation is not that Christ is subliminally substituted for Melite. Throughout the genesis of the novel the hero is ultimately object-less; the fictional realm represents the bounds of a dream within which the (author's) self with its desires is imaginatively projected into an ideal landscape, a heroic story and a cosmic setting; the purpose is not to find another, but to see the selfsame self, to create a mirror. Or how could the final and aesthetically-fulfilled version present a lover who has transcended all the bonds of human affection and stands alone, as

[26] *Herrlichkeit*, III/1, p. 648, 657.
[27] Ibid., p. 668.

the sufficient reason — however attractively qualified — for himself?

In this light, Balthasar's intrusion of Christ is in the first place (that is, structurally) the introduction of a thou, an object for the 'I', a relationship. It is not so much a religious-dogmatic as an ethical act, bending the author's intention out towards the world. But this moral justification does not move the literary critic. The last letter of the 'Fragment' begins not with a universal statement, but with the words, 'Still I sense without finding'.

The most vital aspect of this process of universalisation concerns Balthasar's treatment of the Pietistic tradition. The use of 'heart' in 'the poet's heart'[28] and 'that deeper intensity binding the single heart to the heart of the All'[29] creates virtually Pietistic expressions, as does 'a soul' in 'the divine can only be present . . . when a soul is capable of the act and the mood . . . intensity';[30] and compare the substantivised adjective 'the experiencing one' in 'Thus to be touched and called upon conceals — beyond the reach of all thought — a promise without end, confronting one who experiences it with an absolute demand dischargeable only with payment of life itself.'[31]

I would never deny not only that 'heart' and 'soul' belong to Christian tradition but also that they are in principle usable as abstractions. But here a different principle pertains, a unique and indissoluble context. The statement 'Between these two forms of suffering is the apocalyptic post of the poet's heart' is illegitimate because it purports to know more than can be known, namely, the poet's 'heart'. For his heart does not belong to a (religious) community or institution, but to himself. Instead of 'individual', let us have the correct counterpole to 'universal': 'lyrical'.

---

[28] Ibid., p. 677.
[29] Ibid., p. 654.
[30] loc. cit.
[31] loc. cit.

The distinction between poetic and philosophical statement, which is reflected in linguistic form (most obviously in the difference between poetic and prosaic form), reflects personal intention. There are vital moments when this foremost concern of literary investigation should have become imperative:

'The poet consistently rejects any conception of the *parousia* (as of the Christian faith in general) according to which "the giver of a revelation does everything by himself, and the one who receives the revelation may not even rise up to take it".'[32] The sentence is so formulated as powerfully to suggest that only on the given condition (the quoted clause) is Hölderlin against the *parousia* and Christianity. In itself the condition is quite orthodox. But it comes from a letter (to the 'Fichteaner' Sinclair) in which the Christian God is implicitly identified with the Absolute I; it is thus being used not as a qualification but as a refutation. It therefore cannot be maintained that this is Hölderlin's only reservation.

Balthasar concludes that 'Empedocles' is an attempt at an 'intellectual construction of a figure of redemption parallel to the Christ', an attempt which by its nature inevitably fails. This is true, but raises the pressing question why Hölderlin should have made such an attempt. In stopping short of this question, Balthasar retains the naive possibility that it was an act, however misguided, of Christian piety.

His final section, 'The apocalypse of the spirit', opens with the statement: 'In Christian belief, it is from the spirit sent by him that the ascending redeemer receives glory in the history of the world; and it is good that the earthly form vanishes, or else the spirit could not come.'[33] There follows Hölderlin's poetic interpretation (in 'Patmos') of what is certainly the same belief. But can one describe Hölderlin's vision as 'harsh' in the same way as the doctrine is

[32] Ibid., p. 678.
[33] Ibid., p. 677.

'harsh': 'and there at/Their side, as 'twere a plague, went walking the shade of their dear one'? Even the inflamed imagination of a Christian mystic in some desert could not think of Christ's presence as a 'plague'. Hölderlin's vision represents a pure and macabre intensification which clearly exceeds the Christian's 'it is good that' and passes into the literary critic's domain. But by opening with 'In Christian belief' and then not answering the inevitable question, Balthasar leaves the Christian doctrinal faith hanging over the quoted text.

Just twice Balthasar raises himself up to his full stature, and sternly re-demarcates the line of Christianity. In the dark foreboding of the atheism with which the chapter ends, Hölderlin's 'divine absence' is exposed as a benignly harmonious interpretation of the bitter reality of nihilism: 'this darkest of shadows is inseparable from any kind of thinking based on identity'. But above all, in the finest piece of the chapter, a lengthy account of the parallels between Empedocles and Christ suddenly concludes with the question 'But what divides the two figures?',[34] followed, at last, by the definitive antithesis between analogy and identity. And by 'definitive' I mean that his gradual reconstruction of Hölderlin's reconstruction of Christ has gradually aroused in Balthasar what the creation of God by man should arouse in a Christian: a trace of anger.

So, despite his opening, Balthasar does find a kind of Christianity in Hölderlin. Indeed, this conviction lends to his chapter a note of sorrow, conveying, ultimately, that the poet is denied the personal fulfilment of Christianity (for example, the consolation of a last 'return' to Christ) by forces, both in and outside himself, that, driven on by the might of history, could not be withstood. There is an argument underlying this belief which the methodical vagueness indicated above merely supports, but which is never really stated.

[34] Ibid., p. 675.

It is that Hölderlin's participation in German Idealism is essentially unwilling. German Idealism therefore represents and expresses — as philosophy indeed always must —the blind movement of history against which the individual could not and cannot prevail; the argument emerges in final outline when one recalls the traditional sketch of western philosophy: Hegel, then Marx. So the entire crushing weight of the materialism of modern industrial society waits in the background; and its idea, the absolute rule of man, is anticipated by Hegel and by German Idealism *in toto*.

Thus Balthasar says: 'The further he went the more resolutely did Hölderlin turn his back on the Idealistic philosophy and its destruction, through cold reflection and speculation, of the experience of theophanous reality.'[35] There then follows the fundamental distinction between identity and analogy on the basis of Parmenides-Heraclitus. The argument is, then, that the relationship between (Hölderlin's) poetry and (the Idealistic) philosophy corresponds to the familiar dichotomy between heart and mind, feeling and reason.

But the (implicit) argument goes further. 'If the unsolved philosophical conflict (Idealist against ancient philosophy) reaches to the very centre of the poetic tragedy.... the poet still cannot abandon either of the two poles, because in secret it always has been and always will be the third, Christian position that determines his life and feeling.'[36] Balthasar's hypothesis postulates a triangle of which one angle is 'secret'.

To prove the existence of this third, secret angle, the overt presence of elements of the Christian tradition is really irrelevant. That includes Balthasar's account of the 'transfer' of 'all the Christian forces and motifs' ('glorious', 'holy', 'majestic'). His argument must rest on demonstrating Hölderlin's (Christian) deviation from

[35] Ibid., p. 645.
[36] Ibid., p. 660.

Idealism, and therefore depends absolutely on 'feeling' as opposed to 'reason'.

And indeed, both in the discussion of *Hyperion*, in which Balthasar constantly but allusively associates Diotima, the 'priestess of love', with Christ, and in the crucial section 'Poor love',[37] in which Hölderlin's conception of the 'spirit' is related to the Christian doctrine of *kenosis*, 'feeling' and 'heart' are identified with 'love' and, via the New Testament, via Johannine Christianity, via Pietism, with a 'secret' longing for Christ.

But from whom does the theme of 'love' distinguish Hölderlin? 'Hölderlin contemplates the glory of the ancient world with Christian eyes, and a Christian heart which unquestionably sees and understands it as the glory of love.'[38] The contrast is not with 'objective' Idealism, but with Greece and, specifically, with Parmenides-Heraclitus: 'With Hölderlin the *kenosis* of the One-and-All is *the* poetic theme ... God's cosmic-pantheistic self-depletion.'[39]

Whether or not the assumption that Parmenides-Heraclitus represents Hölderlin's 'ultimate philosophical standpoint' is justified (Spinoza, who so influenced Schelling's turn away from Fichte, goes unmentioned), it is not justified to play off the two poles Idealism-Greece against one another in order to create an illusory triangle Idealism-Christianity-Greece. For Idealistic 'identity' arose out of a breakdown of the analogical ladder, a breakdown that began with Christianity itself and its humanisation of the fiercely numinous Divine, proceeded through the mediæval ensurance (already anticipated in the cousinhood between Christianity and the mystery religions) of the immortality of the soul, and gathered pace in the late Renaissance with its elevation of man, leading finally to an elevation of the individual (Romantic ideal-

---

[37] Ibid., pp. 665f.
[38] Ibid., p. 646.
[39] Ibid., pp. 647f.

ism) undreamed-of by Parmenides and Heraclitus. The elements of Christian tradition that arise inevitably, within the context of German philhellenism, from the contrast between Idealistic and Greek 'identity' do not amount to a third angle of equal value. There is a great danger in identifying the historical individual too closely with the ideas he is involved with. The history of ideas is not geometrically symmetrical, but linear.

Furthermore, the very dichotomy between reason and feeling is nothing less than the first principle of Tübingen Idealism. It was this that inspired the search for a 'real' philosophy to counter the dead abstraction of reason — the legacy of the Enlightenment — and led in the end to 'objective' Idealism. This in turn is directly related to the appropriation of the Johannine Logos-Pneuma-Eros, for that Christology itself arose out of the marriage between Greek abstract thought and the Judaic tradition of revelation. Thus the complex of Christian ideas surrounding Jesus himself — incarnation, revelation, concreteness, sensuality, reality — provided the model for the self-depletion of the Infinite in, through, by, love: 'Phänomeno-logie', 'Logik'.

This means nothing less than the dependence of Idealism on the weakening (humanisation) of the structure of analogy in Christianity itself. Thus Parmenides-Heraclitus are at least closer to Judaic analogy than is Idealistic identity, and were Balthasar's a genuine argument, he would have to espouse identity against analogy! Instead his thought, as it must, performs a circle, via the ambivalent term 'Christology',[40] back to the original distinction between analogy and identity;[41] while the identification of Hölderlin's Johannine idea as 'the alpha and omega of Idealistic thinking'[42] shows clearly that the suggestion of Hölderlin's deviation from Idealism has faded away.

[40] Ibid., p. 665.
[41] Ibid., p. 675.
[42] Ibid., p. 674.

It could, indeed, never have approached the status of an argument without concentrating the (implicit) contrast on Fichte,[43] whose adoption of Kant's critique does not involve Christian tradition, and without the supportive vagueness, above all in the treatment of *Geist*. *Geist* is usually translated as *spirit*, but in Hegel it means both 'spirit' and 'mind', thus comprehending the ratiocinative processes. This has its origin in Kant's 'Copernican revolution', which cautiously proclaimed the supremacy of the (human) subject of reason, as the agent, over the known (and therefore acted upon) object — even when, as in the case of religious knowledge, that object is God. The failure to distinguish Hölderlin from Idealism leaves this Idealistic premiss valid.

Balthasar's attempt to persuade has undeniable power. But this derives from his genuine insight into the crisis of Hölderlin's religious poetry, a crisis which does indeed involve the ambivalence of *Geist* and the conflict between reason and feeling. Christian interpretation is simply too blunt an instrument for its analysis. Balthasar would have had to prove that Hölderlin's deviation from Idealism consists in the attachment of the theme of 'love' to the person of Jesus. That cannot be done. But the use of the contrast between Idealistic and Greek identity to suggest such an attachment reveals the absence of a proper argument. It is not a little deceptive to create the illusion that it only remains mere suggestion because Hölderlin's Christianity is 'secret'. But this deception reflects less the wish to deceive than a struggle between reason and feeling in Balthasar himself. For his 'Hamann' contains an unshakeable criterion.

Balthasar's introductory summary of Hamann's aesthetics is dominated by a single word. Quoting 'The revelation in the flesh is the mid-point of everything',[44] he expands Hamann's 'senses of a

---

[43] Cf. especially ibid., p. 662.
[44] *Herrlichkeit*, II, p. 609.

Christian' into 'those senses which can see, hear and feel God through the flesh'.[45] Nowhere in 'Hölderlin' does Balthasar use the word 'flesh', and nowhere does Hölderlin use it in a religious context. For while 'senses' admittedly refers to the physical sphere, it is most imprecise and has overwhelmingly pleasurable connotations, a fact that only escapes notice through the illusory comprehensiveness of the dualism spirit/senses. Flesh, though, simply will not lend itself to romanticism; if left for a few days it will become extremely unpleasant, as will the *Leib* (body as potential corpse). '"Aesthetic" means the jejune, bodiless attitude, typical of the Enlightenment, which finds the crude, physical, earthly quality of Christianity, its fleshliness, its crucifixion and resurrection and *corpus meum*, too unrefined, preferring to withdraw to ... the "aethereal" edifice of the "purisms of Pure Reason".'[46] *Fleischwerdung* ('becoming flesh') means the same as incarnation; but it is not the same. And Hamann's characteristic contrast is between not spirit and senses, but *Leib-Seele*, body and soul; it occurs nowhere in Hölderlin's work.

In Balthasar's 'Hamann' there is a vital and surprisingly abstract theme which occurs only twice in 'Hölderlin' — at the two moments of denunciation: 'Yet ... the tremendous intensity was, despite all the humility ... objectively hubristic; it restricted the freedom of God.'[47] 'What divides the two figures? ... the relationship of analogy ... freedom in the divine sending, and ... the Trinity.'[48]

Yet this conception of divine 'freedom' is not as abstract as it sounds. It tells what precisely God is 'analogous' to. Looking back to my quotations introducing the theme of analogy, we can sense that the strength lay not in the concept, but in the Hebraic word

[45] Ibid., p. 622.
[46] Ibid., p. 605.
[47] *Herrlichkeit*, III/1, p. 681.
[48] Ibid., p. 675.

(*shekinah*). The mind instinctively went to the Old Testament and its conception of God: analogy to human personality, but more precisely, to masculine will.

Here, then, and not in the 'senses', is the truly irrational refutation of the 'aethereal building' of 'pure reason'; for it is thoroughly irrational to associate the Infinite with masculinity: with competition, rivalry, will to power, the lust and intoxication, the joy, of defeating an enemy; with a jealous god who tramples the grapes into bloody wine with his big graceless feet[49] or lets spittle run down his beard.[50] Were this irrationality ethical, it would not be insuperable. The objection of Romantic idealism — were it ever spoken — would be metaphysical: the tying of the Divine to an idea in its turn tied to perishing physicality. In his introduction to 'Hölderlin', Balthasar spoke of a 'more conscious return to Christ' 'at the last'.[51] What could have been more natural than to make those poems which are the pinnacle of Hölderlin's achievement, 'Patmos' and 'Der Einzige' ('The only One'), the centre of his study, seeing as they also happen to be, more than anything else Hölderlin wrote, devoted to Christ? But Balthasar keeps his distance with broad indications: 'It is by virtue of the unity of word and death that, towards the end, the figure of Christ makes its powerful resurrection.'[52]

Nevertheless, the two poems force the Christian to a decision. For they are the fulfilment of the hymnic form, which evolved out of the elegiac, the lament for Diotima. Therefore the poetry has passed from the forlorn insufficiency of personal grief to the transcendence of religious certainty and truth; this certainty must somehow be vitally related to Christ.

---

[49] Quotation, *Herrlichkeit*, II, p. 620.
[50] Quotation, ibid., p. 616.
[51] *Herrlichkeit*, III/1, p. 645.
[52] Ibid., p. 663.

The two poems are, however, also extremely difficult, and cannot be understood independently of this inwardly long, intense, preceding development.

The transition to the Hymns has gradually eliminated the 'gods of Nature', that is, Nature as the divine. Previously the infinite *Hen kai Pan* was to be worshipped in and through the priestly vessel of human consciousness, which thus itself supplies the last piece missing from the epistemologically-conceived cosmic jigsaw: 'Truly, as heroes need their wreathes, alone in the hearts of/Feeling men do enjoy the sacred elements glory.'[53] But in 'Friedensfeier', some two years later, Nature has been, within the same epistemological structure, demoted to a simile:

> Not he alone, Those unborn and eternal
> Can all be known in this sign; so too doth Mother Earth
> Herself know in the plants, themselves thus Light and Air.[54]

Greece too no longer appears as the poetry's prime concern. For Nature and Greece had really been aspects of the same thing: Nature had been the remaining appearance, and Greece the lost reality. But the change in poetic form does not mean that absence no longer pertains; and it is all the more poignant when Greece does surface, expressing in 'Germanien', but above all in 'Thränen' ('Tears') and 'Mnemosyne', no longer sorrow but a piercing pain. Greece (and not, as Balthasar mildly implied with 'when there came a more conscious return to Christ, no more was left of him than . . .',[55] Christ) is still the object of longing; Christ is related to hymnic presence and certainty.

What certainty has replaced the gods of Nature? What presence has filled divine absence? 'Friedensfeier', with its protracted

[53] Quotation, ibid., p. 655.
[54] SE III, pp. 533, 536.
[55] *Herrlichkeit*, III/1, p. 645.

development to fulfilled hymnic form (it was begun at the same time as the last elegy, in early summer 1801, and not completed till autumn 1802) and its Christocentricity, provides the most natural interpretative bridge.

Critics have long plagued themselves and others with allegorical interpretations of this poem. The presence of the 'cosmic, Germanic, world-historical spirit',[56] of Christ, Napoleon, but also of 'peace' personified, led them to analyse the whole into its parts, and sometimes to seize on a single part and make it the centre of the whole: 'the Prince of the Feast'. Yet 'peace' is not just the apostrophised utopian ideal; it is the very intangibility and insubstantiality of the Divine achieved by the poet. For the Divine is the pacified 'gods', among them not only Napoleon and Christ, but also the Christian God himself.

For what else are we to make of the forms of Old Testament analogy: 'the Lord', 'Father' and 'Son', 'the Master' who steps out of his workshop, and, especially, the consistent use of masculine singular forms? Here, in the hermetic poem, there is no question of Goethean irony. Either they are to be taken as unambivalent Christian statement (Balthasar is too wise for that), or, in view of the hymnic certainty, the poet's religion is founded on a principle antithetical to the principle represented by Napoleon, Christ – and, above all, the Christian God.

For the Christian God is indeed above all, and therefore represents the very principle under which Christ (= striving for unique divinity) and Napoleon (= striving for political 'absolute'-ism) are mere examples to be subsumed. And, in antithetical contrast, 'above all' is – literally – 'Father', Aether, *der oberste Gott* ('the uppermost God') of 'Heimkunft'. Hölderlin, reversing the New Testament, says that we know the Son now: now that we know the

[56] Ibid.

Father.[57] Previously, then, we did not know 'him'. The antithetical principles are those of analogy (old world, hard) and personification (new world, soft); of the way of the world and way of the poet. For Hölderlin has not really eliminated the principle of hierarchy[58] so much as emasculated (harmonised) it; hierarchy is quite acceptable provided that it arises out of the poet's 'innocent' fantasy. Personification, undoubtedly a vital element in Romantic poetry, is here raised to become the very definition of poetry; for if, like a child, the poet can people his own world, then the world peopled by wild will, the adult world, will dissolve.

In 'Friedensfeier', Nature (despite the poem's preface, which is a concession to the public) is not immediately the Divine. The Divine is not 'Father Aether', at least not yet, because the 'Titans' (Napoleon/Christ), or the principle in men's hearts which permits that pair to reign, are not yet 'bound'; men are not yet ready. But the Divine is present in the paradigmatic beauty of the pacification.

To understand, to sense, this beauty one must return to the original dream:

> Lost in the blue expanse, oft I look up to the Aether, and down into the holy Sea, and it doth seem, as though the gates of the Invisible opened before me and I passed away with all around me, until a rustling in the bushes awaketh from the blissful death, recalling me, all unwilling, to where I began.[59]

There is a glimpse of this dream in Balthasar's summary of Empedocles' nature:

> Proceeding from the unconditional intensity of existence

---

[57] ll. 73-75.
[58] l. 28.
[59] 'Fragment of *Hyperion*', SE III, p. 184.

with the divine All, whence his divinity ('I and the Father are one'), Empedocles falls into *kenosis* and, after recognising this ... as mankind's errant alienation from itself, thereupon resolutely devotes himself to death for the sake of love and atonement; that death which achieves a representative reconciliation of time with eternity and opens the prospect of an eschatological promise.[60]

Born of the difference between time and eternity, it is — how can I describe it? — a dream of sheer lightness, nothingness, freedom from all the weight of existence, from the mirror of one's own physicality that is other people; and an infinite surrender.

Thus the antithetical principles of 'Friedensfeier' ultimately go back to the myth of the Fall from innocence which so dominated the thinking mind of this period, but which dominated Hölderlin's poetic career with such unparalled intensity that it remained beneath the surface, where it has escaped the notice of the critics.

Balthasar's thesis that 'identity' à la Fichte-Plotinus is the mere 'theory' must therefore be reversed: it is analogy that belongs to the theory of religious poetry, and the practice is identity. But the issue falls under a more familiar and general problem, that of method in the study of literature. The use of quotation out of context begs the question of the special value of poetry, and of art in general. If the poem's purpose is not really what lies within, the pacification, but what lies beyond — the ideal, the return to the Nature of childhood innocence — then the poem is founded on a buried insight into the unattainability of its ideal, on the question, which concerns none but the self, of 'to be or not to be'. Balthasar's 'eschatology' is really elegiac longing in the form of hymnic certainty. The tension between the appearance of analogy and the reality of identity, which could in itself still possess the universality of a philosophical state-

[60] *Herrlichkeit*, III/1, p. 674.

95

ment, is merely the manifestation of the tension between the appearance of communication and the reality of an ideal which renders other people irrelevant. In thus satisfying an aesthetic prerequisite, that it should not be didactic, the poem satisfies the mightiest criterion of art, in ultimately proceeding from a highest tension: here, that between speech and isolation. Thus poetry is balanced, precisely and briefly, between a communicating past and the silence of the future.

Hölderlin's determined retention and elevation of the priestly stance, which Balthasar pursues throughout, is in direct contradiction with his elimination of any possible religious object. Beauty, however, consists in that elimination, which bespeaks a sensitivity so delicate, so fragile, that all action appears as violence; it expresses 'the poet's infinitely vulnerable soul'[61] like a wild flower amid the grass of an archetypal dawn. The utmost frailty, existing 'in the arms of Nature', knows the utmost safety.

The key to 'Friedensfeier' is the epigram 'The Root of All Evil'.

> All to be one is good and divine; whence cometh the sickness Rife among men that there should One be and none but the One.

The background is the love-affair in Frankfurt and the finally violent interference by the master of the house, the businessman and husband whose motto was '*les affaires avant tout*'. He, the epitome of commercial Frankfurt, and Hölderlin's great enemy, the One God, the despot, have merged into a single principle: the masculine ego, in its 'infinite' striving to be 'absolute' clearly identified with Fichte's Faustian 'I'. God's freedom is, by analogy to the human personality, that of a thou who speaks, conflicts, with an I. Freed from this law, the individual's universe gains an intoxicating potential.

[61] Ibid., p. 666.

But freedom is not only a property of God. Man is 'not just soil and seed (according to the systems of the materialists and idealists), but the king of the field' (quotation, II, p. 613). What a magnificent piece of writing! For Hamann is not opposing one theological-philosophical concept with another. The Enlightenment's dead metaphorical use of language ('soil', 'seed') is exposed by an irreducibly literal image, the 'king', which draws its virility from the Old Testament. What it means to be 'king' — the colour and robes, the golden throne, the sense of manhood, the power of life — we feel (rather than think) through the contrast with the thin and bloodless rational antithesis. Not so much the particular systems as the kind of thinking that produces them is in question. 'Rejection of reason' would be a pallid paraphrase. Nevertheless, man's freedom depends upon 'king'-ship over the question whether man is cause of an effect or effect of a cause; over the very question of human freedom.

Hamann is not anachronistically addressing German 'Idealists', but he is intuitively rejecting Kant and with him, as Balthasar senses, the whole movement from Kant to Hegel which swept up over his death. For what is Kant's critique but the dilemma between cause and effect, 'freedom' and 'senses', metaphysics, ethics and aesthetics performing equidistant orbits around this ever unsolved problem?

At Tübingen, Kant seemed to promise 'free development of all one's powers'. When Hamann describes Jesus as the 'head of our nature and all our powers',[62] he seems to be expressing a similar, but Christian, *Sturm und Drang*. But the difference is not just Jesus; the words *Leib*, 'animal', 'part of the body', 'pulse', 'head', provide a context which gives decidedly physical meaning to 'heart' and 'powers'. The difference is the freedom of a 'body-and-soul'.[63]

---

[62] Quoted, *Herrlichkeit*, II, p. 610.
[63] Ibid., p. 613.

Christian freedom is to know the 'senses' (but let us say, the body and its weight) not as death, but as sin; and thus I understand Balthasar's difficult summary 'freedom to self-determination, yet predetermination to be free'.[64] To accept the body is therefore anything but 'materialism'; yet to see the body as sin is, surprisingly, far more affirmative than the supposed reintegration of the senses which began with the 'harmonious contradiction' of Schiller's postulated 'freedom in the phenomenal world'. Through sin, responsibility passes from the self to another; and the Christian ideas of grace and redemption, expurgated from the enlightened German Idealism, can re-enter the universe. By identifying all men as sinful, Hamann's freedom passes, in prayer, the burden to God.

The general preoccupation with the Fall reflects the extraction of the problem of redemption from death out of God's dispensation and into the jurisdiction of the self. There could not be a more utter contrast than that between Hamann's elevation of mankind and Hölderlin's idealisation of the individual. The former's acceptance of the weight of human existence involves inter-subjectivity not just on the religious but also on the social level, presupposing what is, in sinfulness, the inevitably shared nature of all human beings, above all, physical death; being a little lower than the angels, we are all the ridiculous objects of cosmic pity, and liberated from 'to be or not to be' we can see others as possessing the uniqueness of a 'body-and-soul'. But when the individual is idealised, carried, like Hyperion, aloft into the clouds,[65] each individual is already in himself what mankind in sum is — the abstract structure spirit-senses — and therefore self-sufficient; able on his own account to confront the issue of life and death, he not only rejects God but, fundamentally, ignores other people because they contribute nothing to the metaphysical dilemma. He is not free to be with others; he is preoccupied with his freedom.

[64] Ibid., p. 614.
[65] Cf. *Hyperion* I/55, 2-10.

The 'dialectic' of sex is the 'summit' of Hamann's speculation,[66] and for him 'the senses are centred on the act of begetting and giving birth'.[67] We can add 'as they are for every man'. The distinctive thing about Hamann is that he states it, and that is, that he is free to state it. In the Fall innocence divided into reason and sexuality: 'usurped knowledge is usurped sex, when, according to the will of the Creator, both should have fallen to man out of grace and in faith'.[68] Hamann himself decribes logos and sexuality as 'burning cold' and 'cold fire'. For each is the other; the fall from childhood innocence begets the antithesis between life and death, eternity and finitude, being potential entry into the tumultuous chaos of biological activity, arising and passing away; and the metaphysical dilemma of 'to be or not to be' begets the emotional shrinking-back of 'cold fire'. Balthasar is unwise (in his conclusion) to check Hamann's philosophical liberties, and to admonish[69] his 'inner infirmities'; for this mental and physical exuberance springs from the liberation that only a 'putrid sinner'[70] can experience, and is clearly Hamann's way of praising God, by playing childishly on the face of the earth.[71] 'Do we then not wish to become children, to take to us flesh and blood, take upon us the Cross, like the new Adam?' Small wonder that Christianity, and with it society itself, begin with this myth; for what clearer proof is there that the individual is not self-sufficient than the sexual difference?

Christian freedom, then, is an entry into the irrationality of life which yet accepts that any such entry is sinful; willingly and with enjoyment[72] to sin, yet to be filled with sorrow (not *post eventum*

---

[66] *Herrlichkeit*, II, p. 625.
[67] Ibid., p.623.
[68] Ibid., p. 624.
[69] loc. cit.
[70] Quotation, ibid., p. 604.
[71] Cf. ibid., pp. 622, 631, especially pp. 617f.
[72] Ibid., p. 631.

'guilt')[73] at one's depravity. This is the principle of original sin intuitively maintained against German Idealism. While Hamann's weighed-down world is the 'dialogue'[74] between all-too-human man, the I, and redeeming God, the thou, Hölderlin's 'aethereal' cosmos is palpably on principle deduced from himself. Hence the piercing accuracy of Balthasar's observation that Hölderlin restricts God's freedom 'in the mystery of his suffering' to a 'law'; the mighty theme of the Suffering Servant merely serves to justify the universalised principle of the fall from grace, from oneness with infinite Nature, into time that Hölderlin felt that he had re-experienced in the loss of Susette.[75]

Given the antagonistic principles, masculinity and the flower, given the antithesis between the Christian God (= the will to be Absolute I) and the ideal of unity, given a poetry therefore entirely devoted to superseding this principle of I-ness, identified with Christianity (all this overlooked by the critics because, assuming the antagonistic principles, Hölderlin's are the corrective polemics of 'love' and 'peace'), one might dismiss Balthasar's 'Hölderlin'. For, stripped of Christian tendentiousness, the description of what he himself so well summarises as the 'transfer to the ancient glory, seen as a theophanous Nature-cosmos, of all the forces and motifs of Christian revelatory glory' amounts to no more than a list ('glorious', 'holy', 'divine', etc.) which he has dressed up to avoid the fate he himself has said must meet all such 'speculation about God' 'in the realm of metaphysics': 'dressed up in borrowed, namely Christian, feathers', in the end it 'reveals itself as what it secretly always was: a titanical, Promethean, work of man'.[76]

---

[73] Ibid., p. 624.

[74] Ibid., p. 614.

[75] Cf. *Herrlichkeit*, III/1, p. 665. Hamann's irrational antithesis to the rational antithesis (infinity and finitude) of mathematical logic is to postpone the problem; a procrastination till the Day of Judgement (which, conducted by one to inspire fear, is no rationalistic figure of speech: quotation, *Herrlichkeit*, II, p. 638 ('damnation').

[76] *Herrlichkeit*, III/1, p. 593.

Yet if one looks carefully at Balthasar's 'Hölderlin', one senses that the Christianisation is not an end in itself and therefore wilful, but derives from a true affinity with the poet which has found expression in a venial distortion. Earlier we noted that his universalisation of lyrical motifs yielded elements of Pietistic tradition. Throughout the study there are traces of this softer Christianity, traces, moreover, which bespeak less doctrinal values than an attitude to life. It is the spirit of wondering piety preserved in Bach's chorale preludes, or, in the arias, a flower opening in the scented, intimate mystery of night, a bride waiting for her groom, for the fulfilment of the promise 'I come, I come'. How else could a Christian tolerate the appropriation of God's love in Christ for the sake of intensity, were that love not blended with this love, which 'opens itself to the All in absolute intensity, a feminine role',[77] 'surrendering'[78] to 'the urgent approach of an infinite love in the mystery of the world's being'.[79] The Christ of Pietism, in contrast to the grandeur of the baroque God, has 'treasures within',[80] in the 'heart', such as to console, for life is a dark vale of tears where the soul seeks 'withdrawal from all living things',[81] rejecting the allures of the bright, bright world, 'poor in the eyes of the world', in 'virginity of the spirit'[82] turning away and into itself in 're-flection'.

Balthasar prefaces his chapter on Hölderlin by saying that his was the 'sublimest attempt' 'to unite Christian glory with ancient beauty'.[83] Two pages later he writes that Hölderlin 'contemplates the glory of the ancient world with Christian eyes and a Christian heart'. This reversal indicates that his real sympathy was not — how could it have been? — for Hölderlin's secularisation of 'glory', but

[77] Ibid., p. 671.
[78] Ibid., p. 654.
[79] Ibid., p. 656.
[80] Ibid., p. 674.
[81] Quotation, ibid., p. 654.
[82] Quotation, ibid., p. 656.
[83] Ibid., p. 644.

for the perceiving and contemplative vessel of that glory: the 'eyes', the 'heart', and, above all, the soul, the inner eye, perceiving, wondering, a pure and glad, a child's receptivity, that wanders in the labyrinth of the night and knows nothing of the hammering Cyclopean daylight where an iron will is forging the Industrial Revolution, the death of the spirit. For the world knew him not.

This Pietistic tradition merges easily with that of Catholic mysticism, the gentle sensuality and sorrowful depth of the madonna of the early Renaissance, its Sebastian-Christ with his unspoken 'Father, forgive them, for they know not what they do', with St Francis's *amate*, or, indeed, the feminine wisdom, like Hölderlin's 'Mother Earth' 'all-enduring', of Leonardo's portrait. And is not Balthasar's absorbing of the heretical poet into his all-embracing 'Glory', is not the Catholic catholicism of the entire undertaking, born of the same 'love' as he discovered in this poet who 'sees the glory of the ancient world as the glory of love'? It is that all-forgiving maternal love which had already interceded and bent the straight line of the Law when Abraham softened the will of the Lord as they looked down together over the Cities of the Plain. Not just 'Hölderlin' but the entire *Glory of the Lord* can be seen as an act of faith in the 'spirit', a work, indeed, of 'peace', corresponding (albeit not with Hölderlin's 'secret identification') to a spirit of love and forgiveness which always precedes the interpreter's task. Such an act of faith is nobler, and truer to the poet, than the impersonality of *Literaturwissenschaft*.

Love, then, entwines and softens the Law, Catholic Antigone embraces the knees of Protestant Creon, and Christocentric *Herrlichkeit* answers the Lord's *Kirchliche Dogmatik*. In Hölderlin Balthasar has found what the genuinely orthodox Hamann could not have given him. If my 'venial' sounded patronising, nevertheless he is misguided. He fails to see the implacably mathematical logic of his own words: 'Hölderlin transferred to the ancient glory, seen as a theophanous Nature-cosmos, all the forces and motifs of

Christian revelatory glory.' There is no Darwin yet, and history divides man into two: before Christ 'gods walked among men',[84] and the Divine appeared through Nature, so that man too was divine; now, since the year of our Lord, is darkness, memory, lost life, introversion.

Beneath the idealistic surface, Hölderlin's ultimate creative impulse is a dream, the delight of an intoxication from which all the moral laws of the Christian era, or, as we would say, all inhibitions, have deliciously loosened. The hermetic intensity of the last poetry and its reckless courting of fulfilment of the prayer 'But grant, ye mighty ones! a single Summer/ A single Autumn ... '[85] bear witness to the resurrected hero. The value of intensity of experience is elevated over that of regard for others: 'love thy God', 'love thy neighbour'. And via Nietzsche, Hyperion's 'I will take a shovel and throw the filth into the ditch'[86] is the distant forebear of Josef Goebbels's 'chaff before the breath of God'. Horrified critics will appeal to the novel's structure; but to transcend means not to contradict. This aspect of Hölderlin's idealism contains no moral standard.

The first version of 'The only One' ends with the contrast between 'the spiritual' and 'the worldly'. To seek religion 'in the realm of metaphysics', in the 'spirit'-uality of the Age of Goethe, implies Goethe's 'dismissal of the flat materialism of the European Enlightenment' and is inspired by his 'How hollow and empty we felt in that gloomy atheistic half-light';[87] it presupposes that the greatest enemy is not hostile beliefs, but the scientific materialism that ends all belief. Yet Balthasar's own work is founded upon an ethical standard which, genuinely Christian as it is, he nevertheless shares with Schiller's 'realist', but not with his 'idealist'. Con-

[84] 'Götter wandelten einst . . . ', SE I, 274.
[85] 'An die Parzen', SE I, 241.
[86] *Hyperion*, I/47, 8f.
[87] Quotation, *Herrlichkeit*, III/1, p. 682.

tentment with what ordinary life has to offer, postponement of 'to be or not to be', these are conditions of relationship: whether in religion or society.

MARY AND PETER IN THE CHRISTOLOGICAL CONSTELLATION: BALTHASAR'S ECCLESIOLOGY[1]

John Saward

Hans Urs von Balthasar is a Catholic theologian. He is immensely learned, perhaps the most cultured man of our time, but to regard him as no more than erudite would be to misunderstand him completely. He is a Catholic priest, in communion with Peter's successor, and theology for him is a mission and ministry exercised concretely and faithfully in the Church. Balthasar's attitude to theology is at once contemplative and ecclesial. Indeed, his writings show us the real identity of the ecclesial disposition and the contemplative, for both are characterised by loving obedience to the Catholic truth of the Father revealed in Christ, the incarnate Son, and, under the guidance of the Holy Spirit, proclaimed infallibly by the Church. Obedience is one of Balthasar's major preoccupations and the most striking attribute of his own approach to theology. Obedience, the hallmark of true Catholic theology as it is of all authentic Christian living, is at once christological and Marian. It is christological, because it is a participation by grace in the incarnate Son's obedience to the Father, and it is Marian, because Mary's *fiat*, through the grace which filled her from her conception, is an anticipated participation in Christ's obedience and the perfect model for the obedience of every Christian and so of every theolo-

[1] I would like to dedicate this article to the memory of my teacher and friend, Fr. Cornelius Ernst, OP, who first introduced me to the writings of Balthasar, and whose own essay on Our Lady, 'Mary: Sign of Contradiction or Source of Unity?' (in *Multiple Echo: Explorations in Theology*, London, 1979) has been of great help to me in the writing of this present piece.

105

THE ANALOGY OF BEAUTY

gian. The work of the theologian must involve self-surrender to God in the Church, what Ignatius Loyola calls 'thinking with the Church'. Balthasar explains this as follows:

> [Obedience] ... connects us in faith to the will of Christ in his obedience to the Father, and by the same token connects us to the faithful obedience to Christ of the Church, his Bride, who, in her spirit of faithful obedience, is our mother and educator.[2]

In contrast to the *haereticus homo* (cf. Tit 3.10), who chooses a part instead of the whole truth, his own opinion rather than the mind of the Church, self-affirmation rather than conversion, Hans Urs von Balthasar commends but also exemplifies the *anima ecclesiastica*, 'the soul freed from its egocentric isolation, broadened to the dimensions of ecclesial (Marian) consent',[3] the soul that finds its centre of gravity, not in itself, but in the whole Christ, 'the concrete Christ', Christ in his Church.

All of Balthasar's theology has an ecclesial context. 'Trinity, Christology, and Church form an indissoluble unity both theoretically and practically, theologically and ethically',[4] and his ecclesiology is in permanent coinherence with his treatment of the other doctrines of the faith. Central to his ecclesiology is the idea of the 'christological constellation', in which Our Lady and Peter have a pre-eminent place. What follows is an attempt to introduce this aspect of Balthasar's thought, in particular his understanding of the relationship between the Marian and Petrine dimensions of the Church.

---

[2] *Herrlichkeit*, III/1, p. 466. For Balthasar's understanding of Catholicity, see *Katholisch*, Einsiedeln, 1975, ch. 1 and *passim*.

[3] *First Glance at Adrienne von Speyr*, San Francisco, 1981 (E.T. of *Erster Blick auf Adrienne von Speyr*, Einsiedeln, 1968), p. 53.

[4] *Elucidations*, p. 49.

The Christological Constellation

Balthasar's Christology can be summed up quite simply: the person of Christ must be seen *in relation*. First, we must remember that the person of Jesus Christ is the eternal Son of the Father, the Second Person of the Blessed Trinity, and that in his human nature, as in his divine nature, he exists in his relation to the Father in the unity of the Holy Spirit.[5] Balthasar's Christology hinges on the unconfused interconnection of what the Greek Fathers called the 'theology' of the Triune God and the 'economy' of Jesus Christ: 'Although it is the Son alone who became man, and not the Father and the Spirit, yet in his human form his relation to the Father and the Spirit is also, of necessity, made manifest.'[6] The Paschal Mystery, in particular, must be seen in this Trinitarian context.[7]

Through the Incarnation the eternal Son of the Father has entered the world of *human* relations. Every human being exists, says Balthasar, as part of 'a constellation with his fellow men (*einer mitmenschlichen Konstellation*)'; to be human is to be with.[8] Through the human nature he assumed in the womb of the Blessed Virgin the divine Logos has entered into solidarity with the human race; the one divine person of the Son is the subject of both intra-Trinitarian and inter-human relations. This is what makes him the Mediator, for he is the one *in whom* God and man are reconciled. Now these

[5] *Der antirömische Affekt Wie läßt sich das Papsttum in der Gesamtkirche integrieren?*, Freiburg, 1974, p. 115. [ARA]. It is in this work that the phrase 'christological constellation' is used and in which the notion is explored in most detail. It is also discussed in *The Glory of the Lord*, I, pp. 350-65, in terms of the four archetypal experiences of faith: Petrine, Pauline, Johannine, Marian.

[6] *Prayer*, London, 1961 (E.T. of *Das betrachtende Gebet*, Einsiedeln, 1955), p. 147. On the relation between Trinitarian doctrine and Christology, see the document on *Theologia-Christologia-Anthropologia* of the International Theological Commission, of which Father von Balthasar is a member (*Gregorianum* Vol. 64, 1983, 8ff.).

[7] See 'Mysterium Paschale' in *Mysterium Salutis. Grundriß heilsgeschichtlicher Dogmatik*, III/2, ed. J. Feiner & M. Löhrer, Einsiedeln/Cologne, 1969, especially pp. 223-26 ('Kreuz und Trinität'), and 248f. (the descent into Hell as a *Trinitarisches Ereignis*).

[8] ARA, p. 115.

THE ANALOGY OF BEAUTY

human relations of Christ with his brethren have two aspects, universal and particular. First, the universal: Jesus Christ, the Word made flesh, is the *universale concretum et personale.*[9] Precisely because he is the Word, in, through and for whom all things were made, he imparts his own universality to the concrete human nature he has assumed without depriving it of its particularity. He is a man for all times and places, for all men. He is more than just one man among men; he is the one in whom all the scattered children of God are to be gathered together (cf. Jn 11. 52), the New Adam, the Head of the Body, in whom and under whom all things are to be brought into unity (cf. Eph 1. 10). The fact that his human nature is personalised in the divine person of the Word, and not in a human person, does not cut him off from us. On the contrary, precisely because he is who he is, the divine Word, he is capable as man, in his human nature, of truly inclusive relations with men and is open to all that is human.[10]

In addition to the universality of Christ's human relations, we must not forget their particularity. The Son of God only enters into this universality of human relationship by assuming a concrete, individual human nature, by becoming a man of a particular time and place. And so he is also the subject of concrete, particular human relations. Balthasar writes:

> It is impossible to detach Jesus from the human group which forms a totality with him, even though this statement

---

[9] *A Theology of History*, London, 1963 (E.T. of *Theologie der Geschichte*, Einsiedeln, 1959), p. 89. On the notion of Christ as the *universale concretum*, see G. Marchesi, SJ, *La cristologia di Hans Urs von Balthasar. La figura di Gesù Cristo, espressione visibile di Dio*, Rome, 1977, pp. 33ff.

[10] This has been most forcefully argued by Balthasar's friend, Fr. Louis Bouyer, in his essay in Christology, *Le Fils éternel. Théologie de la parole de Dieu et christologie*, Paris, 1974. In a section entitled 'Le Christ uni à nous par son unité avec Dieu', Bouyer writes: '...loin d'exclure rien d'aucun de nous, il nous inclut tous et toutes les possibilités de notre humanité, dans une réalisation de celle-ci qui en est comme l'universalité concrétisée (p. 479).

does not take away anything from his sovereign position. As soon as one abstracts him (and the doctrine about him, Christology) from it, his figure becomes desperately abstract, even if his Trinitarian context subsists.[11]

The constellation that surrounds Christ includes Joseph, Mary Magdalene, Mary, Martha and Lazarus of Bethany, Nicodemus, Judas, but at its centre, immediately round Jesus himself, are his Blessed Mother, the Baptist, the apostles, pre-eminently Peter and John. 'These figures belong ... to the constellation of Jesus and are consequently *integral parts of Christology*.'[12] We must at all costs avoid an isolationist Christology which would abstract Christ from his concrete human relations. Now, according to Balthasar, we cannot have a full doctrine of the Church unless we see how these historical relationships of the Word Incarnate with his Mother, and with Peter and the other apostles, are, so to speak, 'universalised' by the Holy Spirit and extended to the whole Church to be part of her intrinsic structure and life: Our Lady to be the primordial realisation of the Church in her loving obedience; Peter, commissioned to strengthen his brethren (Lk 22.32), in the office of the Papacy; the other apostles (with and under Peter) in the apostolic succession of the hierarchy. Mary, Peter and John are each of them 'types' of the Church, indelibly imprinted upon her. 'By means of these mediatory figures the "form of Christ" (Gal 4.19) is imprinted upon the whole people of God.'[13] Each in a different way may be said to 'personify' the Church. The key to ecclesiology is thus to be found in the incarnate Son's historical, human relations, which, in a certain sense, are perpetuated within the Church, his Mystical Body, as complementary dimensions of her being and function.

[11] ARA, p. 143.
[12] Ibid., p. 116.
[13] Ibid., p. 189.

We shall now proceed to discuss in turn Balthasar's treatment of the Marian principle in the Church, the Petrine principle, and their interrelation.

Mary's Relation to Christ

Like Christology (and, as we shall see, like the theology of the Papacy), Mariology must be approached by focussing on a *person in relation*. Balthasar warns us against the attempt to seek some abstract and impersonal 'fundamental principle' of Mariology,[14] and suggests instead that we contemplate Mary as a real person in relation to her divine Son and to the Church, his Body and Bride. First, we must see Mary in relation to the person and work of Christ. Balthasar writes:

> At the origin, in the very heart of the Incarnation-event, stands Mary, the perfect Virgin, who 'let it be', who consented physically and spiritually to maternal relationship with the person and also with the work of her Son. This relation might change more and more as Jesus grew and developed his independent personality, but would never be extinguished.[15]

All the Marian dogmas have a necessary reference to Christ. This is above all true of Our Lady's divine Motherhood: Mary is called *Theotokos* because it was God the Son himself, eternally begotten of the Father, who by the power of the Holy Spirit became incarnate from her.

Now the Incarnation took place not only in the Virgin's flesh but also through her faith. She conceived Christ in her womb and in her heart. God wanted the Incarnation of his Son to be assented to freely by mankind and to that end endowed Mary with sanctifying grace from the first moment of her existence. It is the grace of her

---

[14] See *Theodramatik*, II/2, p. 269f.
[15] ARA, p. 116.

Immaculate Conception that enables the Virgin to give her free consent to the Incarnation, as Balthasar loves repeating, on behalf of the whole human race: 'God could not use force on his own creation'.[16] Mary's freely given *Jawort* is prepared for in advance by the 'retroactive' application of the merits of Christ. Through the work of the Holy Spirit Mary's Yes is conformed to the Yes of the Son.

> Mary's word of assent can be a participation in the quality of the Son's consent. This quality can only be bestowed on her in advance by God, not as something alien to her but as the capability for deepest self-realisation. For God is eternal freedom, and, in giving himself, he can only free the creature to highest freedom.[17]

It is sin, not grace, that enslaves; grace is the very soul of true freedom, for it is nothing other than the transformation wrought in us by the presence of the Holy Spirit, and 'where the Spirit of the Lord is, there is freedom' (2 Cor 3.17). In Mary, full of grace, no sinful self obstructs the work of God; through grace Mary is transparent to grace. She 'lets all God's glory through' (Hopkins). Through the Immaculate Conception Mary's Yes is 'disencumbered from the beginning ... so that the earthly/finite ... offers fundamentally no obstacle to the indwelling of God'.[18] Through grace Mary's consent is perfectly free, the expression of her total receptivity and openness to God; in fact, in Mary grace perfects the natural receptivity of womanhood.[19]

[16] *Theodramatik*, II/2, p. '3.

[17] *The Threefold Garland*. The World's Salvation in Mary's Prayer, San Francisco, 1982 (E.T. of *Der dreifacher Kranz. Das Heil der Welt im Mariengebet*, Einsiedeln, 1977), p. 32.

[18] ARA, p. 172.

[19] 'Mary's life must be regarded as the prototype of what the *ars Dei* can fashion from human material which puts up no resistance to him. It is feminine life which, in any case more than masculine life, awaits being shaped by the man, the bridegroom, Christ, and God. It is a virginal life which desires no other formative principle but God and the fruit which God gives it to bear, to give birth to, to nourish and to rear. It is at the same time a maternal and a bridal life whose power of surrender reaches from the physical to the highest spiritual level. In all this it is simply a life that lets God dispose of it as he will.' *The Glory of the Lord*, I, p. 564.

For Balthasar, Marian consent, Mary's openness to God, the absence in her of any self-assertive barrier to grace, is the 'fundamental attitude' of all Christian faith, action, prayer and theology. The perception of this truth is one of many that Balthasar shared with Adrienne von Speyr, and indeed the christological constellation as a whole is one of her most characteristic ideas. In his study of Adrienne Balthasar writes thus of Marian consent:

> Mary, in virtue of her unique election, is the only one capable of excluding from her yes every conscious or unconscious limitation — something the sinner always includes. She is infinitely at the disposal of the Infinite. She is absolutely ready for everything, for a great deal more, therefore, than she can know, imagine or begin to suspect. Coming from God, this yes is the highest grace; but, coming from man, it is also the highest achievement made possible by grace: unconditional, definitive self-surrender.[20]

This self-surrendering consent is not, of course, confined to the Annunciation. It is constantly renewed by Mary throughout her Son's hidden and public life, reaching its climax (though not ceasing) at the foot of the Cross. The 'infinite flexibility' of her *fiat* is shown above all — and this is Balthasar's and Adrienne's great insight — in her courageous going into the unknown, giving herself up more and more to what she does not fully understand. Here she is truly the model for our faith: not fully comprehending, yet believing and saying Yes.

It is essential to this infinite flexibility of Marian consent that time and again it is led over and beyond its own under-

---

[20] *First Glance*, p. 51. For Adrienne's meditations on the interrelationship of Mary, John and Peter, see her *Geburt der Kirche. Betrachtungen über das Johannesevangelium Kapitel 18-21*, Einsiedeln, 1949, pp. 208ff.

standing and has to assent to things which generally seem not to lie within the limits of the humanly possible, conceivable, tolerable, suitable ... More and more is demanded of Mary's understanding, and in this her readiness is extended to be more and more limitless and unresisting. This shows Mary absolutely to be the believer whom the Lord counts blessed (Lk 1.45, 11.28; Jn 20.29).[21]

This never-failing 'readiness' (*Bereitschaft*) to surrender herself to the ever greater demands of God, this unrestricted availability, is not mere passivity or resignation; it has an active quality of attentive vigilance. As we have said, the grace that fills Mary's heart does not destroy but rather sanctifies and perfects her creaturely freedom. Mary truly co-operates in the work of redemption.

Because of its unlimited generosity, Mary's consent can be extended, given over, to the whole Church, to be not only the exterior model for Christian believing, but the *prägende Form* for the Church:[22] the Church is formed, carved, out of her consent. For by her Yes at the Annunciation, at the foot of the Cross, and by her unfailing maternal intercession for us in heavenly glory, Our Lady co-operates in her Son's work of restoring supernatural life to souls. The Church truly lives off the faith of Mary. Her response is 'the principle and exemplar of the response of the entire Church'.[23] Balthasar writes:

> Her person, in her faith, love, hope, has become so supple in the hand of the Creator that he can extend her beyond the limits of a private consciousness to be a Church consciousness, to be what, from Origen and Ambrose, ancient theology was accustomed to call the *anima ecclesiastica*.[24]

[21] ARA, p. 172.
[22] Ibid.
[23] 'Wer ist die Kirche?', *Sponsa Verbi*, p. 169.
[24] Ibid, p. 174.

Our Lady is truly the immaculate heart of the Church. Here, once again, it is instructive to read Balthasar in the light of Adrienne:

> [Her Son] took her with him step by step along the road, preparing her for ever new and greater expansion, so that her spirit might continue to adapt itself to his ever-widening circle. He shaped and formed her so that her individual spirit might become the spirit of the Church.[25]

Mary's Yes is Catholic, expanded and extended to be the foundation of the Church's faith by the work of the Holy Spirit. So inexhaustibly generous is her heart that in a motherly way she gives over her faith to the Church. All that is personal and particular to Mary, her bodily, believing and loving relation with her Son, is made Catholic, universal and ecclesial by the Spirit: this is the intimacy of union to which all men are called as members of Christ.

> Mary's physico-personal experience of the Child who is her God and her Redeemer is unreservedly open to Christianity. Mary's whole experience, as it develops from its earliest beginnings, is an experience for others — for all.[26]

Mary's Relation to the Church

For Balthasar, as for Augustine, Our Lady is the Mother of the Whole Christ; her relation to the Head is inseparable from her relation to the Body, a relation we must now examine in more detail.

The first aspect of Mary's relation to the Church is that, according to Catholic teaching, she is herself a member of the Church. She is

---

[25] A. von Speyr, *The Handmaid of the Lord*, London, 1956, p. 138.
[26] *The Glory of the Lord*, I, p. 340.

114

one of the redeemed through the *praeredemptio* that is her Immaculate Conception.[27] But she is, of course, far more than just one member among many. As *Lumen Gentium* puts it, 'she is hailed as pre-eminent and as a wholly unique member of the Church, and as its type and outstanding model in faith and charity'.[28] Now the great strength of Balthasar's 'constellational' ecclesiology is that it enables us to understand this idea of Mary as the type of the Church in a personalistic and ontological manner. Our Lady is not just a vague symbol of the Church; she is the personal, ontologically primary realisation of the Church. She in some sense 'personifies' the Church.[29] In what precise sense we must now determine.

In his study of St Maximus Balthasar tells us that the theology of the Confessor centres round the concept of hypostasis.[30] Crucial for orthodox Trinitarian doctrine and Christology is the apophatic irreducibility of *hypostasis* to *ousia*, of the question 'who?' to the question 'what?'[31] 'Hypostasis' refers here primarily to the three divine hypostases, but the radical irreducibility of the personal or hypostatic extends itself throughout Christian theology to apply also to human persons created in the image of the tri-personal God. Balthasar, like Maximus, in his Triadology and Christology, in his

---

[27] Cf. Pius IX, *Ineffabilis Deus*: '... intuitu meritorum Christi Jesu Salvatoris humani generis, ab omni originalis culpae labe praeservatam immunem ...' (DS 2803); the Dogmatic Constitution on the Church of the Second Vatican Council (*Lumen Gentium*): 'Redeemed, in a more exalted fashion, by reason of the merits of her Son ...' (n. 53); *Vatican Council 2. The Conciliar and Post-Conciliar Documents*, ed. A. Flannery OP, Dublin, 1975, p. 414).

[28] *Lumen Gentium* n. 53; Flannery, p. 414.

[29] On the dangers of depersonalising the notion of Mary as 'type of the Church', see Cornelius Ernst's essay (n. 1).

[30] *Kosmische Liturgie*, 2nd edition revised, 1961, p. 227.

[31] Cf. Fr. M.-J. Le Guillou: 'L'essence et l'hypostase ne font pas nombre dans l'être de Dieu comme deux entités ou deux formes. Elles n'en sont pas moins irréductibles en tant que raisons ultimes de deux ordres, comme principe *quo* et principe *quod*; le fait qu'elles n'impliquent aucune composition dans la simplicité divine n'enlève rien à leur irréductibilité, mais au contraire la porte à sa formalité maximale (*De potentia*, n. 9, a. 3, ad 4)', *Le mystère du Pere. Foi des apôtres*, Gnoses actuelles, Paris, 1973, p. 117.

anthropology and ecclesiology, always grasps the personal level, the primacy of the question 'who?' For him the primary question to be asked is not '*What* is the fundamental principle in Mariology?', but '*Who* is Mary, and how is she related to Christ and his Church?' Similarly, ecclesiology resolves itself into the question '*Who* is the Church?'[32]

The first and most obvious answer to that question might seem to be: the Church is Christ himself. He is the Head and we are the members, and together we are one person (*heis*) in him (Gal 3.28). Because Head and members (*totus Christus*) are *una caro, unus homo*, St Augustine can even say *Christus sumus*,[33] and in explaining how Christ can merit and make satisfaction for us, St Thomas tells us that Head and members are *quasi una persona mystica*.[34] Now this answer is open to misunderstanding. Pope Pius XII, in his encyclical *Mystici Corporis*, criticised those erroneous views of the Mystical Body in which there is a confusion of persons between Head and members, and points out that Paul 'combines Christ and his Mystical Body in a marvellous union, yet contrasts the one with the other, as Bridegroom with Bride'.[35] The Pope's clarification leads us directly to another answer: the Church is the Bride of Christ. It is on this nuptial mystery that Balthasar has much to say to us.

The union of Christ and his Church is an unconfused union, a union in distinction, a union so intimate that he dwells in us and we in him, a distinction so real that he always remains transcendent over the Church however immanent he is within it. The New Testament describes the union of Christ and his Church in bridal language (Eph 5.21ff.; Rev 21.2ff.) because, in married love, man and

---

[32] 'Who is the Church?' is the title of one of Balthasar's most important essays in ecclesiology (see n. 23). On this subject, see also Y. Congar, 'La personne "Eglise"', *Revue thomiste* lxxi, 1971, pp. 613-640.

[33] *En. in Ps.* 26, 2, 2; PL 36.200.

[34] *Summa theologiae* 3a, 48, 2, ad 1.

[35] DS 3816.

woman attain the deepest physical and personal union (*una caro*) without loss of their identity, precisely in their differentiation and complementarity. The relation of Head and members must be understood as inter-personal and thus nuptial: the Church, Christ's Body, is a Someone, for whom Christ gave himself up (Eph 5.25). Balthasar writes:

> The 'Bride', who, issuing from the wounded side of the New Adam, is at the same time his 'Body' (and only for that reason his 'People'), is both the One (with Christ) and the Other (over against him), in a relation of dependency and freedom, for which there is no analogy in the created sphere, but only in the Trinity.[36]

Once more Balthasar takes us from ecclesiology and plunges us into the Trinitarian mystery, which underlies all others. In the consubstantial Trinity the Holy Spirit is the bond of love between Father and Son, and yet he does not abolish the distinction between Father and Son, nor those between each or both of them and himself. Similarly, when we turn from the processions *ad intra* of the Trinity to the work of the Spirit in the Church, we find that here too, analogously, at the created level, the Paraclete establishes communion without confusion. The communion he establishes between Head and members, and among the members, involves no loss of identity. Bridegroom and Bride are one in their very differentiation.

> The inchoative subject that is the Church is, however, only fulfilled in the mystery of the Holy Spirit, who descends to her as her innermost foundation, and who is capable of constituting the Church as subject in completed form because he is a divine person precisely *as* the unity of love of Father

---

[36] 'Kirchenerfahrung dieser Zeit', *Sponsa Verbi*, 22.

> and Son: unity and union precisely as attesting their eternal opposition. In virtue of this divine *coincidentia oppositorum* he establishes this 'Other', the Bride, an Other, who is nevertheless as such the 'One', the Body . . . [37]

The nuptial relation between Christ and his Church presupposes in the Bride both freedom and dependency, co-operation and receptivity, active obedience and unlimited availability. Now this bridal response of the Church is perfectly realised only in the Virgin Mary, in her freely co-operative and unconditional Yes to the Incarnation and redemptive work of the Son of God. In her consent Mary is already what the Church will be only eschatologically in the wedding supper of the Lamb: 'a bride adorned for her husband' (Rev. 21.2), 'without spot or wrinkle' (Eph. 5.27), *immaculata*. The Church is not faceless; as a Someone, a subject in relation to Christ, she has her perfect realisation in Our Lady, in whose flesh and through whose faith the Incarnation took place. Mary really is the *ecclesia immaculata*.

Now this raises many questions. Foremost among them is: how can one woman be both the Mother of Christ and the Bride of Christ in the sense of being the archetypal and personal realisation of the Church's bridal assent to her Lord? This is one of the two *Fragenkomplexe*, says Balthasar, with which every Mariology must concern itself.[38] While Balthasar's thought on this matter owes a great deal to the work of M. J. Scheeben, he also points to the difficulties the nineteenth century theologian had in expounding his 'synthetic concept' of bridal motherhood.[39] It must be admitted, though, that Balthasar himself is not as clear as he might be about the relation between Mary's real and literal Motherhood and her

---

[37] 'Wer', *Sponsa Verbi*, 202.

[38] *Theodramatik* II/2, p. 266f.

[39] According to Scheeben, Protestantism's error is its failure to grasp the bridal aspect of Our Lady's relationship to God (*Handbuch der katholischen Dogmatik*, Dritter Band, Freiburg, 1933, p. 492f.)

real but non-literal (? analogical-archetypal) role as Bride. Perhaps the following reflections will enable us to explore this great mystery a little more deeply.

First, Our Lady is the New Eve. As Irenaeus says, 'the knot of Eve's disobedience was untied by Mary's obedience; what the virgin Eve bound through her disbelief, Mary loosened by her faith.'[40] At the beginning of the human race there is a man and a woman; at the beginning of the recreated human race there is the God-Man and his Mother. At the Fall there is the disobedience of two human persons; in the Redemption there is the human obedience of the divine person of the Son and the freely co-operative consent of the human person of the Virgin. As Adam was to Eve so, antitypically, Christ is to Mary. Secondly, Our Lady is really and personally what Israel was called to be metaphorically and collectively. The people of Israel spurned Yahweh's covenant love and in their infidelity became like an adulterous wife.[41] Mary, in contrast, through grace, gives the supreme and exemplary act of faith and obedience, a human person's Yes to the Incarnation and work of the Son of God. She makes the bridal response to God that Israel failed to. Thirdly, we should recall that some of the Fathers described the hypostatic union of human nature to the divine Logos as a *matrimonium* or *connubium*; God the Son 'weds' human nature to himself in the bridal chamber of the Virgin's womb. Now this 'wedding' of the Logos and humanity did not take place without humanity's consent; that consent, a truly bridal consent, is given in the freely uttered *Jawort* of Mary, who thus stands before God as the representative of all humanity. As Thomas says of the Annunciation:

> It gave (Mary) the opportunity of obeying freely and she seized it readily, saying, 'I am the handmaid of the Lord'...It brings out that a kind of spiritual marriage (*spirituale matrimonium*) is taking place between the Son of God and human

---

[40] *Adv. haer* 3, 22, 4; PG 7.959A.
[41] See 'Casta Meretrix', *Sponsa Verbi*, pp. 203-305.

nature. The Virgin's consent, then, which was petitioned during the course of the Annunciation, stood for the entire human nature.[42]

'Humanity' and 'human nature' here have two resonances, universal and particular. The *matrimonium* that is the hypostatic union is a wedding of humanity to the divine person of the Logos. Now this humanity is an individual human *nature*, not a human person, not a Someone, and so cannot literally be a Bride. The bridal element only comes in when we see that human nature is given to the Son of God freely, in faith and in love, by the Blessed Virgin. What is more, through the flesh he takes from Mary, the individual human nature he 'marries' in her womb, the Word enters into a nuptial relation with 'all created flesh' (all humanity, the entire race), which is called to be his Bride and to be *una caro* with and in him. In this sense Mary is indeed *Sponsa Verbi*. Balthasar writes:

> When the Church Fathers see the true *connubium* between God and man realised in Christ himself, in the indissoluble union of his two natures, this is not just a purely physical occurrence, with its bridal character solely derived from the side of God and his intention. No, it is a real two-sided mystery of love through the bridal consent of Mary acting for all the rest of created flesh. In Mary's flesh is meant 'all (created) flesh' (Jn 17.2) to which God wills to marry himself; and since Mary is *caro ex qua*, she is also *fides ex qua*.[43]

Christ, the pre-existent Logos, is the Son who chooses his Mother, and Mary in her bridal faith says Yes to that choice. Of course, when we think of the Incarnation as willed and effected, we must remember that it is strictly speaking willed and effected by the

---

[42] *Summa theologiae* 3a, 30, 1.

[43] 'Wer', *Sponsa Verbi*, p. 171. Scheeben points out that the idea of the Logos 'marrying' human nature is more common before Ephesus (431) than after, since it could be taken to imply a personification of the assumed nature and thus the Nestorian heresy of two persons in Christ. Cf. *Die Mysterien des Christentums*, new ed., Freiburg, 1941, p. 310.

whole Trinity: as St Maximus puts it, 'the Father lovingly decreed (*eudokōn*) and the Spirit co-operated when the Son himself effected his Incarnation'.[44] Thus while the *connubium* of the two natures takes place only in the person of the Son, Mary's bridal faith is not exclusively directed to the Logos. The tendency of Catholic tradition has been to see a filial quality in Mary's consent to the Father's *eudokia*, true Motherhood in relation to the Son, and the bridal element has more frequently been appropriated to her relation to the Holy Spirit, by whom the Son is conceived in her womb. Nonetheless, the *eudokia* of the Father is also that of the Son; he truly is the Son who chooses his Mother, and Mary, in free bridal co-operation, says Yes to that choice. She renews that Yes throughout her Son's life on earth and above all at the foot of the Cross. In this way Our Lady is the primary realisation of the Church as *Sponsa Christi*.

One final word by way of clarification of Mary's bridal faith. Balthasar sees Mary as *the* woman, all that woman is meant and called to be, receptive, responsive, co-operative, the answer (*Antwort*) to the Word, the countenance (*Antlitz*) that looks back in love to him.[45] She is thus truly the representative of all created flesh, for the creature in relation to the Creator is intended to be femininely receptive and *capax infiniti*. As Chesterton said, 'Men are men, but Man is a woman'. Socially, as representing Church and humanity, Mary is Bride.[46]

---

[44] *Expositio orationis dominicae*; PG 90, 876C.

[45] *Theodramatik* II/ 2, pp. 260ff.

[46] Once again, when considering the persons of the God-Man and the Virgin, and their relation, we must remember both the social and individual aspects: 'In so far as the man Jesus Christ is an individual human being (*Mensch*), his relation to woman will also be individual; the woman to whom he relates is a definite Someone. On the other hand, in so far as he is the incarnate Word of God and through his existence (*Dasein*) fulfils the commission of the Father to reconcile the whole of God's creation with God (2 Cor 5.19), the "helpmate" to whom he is related will necessarily, as the representative of that humanity (which for God is feminine), have a social aspect. These two aspects, like the two natures of Jesus Christ himself, will be neither simply identical nor separable from one another' (*Theodramatik* II/2, p. 265).

We began this section of the paper by asking (with Balthasar): who is the Church? With the New Testament we gave the answer: she is the Bride of Christ, and we have reflected on the mystery of Mary, who is Virgin Mother, as the primary, personal realisation of the Church as Bride. In this sense she may be said to 'personify' the Church, in her very person to be the 'type' of the Church.[47] Balthasar argues that the contrast so often made between 'christotypical' and 'ecclesiotypical' Mariologies rests on a mistake, a depersonalisation of Christ, Mary and the Church, a false opposition between Mary's person and her mission: 'the more personal and unique Mary's relation to Christ is seen to be, the more it represents the real content of the Church.'[48] In her very person Mary is the first realisation of the Church, 'the real type and abiding centre of the Church'.[49] She is the *Kern* in whom the 'idea' of the Church is fully realised, the Church's immaculate heart, 'the only member of the real pilgrim Church to correspond fully to the ecclesial attribute "immaculate"'.[50] According to Adrienne, 'in her alone the Church is exactly as it should be, the bride without stain or spot.'[51] It is, of course, not only as Bride but also as Mother that Mary is the real type and personal centre of the Church. Just as the Virgin Mother Mary brought forth the God-Man, so now the Virgin Mother Church keeps the faith intact and brings forth new adopted children for God in baptism.[52] Balthasar makes it clear that this typological relation is ontological, actual and personal, and not simply one of exterior resemblance; it should not be taken to imply that in the past Mary exercised the function of Virgin Mother in relation to Christ, but now the Church exercises it in relation to his members.

[47] The classic work on the relation between Mary and the Church is A. Müller, *Ecclesia-Maria*, 2nd edition, Fribourg, 1955.

[48] *Theodramatik* II/ 2, p. 280.

[49] *Engagement with God*, p. 32. Mary is also called the Church's 'personal centre' in *Theo-dramatik* II/2, p. 324.

[50] ARA, p. 150.

[51] *Handmaid*, p. 139.

[52] Cf. *Lumen Gentium*, n. 64; Flannery, p. 420.

This would be again to depersonalise Mary. Being a Mother is not a function but a personal relation. She *is* the Mother of the Word Incarnate, and she exists in that relation beside her Son in heavenly glory. But she is the type of the Church as Mother in an even deeper sense. Because she is Mother of the Head, she is also Mother of the Body and is given as Mother to the loving Church (in the person of John) on Calvary. By her humble Yes (at the Annunciation and by the Cross) she collaborated with the work of her Son in reconciling us all in one body to the Father (cf. Eph 2.16). In her *fiat* the Mother of God, says Balthasar with Adrienne, is the 'womb of the Church', *matrix et mater*, the one in whom the Head is conceived and the Body (by the cross, at Pentecost) is formed. 'The Marian *fiat* . . is a nuptial womb . . . where the Son of God not only can take existence but also institute a truly universal Church.'[53] What is more, even now in heavenly glory Mary is in a maternal relation to the Church. She was, and is now, Mother of the whole Christ, Head and members: she gave human life to the divine Head; she freely consented to the Son's Incarnation and his work of restoring supernatural life to men; now in glory she plays a personal, but of course subordinate and handmaidenly, role in the communication of that life, the filial life of the Son, to his members.[54] She is Christ's Mother and ours, and the life, the grace, the holiness that comes to us from Christ passes through her hands, through her love.[55]

Balthasar and Adrienne speak to us of what is after all the experience of every Catholic: the loving, motherly presence of Mary. All the surprises of God's grace, above all the surprise of believing, the gift of faith, come to us as maternal gifts. The believer, says Balthasar, 'feels the grace that sustains and forms him and keeps

[53] ARA, p. 172.

[54] Cf. Adrienne, *Handmaid*, p. 149f. 'with the overshadowing of the Virgin begin the mysteries of the Mystical Body, which are above all mysteries of the Holy Spirit generated in the womb of the virginal Church' (*The Glory of the Lord* I, p. 327).

[55] On Mary's motherhood in the order of grace, see *Lumen Gentium*, nn. 60–62; Flannery, p. 418f.

him together'.[56] To be in the *communio* of the Catholic Church is to be enveloped by a Mother's love.

Peter in Relation to Christ

Mary, Peter and John are intrinsic to the mystery of Christ and thus to the mystery of the Church, his Body. They are real types of the Church, three complementary answers to the question, Who is the Church? Each personifies the Church or dimensions of the Church: Peter — the apostolic ministry of word and sacrament, John — love, Mary — the Church herself in her innermost essence. Of the three, only Peter has a successor in the strict sense — the Roman Pontiff. We shall now examine Balthasar's theology of the Papacy and the Petrine dimension of the Church.[57]

According to Balthasar, the Pope must be seen above all *in relation*: to the bishops and the whole Church. Now the key to that relation, he tells us, is to be found in Peter's relations to Christ and Mary and to the other apostles in the christological constellation. First, then, Peter's relation to Christ. Here again we must build on Trinitarian and christological foundations. 'In Jesus Christ', says Balthasar, 'the triune God becomes concrete.'[58] Because of the *perichoresis*, the mutual indwelling, of the divine persons in the consubstantial Godhead, the Incarnation of the Son manifests also His relations to the Father and the Holy Spirit. Outside of the Godhead there is another indwelling, that of grace, by which the glorified Christ dwells in us and we in him, and by which, in a special way, he is present ministerially in his apostles and their successors. 'He who hears you hears me, and he who rejects you rejects me, and he who rejects me rejects him who sent me' (Lk 10.46). Among the apostles Peter has an undeniable primacy, so that the Petrine office is *a for-*

---

[56] *The Glory of the Lord* I, p. 363.

[57] 'Since certain of these members possess archetypal experiences which they deposit in the common treasury of the *Communio Sanctorum* for the common use, nothing keeps us from ascribing such an experience to the Church herself.' *The Glory of the Lord* I, p. 350.

[58] ARA, p. 114.

tiori the 'concretion of Christ', his authority and Cross. But then Peter is made concrete in his successors, the Roman Pontiffs. God in Christ; Christ in Peter; Peter in his successors. The Father speaks to us through his Son and Word (cf. Heb 1.1); the Son made man speaks to us through Peter; Peter speaks through the Popes. As the Fathers of Chalcedon said, 'Peter has spoken through Leo'. The Father's Word is uttered concretely in his Church, through his apostolic ministers, with Peter's successor at their head.

The theology of the Papacy must begin with the real person of Peter in the Gospels, in relation to Jesus in the 'christological constellation'. And when we contemplate Peter in the Gospels we find the concurrence of authority and humiliation, power and weakness. He is given an undeniable primacy (cf. Mt 16.6ff.; Lk 22.32; Jn 21.15ff.), but his frailty and folly stand out just as clearly. Peter is, in fact, the most unlikely candidate for the Papacy. The one chosen to be Rock is the most erratic of the apostles; the one commissioned to strengthen his brethren is the weakest of them all; the one elected to lead the flock is the one who denied the Lord. But there is no inconsistency here, as Balthasar brilliantly shows. Peter's whole life is a revelation of God's grace working through human weakness: 'My grace is sufficient for you, for my power is made perfect in weakness' (2 Cor 12.9). Peter is the chosen rock *precisely because* he is, and knows himself to be, the most foolish and weak of the apostles. Peter is a fool of love, purified in the crucible of penitence, one who has been forgiven much and therefore loves much. He knows that he is utterly dependent on Christ, that all is grace, and so he can strengthen his brethren because he knows what it is to be strengthened. And for this very reason the deserter is given primacy, authority, infallibility. The renegade become the rock: that, says Balthasar, is 'the central scandal of Catholicism'; this amazing Petrine paradox is 'the normal means in the real Church by which the work of Christ is maintained through history'.[59] Peter shares in

[59] Ibid., p. 151.

a special way in the power of Christ himself, for how else, as shepherd, is he to protect the flock from wolves (cf. Acts 20.29)? But if he shares in Christ's power, he must share too in his Cross and self-emptying (cf. Jn 21.18). 'The form of office which Christ has instituted in his Church,' according to Balthasar, 'in itself and independently of the person who has occupied it, is the form of the Cross.'[60] The price of being first is to be last: the primate is *novissimus, tamquam morti destinatus* (cf. 1 Cor 4.9). For Peter there is a simultaneity of humiliation and mission, which reaches its climax in his crucifixion upside down:

> This simultaneity is the mode in which the Lord's identity can (subsequently) still take hold in the guilty Peter. It is an imitation beyond and despite failure which is marvellously represented in Peter's crucifixion with feet uppermost: it is the Cross, but in mirror-image, which is the definitive symbol of the hierarchical situation.[61]

It is Christ the eternal High Priest who is present and acts in Peter and the apostles and in their successors, but in the apostolic minister's very conformity to Christ, in his indelible priestly character, he is humbled, shown up, exposed: he is a pygmy in giant's armour, a fool for Christ's sake, a spectacle to angels and men. Peter and the apostles, and their successors, embody in themselves the ever greater demands of Christ and the weakness of his human representatives. Their mission is just this: to give God the greater glory, to reveal the power of Christ in their very weakness. The first are truly, humiliatingly, the last of all.

> Peter was crucified with his feet in the air, resembling yet being totally different, conformed in inversion ... Confor-

---

[60] ARA, p. 290f.
[61] *The Glory of the Lord* I, pp. 566f.

mity is pure grace; it is realised, in fact, in a movement of recoil. But in the history of the world this recoil will never be strong enough to paralyse the grace which conforms him. The prayer of Jesus has triumphed over the 'power of the devil' (Lk 22.31); the power of the devil will have no force (Mt 16.18) over what is built on Peter.[62]

The Pope in Relation

The Pope must be seen as a person in relation (to the bishops and the Church) on the analogy of Peter's relation to Christ and the apostles. This is especially important, Balthasar suggests, when we are considering infallibility. As Gasser made beautifully clear at Vatican I, when the Pope expounds and defines *ex cathedra* the universal teaching of the Church, he does not act as a 'private person', an isolated individual, but as a 'public person' in relation to the whole Church, as shepherd and teacher of all Christians, the one 'in whom the Church's charism of infallibility is present in a singular way'.[63] Balthasar writes: 'This infallibility is equally relational; as a "public person" the Pope takes the definitive decision (and this is true also, by analogy, of the bishops) *in relatione ad Ecclesiam universalem*.'[64] And yet while it is true that we must see the Pope as a person *in relation* (to the episcopal college and the whole Church), we must not forget to see him as a *person* in relation. Only persons, not abstract sees or impersonal functions, can be said to be infallible: it is to the official person, the Roman Pontiff, who represents the universal Church, that infallibility is attributed.[65] Of course, it is not a permanent quality; it is attributable to a personal *act*, of which he is the agent, with the help of the Holy Spirit, in

[62] ARA, p. 130.

[63] DS 3074; *Lumen Gentium* n. 25; Flannery, p. 380. Cf. Gasser's *relatio* at Vatican I, 11 July 1870 (Mansi, 52. 1213A).

[64] ARA, p. 181.

[65] Ibid., p. 180f. Cf. Gasser (1213D).

matters concerning the universal Church. Papal infallibility is relational, personal and actual.

While it is true that we must see the Pope in relation to the college of bishops and the whole Church, we must remember that that relation is 'unconfused' and dynamic; we must not absorb the Pope back into the college as if he were just one member among many, a mere figurehead.[66] As *Lumen Gentium* clearly teaches with Vatican I, the Pope has full, supreme and universal power over the whole Church, which he can always exercise unhindered;[67] he is not only sign but also visible source of the unity of the college and the faithful;[68] his infallible definitions concerning faith and morals are irreformable by their very nature and not by the assent of the Church.[69] Balthasar's great achievement is to interpret these aspects of the theology of the Papacy in the light of the concrete figure of Peter. All that we have just mentioned, all that seems at first sight to distance the Pope from the bishops and the Church, this Petrine 'freedom of action', in fact brings him into even deeper union with the college and the faithful, for *it is a service he undertakes on behalf of the whole Church*. The Pope comes 'forward from the ranks' as a servant, in the service of a slave (Mt 20.25-27), as *servus servorum Dei*, as first only in order to be most humiliatingly last of all. He comes forward not as Lord of the earth (1 Pet 5.3), with Gentile authority (Mt 20.25), but to serve his brothers and strengthen their faith.[70] The ministry of the Pope as Christ's Vicar (his universal teaching authority and power of jurisdiction) is, as it was for Peter, imprinted with the Cross, a ministry of humiliation and exposure of the gap between his own subjective holiness and the

---

[66] See the 'explanatory note' attached to *Lumen Gentium* (Flannery, pp. 423ff.).

[67] *Lumen Gentium* n. 22; p. 375.

[68] Ibid., n. 23; p. 376. Cf. Vatican I, *Pastor aeternus*, DS 3050f.

[69] Ibid., n. 25; p. 380.

[70] ARA, p.175f. As Pope John Paul II said, on his visit to Britain, to the English and Welsh Bishops: 'With you the Bishop of Rome is pastor of God's people, and for you he is the *universal servant pastor*', (28th May, 1982).

objective holiness of the Church, between his human weakness and the solidity of Catholic truth which he teaches. To exercise this humbling service, he needs Petrine freedom of action, the very freedom, says Balthasar, 'which, through the centuries, Conciliarism, Protestantism, Gallicanism, Jansenism, Josephism, Febronianism etc. have contested'.[71] What all these erroneous views fail to grasp is that the Petrine ministry of the Pope involves *risk*, the risk of the Cross.[72] How much safer would a Conciliarist Pope be, comfortably contained within the ranks of the bishops, unexposed to the mockery of the princes of this age. Ironically, all the attempts to absorb the Pope back into the episcopate, all those theories which neglect the asymmetrical quality of the relation between head and members in the college, renew the temptation of Simon Bar-Jona (cf. Mt 16.22f.), repeat Peter's escape from Rome, for they are all a flight from the Cross. The suggestion sometimes made in ecumenical circles that the Pope should be no more than a sign of unity, and enjoy a mere primacy of honour, is profoundly unevangelical, a repudiation of the gospel of Christ Crucified. There is no primacy of honour in the Church, as Jesus makes clear to the sons of Zebedee; primacy and its accompanying authority are exercised only through humbling service.

The Church: Marian and Petrine Dimensions Compared

Balthasar demonstrates clearly the way in which the Church is both Marian and Petrine. It is Petrine: the Petrine office is essential to the Church, and the Pope acts as the representative of the whole Church (*persona ipsam ecclesiam gestante*).[73] Nonetheless, the Petrine Office is exercised by only one individual at a time, while the whole Church is Marian in the sense that Our Lady is the Church's real type, personal centre and primordial realisation as Virgin,

[71] ARA, p. 176.
[72] Ibid., p. 199.
[73] D'Avanzo at Vatican I, 20th June, 1870 (Mansi, 52. 762D).

Mother and Bride. Mary's Yes is the model for the faith of every Christian. Not every Catholic can be Pope, but every Catholic is meant to be like Mary and to know and love her as Mother.

> The form of Mary's faith, which 'lets it be', becomes the determining form, interiorly offered to all being and activity within the Catholic Church, while the pastoral charge of Peter embraces [the Church] in its entirety as its object but is not communicable in its specific unicity.[74]

Mary is the 'enveloping form' of all Church life, the inner shaping principle of the Church as a *communio* of love in the Spirit.[75] Mary envelops the Church with her motherly love by withdrawing humbly to its centre, whereas Peter and his successors, while belonging to the *collegium* and *communio*, stand out from them in exposure, although, as we have seen, that 'coming forward from the ranks' is only a service of the *collegium* and *communio*. In fact, the necessarily masculine ministerial priesthood (the Petrine principle in the general sense) is not an end in itself but is subordinate to, in the service of, the Marian principle.[76] The *ecclesia immaculata* was realised in Mary before one apostle had been called. The apostolic ministry of word and sacrament is intended to enable the Church to become what it already is in Mary: the spotless Bride of the Lamb.

In speaking of the Petrine Office we mentioned the 'gap' between the objectively infallible teaching authority and the subjective weakness of the human being who exercises it. We have said that in the apostolic ministry as a whole the law of grace applies: 'my power is made perfect in weakness'. It is obvious that this cannot be our last word on the matter. The Church must possess both the

---

[74] ARA, p. 171.
[75] Ibid., p. 173.
[76] See 'Wer', *Sponsa Verbi*, p. 165.

'objective holiness' of her structures in the apostolic ministry and the 'subjective holiness' of her individual members, faith, hope and charity realised in act. In the Head and Bridegroom of the Church there is, of course, a perfect coincidence of objective and subjective holiness, but 'this identity must be reproduced in the Church; for the Lord wills to see his Church standing before him, not as a singular, palpable failure, but as a glorious bride worthy of him.'[77] It is in Mary that we see, in a creature and a Christian, the perfect identity of the Church as subjectively immaculate and the Church as objectively infallible.

> In Mary . . . the Church is not only ministerially and sacra-mentally infallible (though she is always subjectively and existentially fallible, always deficient and falling short of the ideal proclaimed). In her the Church is also personally immaculate, and beyond the tension between reality and ideal.[78]

This essay has concentrated on the figures of Mary and Peter in the 'christological constellation' of the Church. As a study of Baltha-sar's ecclesiology it would be radically deficient were no mention to be made of the person who in Christ links the Virgin and the Rock — John, the beloved disciple. He is the one who, at the Lord's bidding, takes Mary to his own home and thus into the apostolic world of Peter. For Balthasar, as for the Fathers of the Church, John is *the* theologian, the most profound expositor of the mystery of Christ. At a time when so many seem attracted by Promethean ideas of the theologian as 'bold explorer' or 'fearless critic', Baltha-sar presents a different model for imitation — the great apostle and evangelist, the man of the Church, who contemplates and com-municates to others the truth that is Jesus in a humble following of Peter as shepherd (cf. Jn 21.15ff.) and by a tender devotion to Mary as Mother (cf. 19.26f.).

[77] Ibid., p. 168.
[78] Ibid., p. 169f.

Hans Urs von Balthasar is without doubt the greatest living Catholic theologian, truly a modern Father of the Church. Although he was not a *peritus* at the Second Vatican Council, his ecclesiology (centred on the 'christological constellation') should be read, so it seems to me, as the profoundest exegesis available of *Lumen Gentium*, especially its understanding of the Petrine (ch. 3) and Marian (ch. 8) dimensions of the Church. The great strength of this ecclesiology is that it is rooted in the dogmas of the Trinity and the Incarnation: just as there can be no adequate Christology which abstracts the incarnate Son from his concrete human relations (Mary, Peter, the other apostles), so there can be no adequate doctrine of the Church which fails to respect the proper balance between the Petrine/apostolic hierarchy and the Marian *communio*. This has considerable importance for ecumenical dialogue, for Balthasar shows convincingly that what Protestantism has called 'the Catholic "And"' (Our Lady, the Papacy) is not a failure in Christocentrism but an expression of Catholic fidelity to the mystery of Christ in its fullness.[79] For just as in the one person of Christ the human will is not swallowed up by, but is freely compliant with, the divine, so too, in the relationship with God which Christ's members enjoy as sons in the Son, divine grace does not overwhelm or destroy creaturely freedom, but rather renews, sanctifies and transfigures it. The freely co-operative and consenting self-surrender of Mary and Peter to Christ are not accidental decoration but intrinsic to the economy of salvation and imprinted on the Church as permanent dimensions of her being and function.

> In Christ, human nature is not ground under by the divine; it is given a chance to co-operate and serve. It is a service made possible and real by grace, but it is an authentic service. Whether we are talking about ecclesial structures (e.g., infallibility, sacramental grace) or man's co-operation with

[79] See ARA, pp.248ff.

grace (e.g., merit, the saints, Mariology), we are really talking about God's free use of man and human realities in Christ. What the Protestant sees as a stress on human capabilities is, for the Catholic, the ultimate sign and high point of God's condescending grace.[80]

---

[80] *Karl Barth*, p. 290.

THE EXEGETE AS ICONOGRAPHER: BALTHASAR AND THE GOSPELS.

Brian McNeil, C.R.V.

Edward Schillebeeckx's two-volume christological study of the New Testament, *Jezus* (1974) and *Gerechtigheid en liefde* (1977)[1] is a massive work that runs to nearly seventeen hundred pages in translation and cites the works of more than eight hundred modern scholars, not restricting itself to 'professional' New Testament scholars but including the work of systematic theologians such as Hans Küng's *Christsein* (1975).[2] It does not pretend to refer to absolutely everything that has been written on the various themes of exegesis, but does claim to guide the reader to 'studies of real significance'.[3] It may therefore seem the more remarkable that Schillebeeckx nowhere refers to the work of Hans Urs von Balthasar, in whose writings scriptural exegesis plays a proportionately much greater role than in the writings of Karl Rahner, who is cited several times. In this, however, Schillebeeckx simply reflects a silent consensus within New Testament scholarship. It is my intention in this essay to offer some observations about Balthasar's exegesis, especially in *Herrlichkeit*, III/2, part II, *Neuer Bund* (1969),[4] and to question the assumption of his irrelevance to contemporary New Testament study.

---

[1] E. Schillebeeckx, *Jezus. Het verhaal van ein levende*, Bloemendaal, 1974 (E.T. *Jesus. An Experiment in Christology*, London, 1979); *Gerechtigheid en liefde. Genade en bevrijding*, Bloemendaal, 1977 (E.T. *Christ*, London, 1980).

[2] H. Küng, *Christsein*, Munich, 1975 (E.T. *On Being a Christian*, London/New York, 1976).

[3] Cf., for example, *Jesus*, p. 62.

[4] E.T. *New Covenant*, forthcoming; references in this essay are to the German edition, with quotations from the English version.

Some of his writing in the 1970s gives the impression that Baltha-sar wishes to have nothing whatever to do with contemporary exegesis;[5] this impression, however, must be balanced by the read-ing of the volume on *New Covenant*. Again and again, the reader who is familiar with the major debates of twentieth-century New Testament scholarship will note nuances of phrasing which show that Balthasar too is aware of divergences within critical scholar-ship, and can accept a methodological approach which does not rest on the *a priori* judgement that all logia attributed to Jesus are authentic. For example, on p. 180, n. 1, he accepts A. Schulz's judge-ment on the inauthenticity of parts of the dialogue between Jesus and the disciples that follows the departure of the rich man (Mk 10.23ff., and parallels in Matthew and Luke). When we turn the page, however, we find a sudden modulation into a key that seems very remote from historical-critical exegesis:

> In the synoptic Gospels, women stand far off and see the crucifixion. These women represent and hint at something that becomes full reality in Mary the mother: accompani-ment into the absolute forsakenness, in which, in order to be truly present, she herself must be forsaken by the son: 'Be-hold your son' (Jn 19.26). John too, who must receive the forsaken mother, represents the Church whose centre is Mary — the Church as second Eve, as the loving bride, springing forth from the slumber of the loneliness on the Cross and from the opened heart, out of which flows what is uttermost; John is nowhere more solemn than in his testi-

[5] See especially *Does Jesus know us - - do we know him?* San Francisco, 1983 (E.T. of *Kennt uns Jesus — kennen wir ihn?* Freiburg, 1980; this book should be read in conjunction with the statement on Christology issued in 1980 by the International Theological Commis-sion). Here he argues in detail the position that lies behind comments such as the follow-ing: '... the diluted, many times filtered image of Jesus which historical-critical exegesis today presents to the student of theology' (commentary on Pope John Paul II's Letter to Priests of Holy Thursday 1979, *Dienst aus der grösseren Liebe zu Christus*, Freiburg, 1979, p. 56).

mony to this event at the extremity. But because the sacraments have their source here, and because the disciples who fled have received communion before the Passion, they too are present, whether they will or not, under the Cross and at the Cross, since they belong to the one body of Christ. John suppresses also the cry of abandonment and the sinking down of the sacrificed Lamb of God into the night; for him, the love that performs everything is so visible that there can never be any doubt of its identity: it is precisely at the point where it 'goes to the end' (13.1) that it becomes most clearly visible as love.[6]

The exegete who reads this passage will tend to dismiss it with the following criticisms.

First, exceedingly few scholars today accept the traditional identification of the beloved disciple, who is the guarantor of the tradition of the community which stands behind the fourth Gospel, with John the son of Zebedee, one of the twelve and subsequently one of the 'pillars' of the Jerusalem community (Gal 2.9). Rather, this figure is to be seen as originally not one of the twelve, and the scenes in which he appears, always having the advantage over Peter (Jn 13.21ff., 19.26 compared with Peter's threefold betrayal, 20.1ff. and 21.7), are indebted to the aetiological concerns of the 'Johannine' community. This applies likewise to the role of Mary in John 19: her presence beneath the Cross is not mentioned in the synoptic Gospels, and is more probably to be attributed to the theological concerns of the evangelist, showing the legitimation by Jesus of his community as the guardian of Jesus' mother, than to his employment of authentic traditions.

Second, the role attributed here to Mary, as one who accompanies her son into his abandonment by God, is not the fruit of exegesis of John 19, but of Catholic Mariology of the mediaeval and post-

[6] *Herrlichkeit*, III/2, pt. II, pp. 182-183.

mediaeval periods. It is, as such, a theological construct which may
or may not be accepted as *theology*, but has no place in the direct
exegesis of the New Testament. The same is true of the phrase, 'the
Church whose centre is Mary': this is a theme dear to Balthasar,[7]
but foreign to the ecclesiology of the fourth Gospel. We remain in
this realm of theological constructs, admittedly traceable to the
patristic age, when Balthasar goes on to speak of 'the Church as second Eve, as the loving bride' that springs from the opened side of
Jesus; modern exegesis tends to agree that the 'blood and water'
that flow from his opened side (Jn 19.34) symbolise the eucharist
and baptism (cf. also 1 Jn 5.8), but it is a *theological* judgement and
not an *exegetical* judgement, when Balthasar understands this as the
birth of the *Church* (using an image more reminiscent of the birth
of Athene from Zeus than of Johannine pneumatology).

Third, to say that the evangelist 'suppresses' Jesus' cry of abandonment (cf. Mk 15.34) is to make unwarrantable assumptions about
his sources. The parallels that exist beteen Mark and John are too
tenuous to justify such a statement. Similarly, every undergraduate
knows that the fourth gospel has no account of the institution of
the eucharist; it is therefore an illegitimate harmonisation of the
gospels to speak of the disciples' 'having received communion
before the Passion' and deduce that therefore 'they too are present,
whether they will or not, under the Cross and at the Cross, since
they belong to the one body of Christ'. This harmonisation draws,
further, on the Pauline theology of the body of Christ, and on the
directly eucharistic interpretation of 'discerning the body' (1 Cor

---

[7] This theme plays an important role in *Der antirömische Affekt*; see also 'Maria in kirchlicher Lehre und Frömmigkeit', in *Maria, Mutter des Herrn*, ed. by Secretariat of German
Episcopal Conference (Die deutschen Bischöfe, Nr. 18, Bonn, 1979), pp. 33-55. The theologian may well object here that to speak of Mary as the personified Church *before* Jesus'
death and resurrection is not implied by acceptance of the dogma of her immaculate conception (or 'anticipated redemption'), and is liable to lead to precisely the mystification
and the undervaluing of the visible Church of hierarchy and sacraments that are found in
Balthasar's essay on 'Frauenpriestertum' (printed in *Neue Klarstellungen*, Einsiedeln,
1979).

11.29); and, of course, a developed eucharistic ecclesiology lies unexpressed beneath these words. Much modern exegesis may seem to overemphasise the diversity within the New Testament: but this passage of Balthasar seems to go to the opposite extreme of implying that there is no *significant* diversity, and that one may make a synthesis that blends the individuality of the distinct writings into a consistent whole.

It is such considerations that lead to the ignoring of Hans Urs von Balthasar's work by contemporary exegesis. The apparent survival of a pre-critical approach to scripture alongside the utilisation of modern tools[8] casts a curious haze over his exegesis, making it difficult to see precisely what is being said; and so, whatever may be said of his contribution to dogmatic theology or to spirituality, his exegesis is likely to be dismissed as an irrelevant sideshow, and his books to remain unread by students. One may indeed conclude that Balthasar is justified in his anxiety that his work on the *New Covenant* will strike the theologian who reads it as 'methodologically unclear, if not hopelessly dilettantic' (p. 9). This conclusion, however, should be questioned.

The exegete whose reactions are as I have described them is not necessarily in disagreement with the theological positions maintained by Balthasar: but he will claim that, *qua* exegete, it is not his business to pronounce on such questions of dogmatic theological interest. His task is to discover as precisely as possible, using the available tools of the historical-critical method, what the gospels say (a task that involves textual criticism) and what the evangelists intended thereby (a task that involves redaction criticism); an aspect of this inquiry concerns the sources drawn on by the evangelists, and hence the authenticity of the logia and deeds ascribed to Jesus. The exegete need not start from a position of faith in the correctness of the faith-judgements of the early communities; *qua*

---

[8] In the analysis of Bernard Lonergan, this would be termed 'residual classicism'.

exegete, he must only delineate what those faith-judgements were, and what they signified in the contexts in which they were formulated.[9] To use a metaphor that is inexact, but helpful, we may say that here the exegete is understood as a photographer.

For Balthasar, exegesis is a theological activity,[10] and theology can be done *only* within the Church of believers: 'the Christ event exists only in correlation to the event of the Church and can be thought and expressed only so; it is only within this situation of reciprocity that the individual can appropriately situate himself in his believing and in his theologising. Outside the circulation of love between bridegroom and bride, between head and body, no one will ever know what theology signifies, and still less, what is the momentum of the glory of the divine love'.[11] This means that the exegete cannot adopt a neutral position that brackets off the questions of faith and theology: his researches must be 'committed'. The exegete is understood here, not as a photographer, but rather (to use another metaphor that is inexact, but helpful) as an iconographer.

Like the photographer, the iconographer intends to make a truthful image; but his criteria of 'truthfulness' are different. He belongs to the community of faith, and his icon expresses the Church's theological conviction that persons (Christ above all, and the saints) and events (e.g., the baptism of Jesus) which had their place in the history of man have an abiding supratemporal significance. He is not interested in the merely historical truthfulness of the saint as he *once* was when on earth, but rather in the theological truthfulness of what he *now* is in heaven.[12] The temporal reality of the earthly

[9] For a theological critique of such presuppositions, see Nicholas Lash, 'What might martyrdom mean?', in W. Horbury and B. McNeil (eds.), *Suffering and Martyrdom in the New Testament*, Cambridge, 1981, pp. 183-98.

[10] 10. Apart from *Kennt uns Jesus* (n. 1 above), see also, e.g., 'Exegese und Dogmatik', *IKaZ Communio* Vol. 5, 1976, pp. 385-92.

[11] *Neuer Bund*, p. 99.

[12] For this distinction between kinds of truthfulness, I am indebted to the lectures on Orthodox iconography by Prof. E. Chr. Suttner at the University of Vienna in the winter semester 1979/80.

existence is not wiped out, nor reduced to a symbol of atemporal truths: it is taken up into the truth of the present life of the Church, for which the icon is a mediation of the presence of the living saint. What does it mean to speak of the exegete as iconographer?

First, the fundamental presupposition of his work must be his sharing the faith of the Church, a faith articulated above all in the christology of the Niceno-Constantinopolitan creed. There can be no division between the 'Jesus of history' and the 'Christ of faith'; the theological problems posed by the Gospels (e.g., the limitations of Jesus' knowledge: cf. Mk 13.32) are to be seen in the context of a kenotic christology that aims to do full justice both to the genuine humanity of the incarnate Son and to the claims of trinitarian theology. Even at the point where these two seem intellectually irreconcilable, and one *seems* forced to 'choose' between the divinity and the humanity of the Jesus who cries out in abandonment on the Cross (Mk 15.34), 'it is, as always, the Spirit who carries out the saving decisions of the Trinity: it is his work that permits the darkness between the Father and the Son to work itself out to the final point, for the sake of the world's salvation'.[13] There can be no 'canon within the canon'; the only hermeneutical principle that can permit an assessment of the relative value of passages of scripture is this faith of the Church.[14]

Second, this means that 'the final form gives the norm'.[15] One may investigate the sources, in order better to understand this final form, but 'anyone who wished to look for acts and events "behind" the interpretative word must necessarily push forward into emptiness'.[16] The reconstructed Jesus of history is a figure empty of

---

[13] 'Alle Wege führen zum Kreuz', *IKaZ Communio* Vol. 9, 1980, pp. 333–42 (here p. 339).

[14] Thus, e.g., Balthasar can speak of a 'lowering of the level of the unique Cross' in the paraenesis of 1 Pet 2.21 (*New Covenant*, p. 177).

[15] *Theodramatik*, II/1, p. 95.

[16] *Neuer Bund*, p. 94.

authority, for in the faith of the Church, the icon of Jesus presented by the Gospels (in a process that includes the 'non-historical' casting of the Easter radiance back over the ministry and teaching) possesses absolute truthfulness: 'to speak aprioristically, if the history of Jesus of Nazareth was correctly understood and interpreted by the post-Easter community, as the superabundant fulfilment of the covenantal love and fidelity established by God in the old covenant, then it was absolutely impossible to comprehend this history, to meditate on it and put it into words, *otherwise* than actually happened, *otherwise* than in the way in which the sacred writers in their naïve openness offered it to us, indeed forced it upon us'.[17] For Balthasar, it goes without saying that the protasis of this sentence is truly fulfilled. Exegesis that would produce results contradicting the Church's teaching (e.g., on the virginal conception of Jesus)[18] is, therefore, impossible *a priori.*

Third, this means that there exists a profound harmony in scripture, both in the Old Testament which looks to Jesus for its future fulfilment, and in the New Testament where, 'with all the personal and material tension between the tendencies represented by the "pillars" (Peter, James, John, Paul), there reigns unity — not primarily on the level of "brotherliness", but in their common looking upwards to the one personal centre of all theologies, to Jesus the Christ of God, the appearing and exposition of the love of the Father.'[19] This principle of unity can be posited at a yet deeper level, in the salvific action of the triune God, which means that 'however much the individual books and words of scripture designate a par-

[17] Ibid., pp. 99-100 (my italics).

[18] Exegesis may, however, show how Old Testament materials have been employed in the infancy narratives: cf. ibid., pp. 52-62. These 'beyond doubt go back, in their core, to historical events that have been long meditated on' (p. 53); cf. also, on the possible historicity of the core of Johannine discourses, *Theodramatik*, II/1, p. 93, n. 7.

[19] *Neuer Bund*, p. 101; cf. also *Der antirömische Affekt* (n. 2 above), where this is exposed in greater detail.

ticular aspect or phase, the whole of the word must always be present in each of them. God's word can reveal itself ever anew from an infinite multiplicity of facets, but it cannot be broken up into fragments. Thus an individual passage too can be interpreted appropriately only in the entire context of scripture, however much one must begin with concern about its particular meaning, its special value as a statement, etc.'[20] Thus, in the strange chronological data of Mark's Gospel, where Jesus continually arrives and departs, Balthasar can find a confirmation of the theological principle that 'the Son has "given an exegesis" (Jn 1.18) in human form of the Father, whom no one has ever seen: as Word made flesh, he has clothed the ineffable in human categories — yet in such a way that through everything that is comprehensible the essentially incomprehensible God shines through.'[21] Similarly, on Mk 5.30f. ('Jesus, perceiving in himself that power had gone forth from him . . .'), Balthasar writes that this is not to be explained by some magic primitivism, but is rather 'an indication of the readiness to pay for the miracle that was *truly* to be worked, with the total loss of power'.[22]

Fourth, following on from this principle, the 'spiritual' interpretation of scripture is no mere relic of the pre-critical understanding, but is a central hermeneutical tool. The same Spirit who inspired the writing of scripture in its christological fullness and unity, inspires its interpretation within the Church today, so that 'for the Christian, there can be only a spiritual interpretation of scripture, one that interprets the (old) scripture (*graphê*) with a view *to* the incarnation of the entire divine Word, and reads the scripture that exists after the incarnation *from* this point, and moreover seeks to interpret what is read out of the Spirit of Christ.'[23] The modern

[20] *Theodramatik*, II/1, p. 102.

[21] 'Die Abwesenheiten Jesu', *Geist und Leben* Vol. 44, 1971, pp. 329-35 (here p. 329; reprinted in *Neue Klarstellungen*).

[22] *Neuer Bund*, p. 72 (my italics).

[23] *Theodramatik*, II/1, pp. 101–102 (his italics).

exegete must therefore be prepared to learn from the Church fathers. For him, as for them, 'what seems outwardly to be a book is inwardly "spirit and life", always standing ready to be used by the living God as he intends, ready to be interpreted and opened up as the unhoped-for, absolutely new word for an individual who loves, or for a group or an epoch.'[24]

It will be seen that this 'iconographic' approach does not banish scholarly exegesis from the Church, but does expect from the exegetes a rather different task from the 'photographic' approach.

What can the exegete learn from Balthasar's exegesis of the Gospels? Undoubtedly, there is illumination to be had on individual passages.[25] But more importantly, the lesson is surely that of the inescapably theological character of exegetical activity, a lesson that is the more vital in our age of specialisation. Balthasar often fights the battle against what he sees as aberrations of contemporary exegesis, but this is not in order to retreat to a secure conservative stronghold, untroubled by the questions of exegetes: it is precisely in order to *harness* scholarly exegesis for the greater battle in defence of the fundamental insights of the Christian faith — a defence that must be undertaken against secularisation, but also against an untheological Catholic conservatism that is equally

---

[24] Ibid., pp. 96-97. This 'readiness' of scripture implies a readiness on the part of the exegete to accept that 'none of the great themes that are broached in the New Testament can ever lose its actuality' ('Aktualität des Themas "Kirche aus Juden und Heiden"', *IKaZ Communio* 5, 1976, pp. 239-45, here p. 239; reprinted in *Neue Klarstellungen*). A parallel example of the ascription of abiding theological significance to a New Testament theme, after the particular historical circumstances have completely altered, is the examination of the question of circumcision in Gal 2 by the systematic theologian Gerhard Ebeling in *Die Wahrheit des Evangeliums*, Tübingen, 1981; his work on Paul shows formal similarities to what I have noted here about Balthasar's exegesis of the gospels.

[25] Besides the examples from Mark already referred to, see, e.g., his discussion of Jesus' petitionary prayers in *Theodramatik*, II/1, pp. 270-75.

deadly for the Church.[26] The journalistic picture of Hans Urs von Balthasar as a reactionary prophet of doom is, precisely, journalistic; the support it claims to find in his writing on exegesis will not bear *theological* examination. His concern, in all the sharpness of his polemic, is to write 'combative theology' (*kämpfende Theologie*) that has its justification in the fact that 'the Word says and demands things of which men want to hear nothing, things that provoke opposition that goes as far as the will to annihilate'; yet 'this combative theology must not forget that it is to be accomplished in the name and the spirit of the Church, with the corresponding dignity, so that it may never descend to the level of worldly wrangling – the tone of doxology must always be able to be heard too'.[27] This programme for theology must include exegesis, but this is possible only if exegesis allows itself to be integrated into the entire enterprise. To use a phrase of Nicholas Lash, there is a 'need to situate academic tasks [of exegesis] appropriately in that broader context of interpretative practice of which they form an indispensable part'.[28]

Balthasar does not offer in *New Covenant* a theoretical account of how exegesis is to be performed: he offers a concrete example. It is, as such, not immediately imitable, for it is logically dependent on his choice of theological concern in *Herrlichkeit* as a whole; even within his own *oeuvre*, one can find different perspectives that govern the exegesis, as in *Theodramatik*, and it is obvious that other theological perspectives than his own are acceptable as legitimate,

---

[26] Balthasar is strongly opposed to the position that 'Christianity is above all a doctrine, a system of "propositions to be held as true"' (*Neuer Bund*, pp. 97-98), especially when this position insulates itself against the questioning of dogmatics and exegesis (see, e.g., 'Exegese und Dogmatik', n. 10 above). See also the 'afterword' to the third edition of *Cordula* (1967), where he speaks of the necessity of retaining the 'neo-Catholics' in the Church (p. 130), despite all his polemics in this book against what he judges to be the inroads of secularisation into the Church.

[27] 'Von der Theologie Gottes zur kirchlichen Theologie', *IKaZ Communio* Vol. 10, 1981, pp. 305-15 (here p. 315).

[28] Art. cit., (n. 9 above), p. 197.

provided that they accept the four principles concerning exegetical activity that I have sketched above. But an icon does not seek to be directly imitable, although part of its iconic quality derives from its standing recognisably within a tradition of iconographic interpretation: it wishes to mediate a presence. If the one who encounters this presence through the icon is himself a painter, he may go on to make his own icon — not a copy, but standing faithfully within the tradition which has enriched the first icon, and to which the first icon itself now belongs. So with Balthasar's exegesis of the gospels, which stands recognisably within a tradition of interpretation: its primary aim is not to be a *model* that other exegetes will reproduce, but to mediate to the reader the presence of the risen Lord to whom the gospels bear witness. If the reader is himself an exegete, he may go on to do his own exegesis, which will be faithful to Balthasar's by standing within the tradition, to which Balthasar now belongs, in its own way. This is, needless to say, a much more difficult enterprise than the assimilation of the principles *either* of scholarly exegesis *or* of dogmatic theology, for it demands the assimilation of both. But if the theological enterprise is not to be fractured into separated disciplines where no real inter-communication on a scholarly level is possible (as has happened in the natural sciences, for example), the effort is necessary. Balthasar is no Simeon Stylites, an object of wonder but not of imitation: his work *invites* imitation, in the sense that I have suggested. His relevance to contemporary exegesis, which (perhaps especially in the Anglo-Saxon world) is increasingly an autonomous discipline, is therefore a challenge to alter the horizons of its work. 'There may, indeed must, be specialisations within the Church's theology — but always in such a way that the whole object of theology, summarised in the Apostolic Creed or in the Niceno-Constantinopolitan Creed, is not lost to view, or even secretly dissolved.'[29] The exegete may be justified in the view that he, *qua* exegete, is not qualified to pro-

---

[29] 'Von der Theologie Gottes . . .' (n. 27 above), p. 315.

nounce on questions of dogmatic theological interest: the importance of Balthasar's work lies in its stringent reminder to the exegete
that he is *not* justified in dismissing dogmatic questions as irrelevant to his own researches.

THE PLACE OF *HEART OF THE WORLD* IN THE THEOLOGY OF HANS URS VON BALTHASAR

Andrew Louth

Heart of the World was published in 1945 and was Hans Urs von Balthasar's first sustained piece of theological writing. By then he had behind him his studies in philosophy and literature which culminated in his vast thesis, *Die Apokalypse der deutschen Seele*, and his studies at Lyons in the Jesuit scholasticate under Père Henri de Lubac, in which he had read deeply in the Greek Fathers, especially Origen, Gregory of Nyssa and Maximus the Confessor. Part of the fruit of those studies had already been published, the rest was shortly to appear, and must already have been nearing completion when Balthasar broke away from such historical studies (though Balthasar had never allowed himself to be a purely historical investigator) to write *Heart of the World*. Five years earlier Balthasar had moved to Basel as a student chaplain, and it was in Basel that Balthasar very soon came to know Adrienne von Speyr — a meeting that issued in Adrienne's conversion to Roman Catholicism in the November of 1940. *Heart of the World* was, then, written out of the initial impact of his friendship with that remarkable woman, whose influence on his own thought Balthasar readily admits. Balthasar has said that, as he prepared Adrienne for reception into the Roman Catholic Church, everything he said found in her a response that seemed to come from the receptiveness of one who had known for ever what he had to tell her, so that the effect of her coming to Catholicism was the unleashing of an apprehension of the dimensions of a faith that had previously been pent up.[1] The

---
[1] *First Glance*, p. 31.

sense of barriers broken down and an almost uncontrollable stream bursting forth is very much the impression *Heart of the World* gives: we can readily believe that this reflects what he had discovered (and evoked) in Adrienne von Speyr.

It is common for a man's early works to foreshadow in significant (and sometimes — with hindsight — unexpected) ways the works of his maturity. In the case of Hans Urs von Balthasar this seems to be strikingly so and the aim of this essay is to explore this a little. But *Heart of the World* also strikes us in another way, for it is not only a remarkable foreshadowing of his later work, in that many of the concerns of that work can already be discerned here, it is also an uncanny crystallisation of the vision of Adrienne von Speyr, as Balthasar later sketched it in his introductory book to Adrienne's writings, *First Glance at Adrienne von Speyr*. A paragraph of *Heart of the World* beginning 'The magic of Holy Saturday . . . '[2] evokes immediately the peculiar quality of Adrienne's vision and one of its most central themes; when we read that, we know where we are. But I shall suggest that there is more than such an echo of Adrienne in *Heart of the World*.

This essay then will have two dimensions: the relationship of *Heart of the World* to the visionary theology of Adrienne von Speyr, and its relationship to the immense theological achievement of which it is the very beginning. Two dimensions — or two poles: for there is no chance of treating first the one and then the other, for Adrienne's influence pervades the whole of Balthasar's theological *oeuvre*, and the themes Balthasar finds in her are the great themes of his own theological vision. Rather we shall start from Balthasar's own account of Adrienne von Speyr's message and then show how all this is developed in *Heart of the World*, and foreshadows the themes found in his mature work. The treatment will be sketchy but (I hope) suggestive; anything else would be beyond the scope of an essay.

---

[2] *Heart of the World*, p. 152.

But first, Adrienne von Speyr. Balthasar's own account of her teaching, somewhat compressed, runs like this. The fundamental structure of her vision is *Marian*: at its heart is Mary's *fiat*, Mary's Yes to God. This 'Yes' and its consequence in the Incarnation yield two fundamental emphases. The first is an emphasis on *obedience*, and on the idea of complete self-oblation represented in the idea of the *vowed life*. What is involved in such a life is obviously endless, but two things in particular are developed: first, the profound nature of sin, which goes beyond any personal sin, for the vowed life leads directly to a participation in the sin of the world, in the sense of the bearing of the weight of that sin; and secondly, the nakedness of the soul before God, implied in such a vowed life and necessary if such a vowed life is to be possible and genuine — a nakedness of the soul before God which can only be realised through the practice of the sacrament of confession. The second fundamental emphasis is *fruitfulness*: the consequences of this vowed obedience are best seen as *fruits*, rather than results or effects or successes. But all this — fruitfulness and obedience — is only possible in relation to Christ's obedience, the obedience of the Son. Mary's obedience was a foreshadowing of that obedience, and only possible in its strength; our obedience is a following or imitation (*Nachfolge* — not *Nachahmung*). And it is the obedience of the Son that discloses the mystery of the Christian life. The obedience of the Son can be viewed in two ways: first, as an unfolding of the intertrinitarian life of the Father, the Son and the Spirit; secondly, as the perfecting of the relationship of the creature to God, something explored in the understanding of the Church as the Body and Bride of Christ. *Two* ways: but inseparable — for life in the Church is a participation in the life of the Trinity. To quote Balthasar: 'In Christ the mystery of love's triune life is open to us; Christian existence for Adrienne takes place within this openness, indeed, strictly speaking, within the Trinity itself: en route from the Father to the world with the Son, led by the Spirit; en route with the Son and the world led home by him, to the Father, led by the Spirit.'[3] Balthasar

[3] *First Glance*, pp. 60.

149

goes on to say that this language may seem too bold, that the language of separation of the Persons may seem to go beyond the safe language of orthodoxy. But he remarks — and in doing so introduces us to another fundamental theme of Adrienne's — 'But one must not forget that Adrienne proceeds from the obedience of the Son of God who humbles himself to be "the servant of Yahweh"; in fact, from the very situation where the trinitarian opposition stands out most strongly: the Mount of Olives, the Cross, the descent into Hell. But it is also precisely there that the mystery of unity is definitively known in the revelation of absolute love.'[4] And he goes on to speak of two ideas that are prominent here: the Cross as a trinitarian event, and the participation of the Father and the Spirit in the event of the God-forsakenness of the Son — and beyond that, of the mystery of our being represented on the Cross in the Son, and how henceforth the Father can only consider and deal with the world through the Son. And we are in the presence of the most characteristic motif of Adrienne: the mystery of Holy Saturday.

Now it requires absolutely *no* effort at all to show how all this is present in and informs the structure and message of *Heart of the World*. The characteristic emphasis on the Trinity and on the Trinitarian dimensions of Christ's mission and especially suffering and death: that is a fundamental *Leitmotiv* in the work. The centrality of obedience, the emphasis on fruitfulness (developed in particular in Chapter IV which is a meditation on the text, 'I am the Vine, ye are the branches'), the descent into Hell and the mystery of Holy Saturday: it is all there. Indeed the movement from the second part of the work called *The Suffering* to the third part, *The Victory*, is the movement from Good Friday to Easter Morning through the mystery of Holy Saturday. Any *explicit* Marian dimension in the work is perhaps muted — a few references — but that does not alter the fundamentally Marian structure of the work.

[4] Ibid., pp. 61.

Let us take a few of these themes and see how they are developed. We begin with the Trinity. *Heart of the World* begins with an evocation of the way in which human existence is fragmented into individuals, each cut off from the other. Men are bound by limits which are impenetrable barriers. Although they seem occasionally to be breached, this is an illusion and the isolation and loneliness of human existence supervene. This, with the idea that human sin is all that binds men together — but does so in order to render the separation and isolation more final — seems to me a view that recalls ideas Bernanos presents in his *Journal d'un curé de campagne*. The doctrine of the Trinity makes its first explicit appearance as something that gives a vision of a wholeness that includes difference but excludes isolation.

> This is a new mystery, inconceivable to mere creatures: that even distance from God and the coolness of reverence are an image and a likeness of God and of divine life. What is most incomprehensible is, in fact, the truest reality: precisely by not being God do you resemble God. And precisely by being outside of God are you in God. For to be over against God is itself a divine thing. As a person who is incomparable you reflect the uniqueness of your God. For in God's unity, too, there are found distance and reflection and eternal mission: Father and Son over against one another and yet one in the Spirit and in the nature that seals the Three of them together. Not only the Primal Image is God, but also the Likeness and the Reflected Image. Not only the unity is unconditional; it is also divine to be Two when there is a Third that binds them together. For this reason was the world created in this Second One, and in this Third One does it abide in God.

> But the meaning of creation remains unexplainable so long as the veil covers the eternal Image. This life would be noth-

151

ing but destiny, this time only sorrow, all love but decay, if the pulse of Being did not throb in the eternal, triune Life.[5]

The first thing that strikes one about this quotation is what sort of a doctrine of the Trinity we have to do with. We are in fact reaching back behind Augustine to the doctrine of the Trinity found in the Greek Fathers. The crucial difference between Augustine and the Greeks (and it is a change Augustine consciously made, for in his early writings he has the Greek theology, derived perhaps from Ambrose or Hilary) is that for the Greeks the Image of God is the Son, who is also God, whereas for Augustine the image of God is something other than God, indeed the highest created spiritual substance, man's soul (and indeed the angels), which is a trinitarian image of the Trinitarian God. God is over against us as Trinity: therefore we are not God. For the Greeks God is over against us as God (the Father), revealed to us as God (the Son) and present in us as God (the Holy Spirit). This characterisation of the Greek patristic doctrine of the Trinity, which has become familiar to us from the writings of Karl Rahner, is presupposed here by Balthasar — and it can hardly be by chance (all his work on Origen, and perhaps more significantly Maximus the Confessor, was already behind him). And like the Greek patristic doctrine of the Trinity what we have in Balthasar is an articulation of Christian vision by means of a modification of Platonic or neo-Platonic terms. The preceding paragraph has worked towards this understanding of the doctrine of the Trinity by means of the neo-Platonic categories of procession and return (*proodos* and *epistrophe* — *Ausgang and Rückkehr*). But whereas, in neo-Platonic thought, return is valued above procession, because procession is a declension in being whereas return is its recovery, this is not so with Balthasar.

> For it is not the rhythm of his creation that it should go out from God by progression and go back to its source in a

---

[5] *Heart of the World*, p. 35.

movement of return. Rather are both these things as one, inseparable, and the going forth is no less unconditional than the return, nor the mission less God-willed than the longing for God. And perhaps the going forth from God is still more divine that the return home to God, since the greatest thing is not for us to know God and reflect this knowledge back to him as if we were gleaming mirrors, but for us to proclaim God as burning torches proclaim the light.[6]

This neo-Platonic dimension in Balthasar's thought seems to me more important than one might expect. Thérèse is seen as correcting a common misconception among the Fathers and scholastics about the relationship between contemplation and action — a relationship which is both stated and (it seems to me) corrected in deeply neo-Platonic terms.[7] There are far more references to Proclus than you would expect in *The Glory of the Lord* and his key-idea of *amethektos metechomenon* runs like a thread through the work.[8] But perhaps most significant — and something we shall come back to — is Balthasar's concern, which he shares with Procline neo-Platonism, with the mystery of generation.

In the passage I have just discussed the doctrine of the Trinity is presented somewhat abstractly and schematically, though the reference to the 'pulse of the life of the Trinity' hints at something more engaged. As *Heart of the World* develops and the Heart, the Sacred Heart, the Heart of the World, is introduced, this is drawn into the context of the doctrine of the Trinity — or rather it is a point of vantage from which the Trinitarian relations are discussed — and experienced.

---

[6] Ibid., p. 33f.

[7] See his *Thérèse of Lisieux*, pp. 138–40.

[8] The Greek phrase is explicitly cited at *Herrlichkeit*, I, p. 293 (E.T. p.305); III/1, p. 948; III/2, p. 12.

The divine Ocean forced into the tiny wellspring of a human Heart! The mighty oak-tree of divinity planted in the small, fragile pot of an earthly Heart! God, sublime on the throne of his majesty, and the Servant — toiling with sweat and kneeling in the dust of adoration — no longer to be distinguished from one another! The eternal God's awareness of his kingship pressed into the nescience of human abasement! All the treasures of God's wisdom and knowledge stored in the narrow chamber of human poverty! The vision of the eternal Father shrouded in the intuitions of faith's obscurity! The rock of divine certainty floating on the tides of an earthly hope! The triangle of the Trinity balanced by one tip upon a human Heart![9]

But the true dimensions of Balthasar's doctrine of the Trinity are revealed as the Son, the Heart, descends into suffering and death, and the Trinity is manifest, distended in the God-forsakenness of the Son. This is foreshadowed a few pages later where we read that the true miracle of the human heart is revealed in the fact

> that the perfect Yes to the Father's will could be uttered in the midst of a storm of impulses impelling the death-tormented Lamb to take flight; that the eternal distance of love between Father and Son (eternally enfolding the one in the other by the embrace of both in the Spirit) could become the yawning gap between heaven and hell, from whose pit the Son groans his 'I thirst', the Spirit now no longer anything but the huge, separating and impassable chaos; that the Trinity could, in suffering's distorted image, so disfigure itself into the relationship between judge and sinner. . .[10]

[9] *Heart of the World*, p. 49.
[10] Ibid., p. 54.

But this is only a foreshadowing of something that is developed more fully later, as Balthasar takes us into the mystery of the Son's God-forsakenness and the way this utter failure and weakness bear fruit in the mystery of Holy Saturday.

We find this touched on, or developed, in several places. Quite a typical one is this:

> You fall into the bottomless; you are lost. Not the faintest shimmer of hope delimits this fear. For in what could you still have hope? That the Father might still pardon you? He will not, cannot, does not want to do it. Only for the price of your sacrifice does he intend to pardon the world: the world, not you. Nothing at all is said about anything beyond your fear. Mercy? But you are yourself God's mercy, and it consists in your own ruination. Someone has to be the scapegoat, and you are it. Indeed, you yourself wanted it this way. Do you want to avert God's lightning-bolt from men? Then it will have to strike you.

> 'Father,' you cry out, 'if it is possible...' But now it is not even possible. Every fragment and shred of possibility has disappeared. You cry into the void: 'Father!' And the echo resounds. The Father has heard nothing. You have sunk too low into the depths: how are those up in heaven still to hear you? 'Father, I am your Son, your beloved Son, born from you before time began!' But the Father no longer knows you. You have been eaten up by the leprosy of all creation: how should he still recognize your face? The Father has gone over to your enemies. Together they have plotted their war-plan against you. He has loved your murderers so much that he has betrayed you, his Only-begotten. He has given you up like a lost outpost; he has let go of you like a lost son. Are you sure that he still really exists? Is there a God? If a

God existed he would be love itself; he certainly could not be sheer hardness, more unrelenting than a wall of bronze. If there were a God, he would have to manifest himself at least in his majesty; you would have to feel at least a breath of his eternity; you would at least be allowed to kiss the hem of his garment when, in his sublimeness, he walked away over you, perhaps crushing you heedlessly underfoot. Oh, how gladly you would allow yourself to be trampled by that adored foot! But, instead of gazing into the pupil of God's eye, you stare into the void of a black eye-socket. And so you stagger over to men; now that eternal love is dead and the chill of the world's expanse wraps you in its ice, you seek some measure of life in men's animal warmth. But these are asleep. Let them sleep; let even the beloved disciple sleep. They would never understand that God no longer loves.[11]

As Balthasar's Christ stares 'into the void of a black eye-socket'(in die Leere einer schwarzen Augenhöhle), we recall Jean Paul's Christ in *Siebenkäs* who, searching beyond the world after the divine eye, felt it staring back at him 'with an empty, bottomless eye-socket' — 'Keep shouting, discordant tones, destroy the shadows with your cries; for He is not.' (mit einer leeren bodenlosen Augenhöhle' — 'Schreiet fort, Misstöne, zerschreiet die Schatten; denn Er ist nicht.) There is no God, God is dead. Long before Jean Paul was dragged on to the theological scene in the sixties, there are echoes of him in Balthasar's *Heart of the World*. And this is picked up still later in the book:

Immeasurable emptiness (not solitude) streams forth from the hanging body. Nothing but this fantastic emptiness is any longer at work here... There is nothing more but nothingness itself. The world is dead. Love is dead. God is dead.[12]

[11] Ibid., pp. 109–10.
[12] Ibid., p. 150.

It is Good Friday. And we descend into Hell, enter into the chaos of Holy Saturday.

Chaos. Beyond heaven and hell. Shapeless nothingness behind the bounds of creation. Is that God? God died on the Cross. Is that death? No dead are to be seen. Is it the end? Nothing that ends is any longer there. Is it the beginning? The beginning of what? In the beginning was the Word. What kind of word? What incomprehensible, formless, meaningless word? But look: What is this light glimmer that wavers and begins to take form in the endless void? It has neither content nor contour. A nameless thing, more solitary than God, it emerges out of pure emptiness. It is no one. It is anterior to everything. Is it the beginning? It is small and undefined as a drop. Perhaps it is water. But it does not flow. It is not water. It is thicker, more opaque, more vis-cous than water. It is also not blood, for blood is red, blood is alive, blood has a loud human speech. This is neither water nor blood. It is older than both, a chaotic drop. Slowly, slowly, unbelievably slowly the drop begins to quicken. We do not know whether this movement is infinite fatigue at death's extremity or the first beginning — of what? Quiet, quiet! Hold the breath of your thoughts! It's still much too early in the day to think of hope. The seed is still much too weak to start whispering about love. But look there: it is indeed moving, a weak, viscous flow. It's still much too early to speak of a wellspring. It trickles, lost in the chaos, direc-tionless, without gravity. But more copiously now. A wellspring in the chaos. It leaps out of pure nothingness, it leaps out of itself. It is not the beginning of God, who eter-nally and mightily brings himself into existence as Life and Love and triune Bliss. It is not the beginning of creation, which gently and in slumber slips out of the Creator's hands. It is a beginning without parallel, as if Life were arising from Death, as if weariness (already such weariness as no amount of sleep could ever dispel) and the uttermost decay of power were melting at creation's outer edge, were beginning to flow, because flowing is perhaps a sign and a likeness of weariness which can no longer contain itself, because everything that is strong and solid must in the end dissolve into water. But hadn't it — in the beginning — also been born from water? And is this wellspring in the chaos, this trickling weariness, not the beginning of a new creation?

The magic of Holy Saturday. The chaotic fountain remains directionless. Could this be the residue of the Son's love which, poured out to the last when every vessel cracked and the old world perished, is now making a path for itself to the Father through the glooms of nought?. . .[13]

Two themes, at least, are intertwined here. There is the theme that in the God-forsakenness of the Son, the Chaos that stretches between the Father and the Son is the Holy Spirit, and that this provides the principle for the new life that is the fruit of the Trinity's embrace of the world in all its sinfulness and fallenness. But there is, too, the exploitation of the theme of the mystery of birth. The mystery of birth is central in Balthasar's understanding of the Trinity, of the creation and of the re-creation, as this passage makes clear. Just how important it is in Balthasar's understanding emerges in *Herrlichkeit* III/1 (*Im Raum der Metaphysik*), where the development of the final section begins with the remark, 'If one surveys western metaphysics as a whole, one must wonder how little the riddle of propagation — not only of organic natures, but above all of man, who is spiritual — has disturbed the philosophers.'[14] It may not have disturbed philosophers, but it has fascinated Balthasar, at least from the time of *Heart of the World*.

[13] Ibid., pp. 150-2.
[14] *Herrlichkeit*, III/1, p. 945.

All these passages have been cited to illuminate the place of the doctrine of the Trinity in the development of *Heart of the World*. But they force on us another idea that is also fundamental in Balthasar's theology: that of substitution, and substitutionary atonement. 'Stellvertretung' would be the German, but in *Heart of the World* Balthasar does not use much technical language, though once he refers to Christ as *stellvertretende Sühne*. And although 'substitution' is narrower in meaning than 'Stellvertretung', it is, I think, the word needed in English. For Balthasar Christ stood in our place, bore the suffering and death that was our lot, was 'made sin' for us. It is the lack of such a doctrine of substitution that is one of the things Balthasar holds against Karl Rahner. 'It is not to the point if Rahner, where he deals with the Cross, indulges in continual polemic against a legalistic doctrine of satisfaction (misjudging thereby Anselm's ultimate intention), for it is a matter of the interpretation of the New Testament expression, that Christ bore our sins on the Cross': so Balthasar complains against Rahner in *Cordula*.[15] Balthasar, on the contrary, delights in the sort of language such a legalistic doctrine of satisfaction makes its own. So, for instance, from the passages just quoted, Balthasar speaks of the Trinity being distorted in the Passion into the relationship between the judge and the sinner.[16] The relationship of judge and sinner is a distortion, but it is real none the less. He says, too, 'only for the price of your sacrifice does he intend to pardon the world'.[17] Christ is the scapegoat (*Sündenbock*). 'The Father has gone over to your enemies … He has loved your murderers so much that he has betrayed you … He has given you up … let go of you …'[18] He is very keen on language of the Father betraying the Son: he speaks of the moment when the Father in disguise joins the 'traitors, and the

---

[15] *Cordula*, Einsiedeln, 1966, p. 91; and cf. the excursus on Rahner's soteriology in *Theodramatik* III, pp. 253–62.

[16] *Heart of the World*, p. 54.

[17] Ibid., p. 109.

[18] Ibid., p. 110.

heart is left, alone'; [19] or of the language of the Judge condemning, and exacting the penalty from, the Son: 'what if the imperious command of the angry Judge should blaze against me with terrible threats?'[20]

This insistence on the reality of substitution, a reality that presses the notion to the point of paradox, is something that continues to mark Balthasar's theology. We have seen that it is part of his long-standing criticism of Rahner's theology. In his own attempt at a dogmatics — *Theodramatik* — there is an extended discussion of this theme in which in his historical survey[21] he develops first the patristic theme of an *admirabile commercium* between God and man in Christ, and then moves on to discuss two ways in which the theology of the atonement is approached in modern theology. These two ways focus on the themes of *solidarity* and *substitution* ('*Substitution*' is the German word used here). 'Solidarity' is the word modern theologians, he feels, are happiest with: it avoids the language of sacrifice and redemption which is felt to be incomprehensible to modern man. But Balthasar finds this word too shallow, too frail to bear the weight of the Christian understanding of the atonement. So he turns to an examination of the language of substitution — something developed especially in Protestant theology to which Balthasar gives his (for him unusually) sympathetic attention. Luther, Calvin, and the Protestant scholastics are discussed, and then modern theologians such as Barth, Pannenberg and Moltmann. Balthasar clearly finds in the radicalism of the language of substitution something that approaches more nearly what is needed to convey the radical nature of what God has done for us in Christ. In a concluding section, Balthasar attempts to meet the charge that the language of sacrifice and substitution is no longer comprehensible by drawing on the work of René Girard where he

[19] Ibid., p. 53.
[20] Ibid., p. 71.
[21] *Theodramatik* III, pp. 224–94.

finds the idea of the scapegoat given a new relevance. He also seeks support for this approach in the work of Sergei Bulgakov and A. Feuillet.

We have noticed how Balthasar draws on Barth as he develops the notion of substitution: the parallel with Barth is confirmed in the way Balthasar views the relationship between the Cross and the Resurrection. For Barth the Resurrection is the revelation of what has been achieved in the Cross (though it is revelation that can *only* be seen in the light of the Resurrection — so he can hold it against Bach's St Matthew Passion that it is a treatment of the Passion without any reference to the Resurrection).[22] Something similar is true for Balthasar: 'Where did I triumph if not on the Cross? Are you as blind as the Jews and the pagans to think that Golgotha was my downfall and my failure? Do you believe it was only later — three days later — that I recovered from my death and climbed up laboriously from the pit of Hades to appear among you once again? Look: this is my secret, and there is no other in heaven or on earth: My Cross is salvation, my Death is victory, my Darkness is light.'[23] And later in the same chapter: 'This was my victory. In the Cross was Easter. In death the grave of the world was burst open. In the leap into the void was the ascension to heaven. Now I fill the world, and at last every soul lives from my dying'[24] — a passage that links his understanding of substitution with his understanding of death and resurrection. Of course for Barth this doctrine of substitution means that holiness is no longer any concern of man's: man's existence is worldly, and the world has been redeemed by Christ (or that is what I take him to mean). One of the things Barth finds puzzling about Balthasar is his interest in such people as Thérèse and Elizabeth of Dijon.[25] Balthasar is indeed concerned with holiness,

---

[22] *Church Dogmatics* IV/2, Edinburgh, 1958, p. 280.
[23] *Heart of the World*, p. 175.
[24] Ibid., p.181.
[25] *Church Dogmatics* IV/1, Edinburgh, 1956, 858-9.

and can talk about mysticism — but for him both these are capable of being misunderstood, and a proper grasp of what Christ did can prevent that misunderstanding. Balthasar's understanding of holiness has its own characteristic stress. The passage last quoted continues: 'And wherever a man decides to forsake himself, to give up his own narrowness, his self-will, his power, his blockaded resistance to me, there my Kingdom flourishes.' That gives the tone of the holiness that is, for Balthasar, demanded of the Christian. It is concerned with fruitfulness, not results or achievement. It demands great effort, but it is an effort of preparation — preparation for God. In another place he says (of Mary Magdalene — the type of the Christian — at the tomb): 'And so you stare into the void. For in fact the grave is empty, you are yourself empty, and are, therefore, already pure, and only this staring spasm keeps you from looking behind you.'[26] We are reminded of Adrienne von Speyr and her emphasis on *Ausräumung*: an *Ausräumung*, a draining out, emptying out, so that our life can be Christ's. And the keynote here is obedience: 'it is not ecstasy that redeems, but rather obedience', as Balthasar puts it.[27] In this context it is perhaps worth recalling how Balthasar in *First Glance* twists round the definition of mysticism as an experiential perception of the reality and being of God (*cognitio experimentalis Dei*), so that mysticism, in that sense, is primarily realised in Christ and only through him realised in us: realised in Christ 'in his existence (and his consciousness), his suffering and Resurrection, his presence in the Eucharist and other sacraments'.[28] One is reminded of Barth's comment on 'experience' in a discussion with some Swiss Methodist preachers: 'I do not deny the experience of salvation . . . But the experience of salvation is what happened on Golgotha. In contrast to that my own experience is only a vessel.'[29]

[26] *Heart of the World*, p. 159.
[27] Ibid., p. 55.
[28] See *First Glance*, p. 86.
[29] Quoted in Eberhard Busch, *Karl Barth*, London, 1975, p. 447.

One could go on. There is much more that could be said — and much that is difficult to articulate. The very language and structure of the work are significant. The relation of God to man, of Christ's redemption and our response, is so close that they cannot be separated — and so the book is in some ways repetitive, though it is the repetition of a spiral, not of a circle. Also the style is appropriate to a mystery that entices us and involves us: it comes as no surprise that when Balthasar eventually writes a dogmatics it is called *Theodramatik*, or (perhaps it is the same thing) when Balthasar focuses his concern with beauty and form on one art form, it is drama. But enough has been said to show how the fundamental perceptions of Balthasar's theology have already crystallised in this early work, so that *Heart of the World* can be seen to contain *in nuce* not only the characteristic themes of his theology, but also the style which is inseparable from the apprehension of these themes.

SOME REFLECTIONS ON HANS URS VON BALTHASAR'S CHRISTOLOGY WITH SPECIAL REFERENCE TO THEODRAMATIK II/2 AND III.

Donald MacKinnon

The topic of Hans Urs von Balthasar's treatment of Christ's person is one that is almost as wide as his entire *oeuvre*. If he has delayed to the last volume but two of *Theodramatik*[1] to offer a systematic account of his reading of traditional Christology in its strengths and weaknesses and to present his own vision of the object of his faith, both in the shorter and in the longer works of his extraordinarily wide-ranging pen he has given his readers an example of sustained theological activity, animated by a remarkably independent judgement, with very few parallels in the present century.

The reader who comes to the systematic exposition contained in *Theodramatik* II/2 with some knowledge of the author's previous writings is better able than the novice to appreciate the sustained visionary quality of his achievement in this section of his work. Although the material with which we are concerned occupies less than three hundred pages, it is marked at once by density of argument, exceptional learning that is always made to serve and never to obscure the author's central purpose, and a visionary perception whose depth is assured by the rigorous intellectual discipline by which the author has himself achieved it. Of course the section is not complete in itself and the reader would be well advised to take the pages in the next volume of the work[2] that treat of the doctrine

---

[1] *Theodramatik*, Bd. II, *Die Personen des Spiels*; Teil 2: *Die Personen in Christus*, Einsiedeln, 1978.

[2] *Theodramatik*, Bd. III, *Die Handlung*, Einsiedeln, 1980, especially pp. 295-395.

of the Trinity in very close conjunction with it. Again these latter pages remind the reader even more forcefully than the first-mentioned section that the topic of *kenosis* is of pivotal significance in Balthasar's work. Anyone who knows his monograph on the Paschal mystery[3] will find here the theological context of that essay fully articulated.

There is a great division between contemporary writers on the kind of issues that here occupy Balthasar's mind, and that is their awareness or their disregard of the fact that in the terrible twelve years, 1933–1945, six million Jews were deliberately murdered. The refusal to reckon with this appalling fact gives to any treatment of fundamental theological issues a sort of shallowness that no modernist expertise can conceal. In the pages of his work with which we are here concerned there is comparatively little that treats directly of these horrors; but the nervous tension of the whole argument bears witness to the author's passionate concern to present the engagement of God with his world in a way that refuses to turn aside from the overwhelming, pervasive reality of evil. It is not that Balthasar indulges in any facile cult of pessimism; for one thing he is too well schooled in the great traditions of European literature for such triviality. It is rather that he insists on a vision that can only be won through the most strenuous acknowledgement of the cost of human redemption.

It would be tempting here to refer to his important work on Karl Barth's theology,[4] and there is no doubt that the Catholic has put himself to school with the greatest master of Reformed theology of this century to very good effect. The lessons that he learnt through his remarkably penetrating study of Barth's work were permanent. But more immediately significant is a very small volume of medi-

---

[3] 'Mysterium Paschale' in *Mysterium Salutis* III/2.

[4] *Karl Barth, Darstellung und Deutung seiner Theologie*, Cologne, 1951.

tations for the fourteen Stations of the Cross.[5] At the outset of the first volume of *Theodramatik*[6] Balthasar speaks of the dramatic dimension which he wishes to restore to theology and indeed the whole work is unified by that defining task. But the reader who would want to get inside the author's understanding of the dramatic would be well advised to study these brief but extremely pregnant meditations. Again and again he will be reminded that the tragedy which reached its crisis in Pilate's Praetorium is one that is still being played out in this present century. There is a line traceable from that hall of judgement to the death camps of twentieth century Europe where millions of the Jewish people perished in circumstances of unspeakable indignity. It is a fact that Christians' sense of Jewish responsibility for Jesus' condemnation and execution has contributed more than the average Christian believer can begin to conceive to help create the climate of feeling and imagination in which these horrors were possible. It is not morbid to insist that if we are still to have Christian theology, it must be the work of men and women who never allow themselves to forget these things. Balthasar has written an interesting book on the influential Jewish thinker, Martin Buber;[7] but it is in these meditations that he allows his imagination to be overwhelmed by the reality of the drama in which he knows himself to be involved. It is not that he allows his commitment to faith in Christ's Resurrection to be undermined; it is rather that he would insist that where this *ultimate* victory is concerned, we should not forget the profound lessons to be learnt from the reply of the Duke of Wellington to a gushing woman, who had spoken to him of the supremely exhilarating experience of a victory: 'Madam,' the Duke replied, 'a victory is the most terrible thing in the world, only

---

[5] *The Way of the Cross*, London, 1969 (E. T. of *Der Kreuzweg der St.-Hedwigs-Kathedrale in Berlin*, Mainz, 1964).

[6] *Theodramatik* I.

[7] *Martin Buber and Christianity*, London, 1961 (E.T. of *Einsame Zwiesprache. Martin Buber und das Christentum*, Cologne/Olten, 1958).

excepting a defeat.' There is not a little on the subject of analogy in theological discourse in the two volumes with which we are chiefly concerned, lessons whose significance for the understanding of the whole work might indeed have been made clearer; but the powerfully argued pages that Balthasar devotes to the relations of the Trinity to the Cross show that he is acutely aware that Crucifixion and Resurrection, to be properly understood, must be treated as part of the doctrine of God himself. This though he protests vehemently against any diminution of divine transcendence such as he finds in 'process-theology'. The frequency with which he recurs to the topic of the relation of the immanent to the economic Trinity shows that for him the latter is the expression of the ultimacy of the former, or it is nothing. His criticisms in this connection of the work of Jürgen Moltmann might indeed be judged unfair to the best writing of a theologian who is in many important respects closer in feeling to Balthasar than many other contemporaries. But it is the centre of Balthasar's own vision that is at issue here. If he loses a fundamentally theocentric concentration, then it is his Christology that is imperilled and indeed the understanding of Christ's work.

Perhaps the complexity of these paragraphs goes some way to conveying the texture of Balthasar's work. There is a remorseless emphasis on the concrete; he will not turn aside from the darkest realities of human history and in this emphasis he draws most powerfully on the resources he finds in the Scriptures. He is very well read in contemporary and recent critical study; but when he says that Christology lies between exegesis and dogmatics,[8] he understands exegesis in a way that is essentially his own. It would not be unfair to say that this conception of interpretation receives its clearest definition in the use he makes of the fourth Gospel. His great learning in the world of European literature gives him a sensitivity to the way in which in that Gospel concepts interpenetrate

[8] *Theodramatik* II/2, pp. 92ff.

one another, reflected sometimes in the deliberate ambiguity of the author's language. But it is with the conceptual interpenetration that Balthasar is concerned. It is not that he is not inflexibly aware that crucifixion is one thing, exaltation another, or that humiliation remains horrifying, while in vindication there must be a note of triumph. He does not suppose that, by his use of the concept of *doxa*, the fourth Evangelist obliterates the distinctions on which he elsewhere strongly insists; it is rather that by his use of this concept he enables his readers to grasp an order in which they are found so inseparable that indeed they interpenetrate one another. That order is ultimately expressive of the very being of God as he is in himself, transcribed into terms of an engagement with his creation, that is at once his own initiative and at the same time fulfilment and promise.

The focal point of Balthasar's whole exposition is found in the concept of *Sendung* or mission. Like *doxa* in the fourth Gospel it is a focus of conceptual interpenetration. In his presentation of its content Balthasar ranges widely, quick for instance to bend to his use Paul's self-revelation in his second letter to the Corinthians, finding in the apostle's understanding of his own restless existence intimations concerning the *kenosis* of his Master. Certainly *kenosis* remains profoundly significant for Balthasar; indeed it dominates his imagination in the many passages in which he gives free rein to his mastery of his own language and recaptures the emphases of the earlier monograph on the Paschal mystery. Yet in the present work, mission is a more inclusive concept than self-emptying and demands in its use a more searching discipline. Thus Balthasar makes use of it to great effect in a long and rigorous treatment of the problems of the limitations of Christ's human knowledge. Again like the concept of limitation itself, of which he makes hardly any use, the concept of mission presses beyond poetry into ontology. To write in these terms is not to belittle the work of the poets; in this work Balthasar is arguably more indebted to Sophocles and Calderon than to Plato and Suarez! Such language is admittedly an exaggeration; but it is with the dramatic dimension that Balthasar is concerned in this work, and part of the power of the concept of mission is that it enables him to integrate that dimension with the ontological styles of the older traditional theology. Sometimes he writes as if the uninformed use of the concepts of substance, essence, nature, etc., betrayed the user into a misunderstanding of the stillness of God, a radical misrepresentation of his transcendence. Yet theology is ontological, or it is nothing. Further for a writer whose perspectives are as remorselessly theocentric as Balthasar's, there is something frivolous in any aversion from an underlying and dominant concern with what is. Moreover the reference earlier in this essay to the significance of Auschwitz for Balthasar on his knees on Good Friday should suffice to make plain that for him God's engagement with his world must reach in different ways the very substance of both alike, or else the very idea of it must be dismissed as 'sound and fury signifying nothing'.

Again the first outline of this concept of *Sendung* has served to show the daunting complexity of the author's method. Yet it is a complexity that is all the while deployed in aid of a fundamental simplicity which will be found in the end, but which, because it is the simplicity of the Triune God, will only be approached when we have made our own his ways with his creation in Christ and come to affirm those ways as expressive of that which is sheerly ultimate. In his treatment of the Gospel narratives there is in Balthasar a refreshing absence of the Philistine and in consequence a readiness to take with the utmost seriousness the many references in the synoptic Gospels to the Spirit. He is never uncritical; yet he is sharply aware that the writers are representing very often in significantly different ways a history that is grounded uniquely in God. In my judgement he would have helped himself by bolder use of the concept of limitation, implicit in that of mission, central for Balthasar because it is for him ultimately a Trinitarian concept. He is fully justified in extrapolating this concept of mission from the levels at which he finds it used descriptively in the New Testament, into the being of God as he is in himself. But as his treatment of the problems of Christ's human knowledge well brings out, an understanding which virtually identifies Christ's human knowledge with his self-conscious response to his mission demands use of the concept of limitation to indicate both the context and the manner of that self-restriction. His use in this connection of the notion of autonomy is admirable and encourages the reader to meditate on its presence in the *perichoresis* of the persons of the Trinity. But their very distinction demands limitation as the context which mission marvellously transcends.

Balthasar is not a philosopher in the professional sense, though his early essay on truth and his (earlier) study of the history of German Idealism — *Prometheus*[9] — show him more than ordinarily knowledgeable in this area. Moreover the notion of dialectic is one with which he is clearly fascinated, contrasting, in *The Glory of the Lord*, the dialectic of Plato with that of Sophocles, and sensitive to the ramifications of Barth's theological dialectic in his massive study of that theologian. One can trace also here the influence of Erich Przywara, although Balthasar's own understanding of *analogia entis* is inevitably affected by his familiarity with Barth's critique of his own master. His own dialectic is indeed (like Barth's) theological rather than philosophical; certainly he continually refers to Hegel; but a great gulf divides his Christology from that articulated (as it were) under Hegel's guidance by Hans Küng in his *Menschwerdung Gottes*. It is indeed partly in bringing out these differences that his own theological dialectic is most obviously in play with its insistence that the 'self-emptying' involved in the processions within

---

[9] Thus the title of the second edition of the first volume of Balthasar's three-volume work, *Apokalypse der deutschen Seele*, Salzburg, 1937-39. *Prometheus. Studien zur Geschichte des deutschen Idealismus* was published in Heidelberg, 1947.

the Godhead is understood as the ground of Christ's *self-kenosis* in the Incarnation. That *kenosis* is a totally gratuitous act which, however congruous with its foundation, would still forfeit the mystery of its totally free creativity, if it were regarded as a necessary consequence of the divine 'situation'. And here of course the importance of autonomy in Balthasar's theological structure should be emphasised.

It is part of Balthasar's genius as a theologian that he has recognised, in Christian history, an ongoing tragic dialectic. He compels the student to bracket together the argument of Christ with Pilate and that of Antigone with Creon in Sophocles' play. Of course the former raises explicitly metaphysical issues. 'What is truth?' But, as in any drama, it is the total action that is to supply the sense. Jesus indeed is innocent; he has come to bear witness to the truth, to reveal the poverty of Pilate's judicial integrity, the lie at the heart of Caiaphas' statecraft. But the truth lies beyond their weakness and their guilt; it is there in what Jesus by his innocence, and by his condemnation in spite of that innocence, even because of it, makes of that weakness and that guilt. It is a dialogue, which is more than any sort of argument, one that is all the time creating the situation, which will give it sense. The irony is devastating, even horrifying, were it not that Jesus leaves the Praetorium carrying his own cross (John makes no mention of the Cyrenian). But is Jesus here creator *tout simple*? And the answer must be no. For here as everywhere the concept of *Sendung* must have the last word. Judgement is given to him as Son of Man; but it is something given and received. His creativity resides in the total pervasiveness of his *Auftrag*. Indeed Balthasar identifies him with that *Auftrag*, and his handling of the difficulties involved in that identification shows his relative weakness as a philosopher. How can anyone *be* his Mission? What of the difficulties of analogy involved in such predication? Balthasar finds a heuristic key in the working of grace in the lives of the saints, drawing here on his study of Paul's *apologia pro vita sua* in his second letter to the Corinthians, his own essays on Thérèse of Lisieux, and Elisabeth of Dijon, and fittingly recalling the work of the revered Scottish theologian, the late Professor Donald M. Baillie of St Andrews University.[10] But Balthasar has gone a long way beyond Baillie, and he knows it. He is much nearer to the Russian Sergei Bulgakov in his final Christological perspectives than to the Scot.[11] He is reaching after the concept of an act altogether without parallel, constitutive of a series of relationships which are, for all their multiple differences, transformed by that act into what otherwise they could in no sense have been. He admits when he comes to treat of the 'hypostatic union' that the conceptual apparatus of its initial formulation breaks down. He writes illuminatingly of Christ's self-consciousness, probing the paradox of duality, clearly hoping that in *Sendung* he has a conceptual instrument strong enough to disclose a transcription that is in the deepest sense ontological in character, as if here is the *Anknüpfungspunkt* of divine and human in Christ. But to grasp this our concept of the divine must be transformed by finding the very being of the Trinity bodied forth for us by, because totally present in, the agony and dereliction of Gethsemane and Calvary. And here Balthasar makes effective use of A. Feuillet's excellent study of the Gethsemane narrative.[12] 'Father, if it be possible.' It is Balthasar's achievement to insist that any valid Christology must press from drama to ontology at that point and place: and this not by eliding the dramatic, but allowing the ultimate to open itself to our awareness as love there, and not elsewhere.

It is arguable that a greater philosophical expertise would have helped his exposition. In the early *Prometheus* he showed knowledge of Kant, including his *opuscula* on theodicy and the 'last

[10] *God was in Christ*, London, 1948. This though Balthasar would certainly accept Barth's criticism of Baillie's work in KD IV/2, 1955.

[11] *Du Verbe Incarné*, (F.T. Paris, 1943).

[12] *Theodramatik* III, p. 292 and elsewhere. Feuillet's study is entitled *L'Agonie du Gethsémani, enquêtes exégétiques et théologiques*, Paris, 1977.

things'. But his insistence in *Theodramatik* (and elsewhere) on the mystery of 'the hour' would have been given sharper point by reference to Kant's profound examination of the limitations of characteristically human knowledge, in particular his treatment of time and causality, and other aspects of his doctrine of categories. The concept of receptivity is one Balthasar surely needs, and through Kant, he might have found his way to the notion of a receptivity which is as far from abject, passive acceptance as autonomy (manifestation of the reciprocal love of Father and Son) is from blind obedience to despotic command.

Certainly we do not have here the last word on the problems with which Balthasar is dealing; but we have one of the profoundest contributions to Christology made by any theologian since the second world war. 'God so loved the world that He gave his only begotten Son.' It is enough in the end to praise the work briefly commented on in this essay by saying that its author is among those very few theologians who have devoted superlative scholarship and talent to constrain their readers to attend to the height and to the depth of that love. In the end no more (and no less) should be asked of the one who dares probe the mystery of Christ's person. The opposition in christological reflection between procedure *von unten* and procedure *von oben* is revealed in Balthasar's work as almost totally misleading, even destructive. We have to move to the deepest level (the word *Verlassenheit* occurs again and again in the paper we have been surveying) where Christ is forsaken by mankind and by his Father, using the opening words of Psalm 22 to express a total abandonment, in agony of body and mind, to an ultimate human insignificance. And this climactic *kenosis*, or rather final stage of his self-emptying, is 'the hour' that across the to and fro, the changing relationships of his ministry, is always steadily approaching, yet never to be anticipated, in the end to be received, as if (to use traditional language that Balthasar does not hesitate to employ) the *status exinanitionis* were as much a matter of

173

gift as the *status exaltationis* itself. We are forced by the subtle, strenuous movements of his argument to find really present in these movements the ultimate Trinitarian *diastasis* of Father and Son in the unity of the Holy Spirit. 'God so loved the world that He gave.' In the simple profundity of these familiar words the heart of the matter is concentrated, and by them we are bidden hold depth and height together. And if we follow their imperative, reflection on the love of Christ in the concrete of its expression (and here again I refer to Balthasar's meditations on the Stations of the Cross) will pass for those who have begun to learn the inwardness of the Paschal mystery, into a theology in the profoundest sense, an essay that does not shrink from daring to speak, in human terms, of God as He is in Himself.

APPENDIX

The above essay was completed in April 1982, and since then has remained unaltered. Towards the end of the year 1983, the fourth volume of Hans Urs von Balthasar's *Theodramatik*, entitled *Das Endspiel*, was published, and although it would be out of place to deal here with the author's eschatology, there are sections in this volume which require, which indeed demand, mention in view of their pivotal importance for the subject-matter of this essay.

Thus on pp. 104ff. of this fourth volume Balthasar states explicitly 'Der Sohn ist trinitarische Offenbarung', and in the next sentence, quoting from the mystic Adrienne von Speyr, to whose writings he owes a profound debt, he continues (the translation is my own): '(Christ) builds on earth an extrapolation of the Trinity; he lives a perfectly trinitarian existence, although he becomes man among men.' Later in this same passage, Balthasar again makes his own what he has learnt from Adrienne von Speyr, and draws out the dynamic interpenetration of the persons of the Trinity in their *ewige Einheit wie Differenz*, in the mission of Jesus. Of course the dense theology of this passage and its cognates demands to be undergirded by the concept of exegetical method which it is part-task of the whole work *Theodramatik* to supply; but the passage to which I have referred illustrates the power and spiritual dexterity with which Balthasar surmounts the facile distinction between so-called 'from below upward' and 'from above downward' procedures in Christology.

In another passage entitled *Der Abstieg des Sohnes* (pp. 221-243) the interpenetration of a profound Passion-Mysticism with an unflinchingly metaphysical Trinitarian theology seems to reach what I can only call a height of lyrical rigour, that is surely unique in modern theology. A summary of this section might easily suggest a self-indulgent love of paradox. Yet the disciplined interpenetration of the ontological and the dramatic dimensions of his subject enables the reader to glimpse within the Father's abandonment of his Son, made concrete in the desperately human passion of Jesus, the ultimate joy of the Trinitarian processions as in themselves really and objectively present in 'the hour of darkness'.

Of course Balthasar is quite unafraid of the traditional distinction between immanent and economic Trinity. Certainly he will not allow the former to be swallowed up in the latter. Rather it is the former in its sheerly ultimate transcendent status that is through Christ engaged with the bitterness of human history. But any interpretation, let alone summary, of these twenty-odd pages is no substitute for their close reading; for at this point the author has achieved a level of theological perception only possible to one who is at once metaphysician, logician and poet. I will not say here exegete; for there is a place in which the exegete (and Balthasar commands the skill of the exegete and practises his own style of exegesis) must yield to the poet.

We are familiar in contemporary theology with those who argue that the traditional scheme of Trinity and Incarnation must give place to a theology at once tidier, more easily assimilable and in every respect less demanding. It is thus suggested that, for instance, the *homo-ousion* was the solution of a problem that could only have arisen for students of Greek metaphysics. (An analogy might be found in the suggestion of the late Professor W. K. C. Guthrie that a notorious contradiction in Aristotle's *de Anima* could be avoided by identifying the *nous poiētikos* with the *prōton kinoun akinēton* of the *Physics* and *Metaphysics*.) Such a view of the *homo-ousion* as speculative indulgence displays a cavalier indifference to the sort of questions thrust on the reader's attention by the New Testament material, and however much the traditional scheme needs radical *approfondissement*, at least it advertises those questions, even suggesting riches of understanding to be gained by a refusal to dismiss the unique, or to bypass the demanding road of conceptual reconstruction.

Certainly there are other theologians who in very different ways have suggested and argued that the traditional scheme needs not to be jettisoned but rather to be renewed by a kind of boldly innovative acceptance of its implications. Above all, as Hans Urs von Balthasar most clearly sees, the tragic dimension of the Christian story in its concrete, historical detail needs to be integrated with the inevitably ontological styles of traditional theology. And here the reconstitution of the doctrine of the Trinity beckons even as it also, by its very profundity, deters the enquirer. Yet once the historical traditions embedded in the Gospel are received in their unquestionably tragic quality, the student finds himself thrust towards the mystery of the relational unity of Father, Son, Holy Spirit. Many have remarked on the authentically tragic style of the climactic dialogue of Jesus and Pilate in John 18 and 19. But this same style suffuses whole areas of the Gospel tradition, and its continuous context is the relation of Son to Father: the enigma that is at once the ground of Jesus' being, and the source of the frequently elliptical, yet always searching, quality of his teaching, his actions, his answers. It is in the upper room, in Gethsemane, and on Calvary that the deed which unites Heaven and earth finally envelops the central figure of the Gospel story. But the ground that is constitutive of that deed in form and in detail alike is the threefold God who is here engaged in his unfathomable unity, for the redemption of mankind.

Certainly Balthasar is not alone in finding the reconstitution of the doctrine of the Trinity of supreme importance for characteristically Christian theology. One thinks inevitably of Jürgen Moltmann's *The Crucified God* and its recent sequel, remembering also the author's significant dialogue with the Jewish scholar, Rabbi Pinchas Lapide. There is the remarkable work of the San Salvadorean Jesuit, Jon Sobrino, who subtitles his *Christology at the Crossroads* a 'Latin-American approach', who most certainly displays and acknowledges Moltmann's influence, but whose insight and originality are alike beyond question. There is the massive study *Gott als Geheimnis der Welt* in which Professor Eberhard Jüngel has given sustained, if sometimes difficult, expression to the idea sketched in his earlier monograph *Gottes Sein ist im Werden*. There are also great riches to be mined from the even more massive work of Edward Schillebeeckx. Certainly there is already here a literature that calls urgently for comprehensive study and evaluation, and that in the light of earlier essays in the same direction by writers as varied as Charles Gore, Henry Scott Holland, R. C. Moberly, Frank Weston, Peter Taylor Forsyth, Oliver Chase Quick, and Sergei Bulgakov.

But it would be altogether out of place to conclude this appendix on a bibliographical note, especially as in the writer's judgement Balthasar, in the height and depth of his intellectually disciplined, theologically informed and profoundly cultured spiritual perception, is in many respects his kinsmen's 'master in Israel'. The subject of the essay to which I have added this appendix is his Christology. It was already clear before *Das Endspiel* appeared that although his treatment of the doctrine of Christ's person was of first-order importance, his theology was theocentric rather than Christocentric. His Christology was grounded in his understanding of the Trinitarian being of God, even if the latter was only approached across the former. It would be an over-simplification to speak of the former as epistemologically, the latter as ontologically, prior. Rather it is one of Balthasar's deepest insights to find the latter conveyed with the former in such a way that even if the Trinitarian being of God is the ground of the incarnate life of Christ, the former is totally engaged in and with the latter. Here his unique sense of the interpenetration of the central moments of the Christian mystery is crucially significant.

It was by reason of the light thrown by the last volume of *Theo-dramatik* on Balthasar's thought in this respect that I have thought fit to add this appendix, regretting the need to ignore the theodicy to which much of the volume is devoted, but still insisting in conclusion that at no point in this massive work is the student allowed to forget that its author is one of those Christian theologians who never, as they treat of the mysteries of their God, allow their reader to forget that this century is marked indelibly in history as that of Auschwitz, Maidanek and Treblinka.

AFTERWORD

John Riches

Balthasar as a theologian stands alone. A volume of essays celebrating Balthasar at 80 must reflect the singularity of this theological colossus whose work may have inspired awe but has in practice till now evoked few positive echoes outside his immediate circle: de Lubac, Ratzinger, Bouyer. Our intention has been to encourage discussion, to open up to an English-speaking readership some of the themes and perspectives which are formative of Balthasar's theology whose major work is only now gradually appearing in English translation. Above all it is to introduce into our own theologising and reflection some of the breadth and sharpness of Balthasar's own knowledge and vision. No theologian living could claim to have a wider knowledge both of the Grand Tradition of theology and of the great works of literature and poetry which have been such important vehicles of that tradition in the modern world: Soloviev, Hopkins, Péguy, Bernanos, Claudel. . . Few have a theological vision more deeply informed by the drama of the *Triduum Mortis*, as that which illumines our understanding both of the divine Trinity and of the human condition, its sinfulness and its untold possibilities.

To speak of Balthasar's vision of the drama of the *Triduum Mortis* is to indicate, at least schematically, what it is that marks him out from his contemporaries: his concern with the aesthetic and the dramatic, to which in turn the first two parts of his projected trilogy are devoted. From his earliest theological works, notably *Heart of the World*, his volume of meditations published in 1944, his theological endeavours have had their centre in the essential Christian mystery of the Cross and Resurrection. And if his theology — properly understood — is *aesthetic* it is because it consists in reflection on what it is that enables us to *perceive* the drama of the Cross and the *descensus* and the Resurrection as the revelation of the divine glory. Such reflection is not restricted to the subjective conditions of the possibility of such perception; rather, any thought about what it is that enables *us* to see the divine glory is intimately linked to questions about the object of such perceiving. What is it about *what* we see — the divine *Gestalt* of the incarnate, crucified Lord — that enables us to see in this figure, as nowhere else, that triune majesty?

Such questions were prompted in part at least by his early training as a *Germanist* which led to his studies of the German idealists in *Prometheus*. What is it, he asks, that distinguishes the great work of art — and that enables us to distinguish the great work of art — from its many fellows in its genre? And what is it that in the human field enables love to transcend *Eros* and to recognise and hold fast the beloved's uniqueness within the species, even after the erotic fancy has faded? And what do such reflections teach us about the incomparable quality and character of the saints, 'in whom the uniqueness of the one God is expressed — again and again?'[1] Thus his work throughout is characterised by a search for the irreducibly specific character of whatever falls beneath his gaze, just as it is marked by a sharp polemic against those tendencies in contemporary thought which dissolve the object, which stand in the way of all attempts to see it whole, to see it as it is. And precisely because such contemplation brings us face to face with what it is we contemplate, it should not be thought of as something distanced but rather, as in the meeting between the lover and the beloved, as that which leads into the 'great adventure' in which the life of the beholder is shaped and formed by what he sees.

[1] 'Theology and Aesthetic', *Communio: International Catholic Review*, Vol. 8, No. 1, 1981, p. 63.

Balthasar's theology is marked out, that is, by his own conviction that in the great works of art, literature and music we do indeed perceive something of the truth and reality of *being*. Thus it is clearly of great interest to enquire after Balthasar's own understanding of and indebtedness to the great figures of the German tradition of letters with which he has engaged. If Balthasar stresses the analogy between such work and its perception of reality and that of Christian faith and theology, how far is he ready to accept the insights, to allow his own vision of God, man and the world to be shaped by what he learns from them? It is not simply questions of the formal similarities between literature, art and music, and theological perceiving that interest Balthasar (though such questions do concern him in Vol. 1 of *The Glory of the Lord*) but of the *content* of such widely varied visions.

Here the Simons, father and son, have pressed questions on Balthasar from rather different angles. Why, writes Ulrich Simon, does Balthasar draw back from an acceptance of Goethe's *Mediation of Antiquity*, of his Christianised humanism which celebrates the reflection in nature of the transcendent glory of the divine? Balthasar clearly feels a deep sympathy for Goethe, sees him as rejecting, after his Italian journey, the search for identity with being with its Faustian emphasis on action untrammelled by conscience and turning instead to a vision of the world, albeit hardly won, which is continuous with the great tradition from Homer, Plato, Denys, Maximus, of the *analogia entis*. Such a vision has room for a cosmic triumphalism — so removed from a dully northern Protestantism — which can find its expression or reflection in the processions, feasts and carnivals of the Catholic south. Above all, Goethe sees in the artist's imaginative and creative shaping of his work the point at which the analogy between the divine reality and the reflected glory of nature is to be grasped most clearly. It is in the ordering of the confused world of nature — better in his perception and release of the hidden Paradise in such confusion — that the artist most closely resembles the supreme Artist. And yet in the end Balthasar's vision of the divine glory is not Goethe's. The uniqueness of the Christian vision, for all its continuity with the vision of Antiquity, must be asserted.

If Ulrich Simon suggests that Balthasar perhaps draws back too quickly in taking into his view of things the Goethean vision of grace and nature, then Martin Simon by contrast is more ready to accuse him of succumbing to the pagan charms of Hölderlin. Here the issues are complex, involving central questions of interpretation of Hölderlin's work: how far can Hölderlin, in his treatment of classical themes and motifs be seen to be continuing the tradition of the analogy of being, as did Goethe? Martin Simon disagrees importantly with Balthasar. If the outward form of Hölderlin's work, notably in 'Friedensfeier', suggests the classical perspective, what the poet sees is his sense of identity with being beyond all the contingencies of physical and indeed social existence: 'Born of the difference between time and eternity, it is — how can I describe it? — a dream of sheer lightness, nothingness, freedom from all the weight of existence, from the mirror of one's own physicality that is other people; and an infinite surrender' (p. 95). Moreover, suggests Martin Simon, this is really what attracts Balthasar to Hölderlin as opposed to the more orthodox Hamann with his authoritarian Father God. For there is a common strand of spirituality underlying pietism (as contrasted with more authoritarian forms of Baroque piety) and Catholic mysticism which unites Balthasar and Hölderlin. And is not Balthasar's absorbing of the heretical poet into his all-embracing *Glory*, is not the catholic Catholicism of the entire undertaking, born of the same 'love' as he discovered in this poet who 'sees the glory of the ancient world as the glory of love' (p. 102)?

What these two essays do is both to point out the real need for a full and sustained treatment of Balthasar's criticism and reception of the poets, not least of those who stand outside or at a distance from the Christian tradition, and to show the fruitfulness of an informed and sensitive engagement with the poets such as Balthasar offers. There is of course much more in the corpus of Balthasar's writings which needs to be noticed: his treatment of the Christian poets, Dante, Hopkins, Péguy in Vol. 3 of *The Glory of the Lord*, as well as the discussions of the classical poets, Homer and Virgil, above all in Vols. 4 and 5. There are of course dangers in all this; but the study of Hopkins in Vol. 3 shows I think how much has been lost to Christian theology by the divorce which has occurred — in the name of precision, of clarity, of truth? — between literature and theology. It shows too I think the point at which Balthasar clearly distances himself from Hölderlin's search for union with being beyond all the particularities of finite existence. The dispute between poetry and philosophy may be as old as Plato, but the total disregard of literature and poetry by theology is of particular balefulness in an age where philosophy has been largely purged of its metaphysical instincts and where it has been the poets and the artists who have kept the metaphysical *thaumazein* alive. The vigorous debate which Balthasar conducted with Barth on the *analogia entis* and the *analogia fidei* is played out here in a different mode which reveals much about the delicate tension which runs through the whole corpus between his real sympathy for the metaphysical tradition from Homer onwards and his insistence on the distinctness and uniqueness of the self-revelation of the Triune God.

It is noteworthy that Balthasar, for all his great interest in the metaphysical tradition, has never himself been much given to engaging with the works of philosophy of religion. Thus while he can properly point to Austin Farrer's *The Glass of Vision* as evincing a shared interest in the relations between art and poetry and theology, there is a much larger gap between him and more recent British practitioners of natural or metaphysical theology with their debt to Aristotle and John Locke. His own excursions into the fields of metaphysics in *The Glory of the Lord* Vols. 4 and 5 locate him within a tradition reaching from the myths through Plato and the tragedians to the great flowering of German Idealism after Goethe. Yet if it is here that his interest is kindled, the engagement with this tradition is critical and Balthasar is rightly sensitive to those who simply dismiss his theology as Platonising. The issues are sharply set out in Father O'Donaghue's perceptive review of Vol. 1 here reprinted. (It was, it should be noted, Father O'Donaghue who made the approach to T. & T. Clark which led to the present translations.) Balthasar's indebtedness to Plato lies not least in the perception that 'every experience of beauty points to infinity'; in his affirmation that there is therefore an *analogy* between the application of the categories of aesthetics, ethics and logic in the natural order and their application to revelation. But such claims must run the gauntlet of Kierkegaard's charge that to speak in these terms 'is to submit Christ to my inner idea or sense of the beautiful. "Either Christ shatters my conception of the beautiful or he fulfils it." If he shatters it, as Kierkegaard and Barth affirm, then what place is there for a theological aesthetics in Balthasar's sense? If he fulfils it then theology will be much more beholden to Plato and the Greeks than Balthasar himself seems prepared to admit' (p. 00).

To argue thus is of course to uphold Barth's final judgement in his debate with Balthasar, that there could be no compromise between the *analogia entis* and the *analogia fidei* — this despite Balthasar's claims to the contrary in the Preface to the Second Edition of his book on Barth. It is, further, to suggest that theology must in the end, willingly or otherwise, pay its tribute to philosophy. Where this comes home — so O'Donaghue — is in Balthasar's acceptance and assimilation of the Dionysian mystical tradition running through to John of the Cross. It is above all in a neo-Platonism that shows itself as eloquence rather than analysis, as an inner glow rather than a conceptual network.

If there is a tendency here — but only a tendency — to portray

Balthasar as more the theologian of the heart than the mind, of a heart which burns in the great adventure of the dark night of the soul, then Rowan Williams in his study of Balthasar and Rahner points to certain very clearly articulated theological differences which have marked Balthasar out both from his contemporary Catholic colleagues and indeed from a particular metaphysic or *Geistphilosophie*. This debate may indeed provide some of the answers to questions raised throughout the papers so far discussed.

Williams places the debate between Rahner and Balthasar — which caused a scandal in the late sixties and seventies — within the wider context of philosophical and metaphysical differences which reach back as far as Balthasar's review of Rahner's *Geist in Welt*. In that work Rahner advocated a doctrine of the *Vorgriff* of the mind/spirit. The mind's prior understanding of the unlimited possibility of being is the condition of the possibility of concrete, particular acts of understanding. Moreover such prior understanding paves the way for our understanding of God and is thus a 'kind of universal *praeparatio evangelica*, a tacit expectation of hearing loving self-communication, in the radical openness of the human spirit's love and searching' (p. 00). Divine revelation in Jesus Christ comes as the complete realisation of such human potential — a *potentia oboedientalis* of a strangely connative kind! If Lessing contrasted orthodoxy's desire to possess dogmatic truths with the human spirit's search for the truth, here Rahner, similarly critical of Catholic *Schultheologie's* preoccupation with the appropriation of propositional truths, sets out a scheme which would enable us to see the divine self-revelation as peculiarly appropriate to the questing mind.

Balthasar's objections to such a scheme, as leading to some kind of doctrine of 'anonymous Christians' — those who already in their openness and searching betray the virtues of faith, hope and love — are twofold: that in his concentration on the knowing subject Rahner is in danger of ignoring the important dimension of inter-subjectivity in human knowing; that further the concentration on the subjectivity of the agent intellect and its pre-apprehension of the limitlessness which 'underlies' concrete existence may suggest 'a void of purely negative indeterminancy' rather than make possible any affirmation of *esse* as plenitude. By contrast Balthasar suggests that a more fruitful line of approach lies via the experience of the *Gestalthaftigkeit des Wesens*.

This might mean: (i) being is to be apprehended primarily in the endless *variety* of particular forms; only by attending to such variety is it to be grasped as gratuitously creative; or (ii) attention to the *Gestalthaftigkeit des Wesens* alerts us to the sense in which beauty is a fundamental determination of all being, viz., that to exist concretely — *da-zu-sein* — is to exist as the concrete expression of an idea, as its *Ausdrucksleib*. This latter view, which finds its sympathetic exposition in Hopkins's Scotism, his doctrines of *quidditas* and inscape, points indeed to the source of all being as creative and infinitely fecund. It is perhaps here that we see most clearly the point at which Balthasar's perspective, informed by his reading not only of Plato but of among others Goethe and Hopkins, causes him to challenge the inwardness and abstract nature of Rahner's thought and to turn again to the contemplation of the world's richness, its *grandeurs et misères* which may receive further enlightenment and elucidation from the divine *Gestalt* of the revelation which is lived and acted out by the Son in obedience to the Father's mission.

This is the point to enter a protest at those elsewhere who have tended to see Balthasar's work as fundamentally conservative, as a refusal to come to terms with the crucial questions raised by the Enlightenment and susbsequent reactions to it. It would wholly mistaken to see Balthasar's criticisms of Rahner's essay as simply a refusal to attend to questions raised by the Enlightenment. As Charles Taylor has suggested, there were two major contrasting reactions to the objectifying character of Enlightenment thought, expressed respectively in the ideals of radical freedom and integral expression. Kant protested in the name of the moral freedom of the individual against the reduction of human conduct to the sum of a person's desires. Others, like Herder, protested against the way in which views of the human person as compounded of different elements: soul and body, reason and feeling, caused people to lose sight of its unity with itself, with nature and with the society and culture to which it belongs. For Herder human life 'was seen as having a unity rather analogous to that of a work of art, where every part or aspect only found its proper meaning in relation to all the others. Human life unfolded from some central core — a guiding theme or inspiration — or should do so, if it were not blocked or distorted'.[2] Rahner's theology has its roots in Kant's explorations of the conditions of the possibility of human cognitive, moral and aesthetic experience, as mediated to him via Catholic theologians like Maréchal; Balthasar has indeed written powerfully and perceptively on Kant, notably in his early studies of German Idealism, *Prometheus*. Yet the same volume shows his deep knowledge of and creative engagement with the tradition stemming from Herder. This is not to suggest that Balthasar's work is simply indebted to Herder but rather to indicate the breadth of his engagement with the German Idealist tradition and, behind that, with the Enlightenment.

Certainly the notion of expressive unity runs like a *Leitmotif* through his work. It is, as we have seen, of major importance in his work on the analysis of faith. The problems of Scholastic theology, it might be said, lay partly in its isolation of the act of faith from its history in the life of the believer in the Church; partly in the way in which responsibility for such an act had to be apportioned between the reason and the will. Balthasar, insisting that explicit confession of Christ is central to the life of faith, sees such assent as part of a history where the believer is taken up into a living relation with the

[2] C. Taylor, *Hegel*, Oxford, 1975, p. 2.

Godhead and where the life of the Godhead takes form and shape in the life of his saints. As such, faith is not simply the assent to propositions whose sense is as yet dimly perceived; it is a deepening appropriation of and being appropriated by the form, the *Gestalt* of revelation where the whole person is conformed to the Beloved.

But again, the life of the believer is not to be seen in isolation. Faith is not a relation between an alone and an Alone. It occurs, as John Saward reminds us, within the community of the faithful, the Church which in turn is rooted in a history which has its rise in the concrete, particular relations of Christ's Incarnation. If the Word is incarnate as a man, then it is incarnate as one whose very being is a being with others, whose particular relations form a constitutive part of what and who he is (though this without losing sight of the universality of his humanity in its relation to the divine Logos and Creator of humanity). In this sense the Church has indeed a *Gestalt* which reflects the particular constellation of relations into which Christ entered with Mary, Peter, John, Paul. For Balthasar such relations are a permanent feature of the reality of the Church, precisely because they are integral to the incarnate reality of Christ. While this then, for Balthasar, firmly establishes a hierarchichal principle in the Church, it is one which is tempered both by its correlation with other poles of this constellation: the Johannine, Marian and Pauline; and also by the binding of that hierarchical principle to the concrete story of Peter, whose strength is based on weakness, who is set over the Church as its servant and whose own crucifixion, upside down, demonstrates his identity with the Lord. And on such identity with the incarnate Word, achieved despite the rejection, denial, the brokenness, the Church is to be founded; through such identity the reality of the crucified Lord is present to the world; against such the 'power of evil' cannot prevail. And it is moreover within a community of faith so structured that it is possible for the rich variety of individual spiritualities to flourish that Adrienne so richly documented.

Again, it is a recurring theme of Balthasar's writing that we must see things whole: not simply, that is, reduce them to their constituent parts but learn to see them for what they are. Scripture then is to be read not simply as a source book for the events and community history which underlies it but as itself — so Brian McNeil — an icon of those events and their central figure Jesus. It is, that is to say, the necessary, inevitable result of the Church's reflection on the life, death and Resurrection of Jesus, a reflection which — like an icon — embraces not only the temporal significance of those events but sets the incarnate Christ within a supra-temporal context and mediates to the believers the presence of the living Christ.

Hence exegesis cannot be simply analysis of the constituent sources of the biblical *Gestalt*, though such an analysis may properly inform our understanding of the scriptural icon; rather it must itself be iconography, as it reflects on and itself mediates the presence of the living Christ in the biblical *Gestalt*. In this sense it is imitative rather than reductive, whereby true imitation presupposes a proper appreciation of the scriptural form. Yet the imitation can occur only — so Balthasar — within the community of faith and this means in accordance with the canons of the Church, precisely because Scripture itself is a mediating form compounded as it were of the revealing word and its witness to itself in the testimony of the Church. In this sense then all true exegesis is spiritual, assisted and enabled by the Spirit in the Church.

Such a contemplative vision of things equally makes him the more receptive to the narrative elements of the Christian story. It is hardly possible for those schooled in recent works of critical theology to read Balthasar's christological meditations, *Heart of the World*, without a sense of shock at the unashamedly mythological character of the writing. Just as Barth stressed the centrality of the Son's journey into a far country for Christian theology, so Balthasar stresses not only the descent of the Son among us but his further journey on Holy Saturday into the God-forsakeness of Hell. Here, as Andrew Louth shows, Balthasar is endebted not only to the work and vision of Adrienne von Speyr but also to Greek patristic tradition and its neo-Platonic strains of thought. Not that Balthasar takes over the thought of Plotinus and Proclus without filtering it through the specifically Christian insights which are to be drawn from the *descensus*. The neo-Platonic scheme of procession and return, with its emphasis on the restitution of being which occurs in return, is reversed. 'And perhaps the going forth from God is still more divine than the return home to God, since the greatest thing is not for us to know God and reflect this knowledge back to him as if we were gleaming mirrors, but for us to proclaim God as burning torches proclaim the light.'[3] This theme is developed in the meditations on the descent of the Son into suffering and death, on the mystery of the fact 'that the perfect Yes to the Father's will could be uttered in in the midst of rebellion by a Lamb condemned to death …. that the eternal distance of love between the Father and the Son, which yet eternally enfolds the one in the other in the embrace of both in the Spirit, can become the yawning gap between Heaven and Hell so that the Son groans, "I thirst", and the Spirit is no more than the great separating and impassible Chaos.'[4] And moreover such manifestation of the divine in the other, and not only the other but in that which is strictly *opposed* to it, is precisely a manifestation of the creativity and the regenerative power of God. Here in the very heart of human sinfulness, the drama of God's love is played out and the Church is born.

And so we come back to the starting point of all Balthasar's theological reflections: his meditation on the mystery of Christ's Cross and Passion, his *descensus* and Resurrection. What informs such meditation is, as Donald MacKinnon stresses in his own reflections, first, Balthasar's refusal 'to turn aside from the overwhelming, pervasive reality of evil', a reality terrifyingly manifested in the

[3] *Heart of the World*, p. 33f.
[4] *Ibid.*, p. 54 (translation revised).

destruction of the Jews in Nazi Germany. Such a refusal makes him critical of certain forms of Christian universalism which fail to acknowledge or do justice to the *Agonie* which is the cost of human redemption. Yet for all that they are not, as MacKinnon reminds us, to be confused with any facile cult of pessimism which would disregard the redemption so hardly won. And it is, second, their unreservedly theological character.

Balthasar's own most sustained theological reflections are to be found in the second part of his projected trilogy, *Theodramatik*. There he sets such thinking firmly in the context of the divine dealing with the world, the drama which finds its culmination and denouement in the ultimate humiliation of the Cross and the *descensus*. This emphasis on the divine drama of salvation is exhibited not least in the way Balthasar deploys the notion of *Sendung*, mission, in a treatment of Christology which betrays few inhibitions about making use of traditional, more obviously ontological categories. For what interests Balthasar here is not a simple replacement of traditional christological categories of nature, essence, substance with the more nearly poetic category of mission, but rather the theological insight which can result from the conceptual interpenetration of such varied categories. Here 'the concept of mission presses beyond poetry in ontology.' Or again, Balthasar's theology is rooted in his own meditations on the Cross, as in *The Way of the Cross*, where he 'allows his imagination to be overwhelmed by the reality of the drama in which he knows himself to be involved' (p. 00). And it is the dialectic which is thus created betwen traditional treatments and his own imaginative appropriation of that drama which yields the theological gains.

And such theological gains are ontological, indeed trinitarian. They serve, as all true theology must, to plumb the mystery of being, to perceive, however darkly, what is, and how it is. Hence it is that the notion of the Son's mission by the Father, of his going forth into the darkness of humiliation and death, may shed light on the relations of the persons of the immanent trinity, indeed may lead to a reversal of the neo-Platonist schema of procession and return when the humiliation of the Son is itself seen as part of the Father's giving. Not that the kenosis of Word in the incarnation is to be seen as identical to the inner-trinitarian 'kenosis' of the processions; the immanent trinity is for Balthasar the transcendent theological reality, such that the kenosis of the Son in his *status inanitionis* provides only analogies for the reality of inner-trinitarian relations. But by such analogies we may be led into the mystery of the divine source of all being as he reveals himself to us in the giving of the Son.

Perhaps in the end it is in this calling of theology back to its proper task of the unravelling of being, of the tracing out of the lineaments of the reality of the incarnate, crucified, descended and risen Lord, that Balthasar's most valuable contribution will be seen to have been made. Such a call is delivered with all the authority of one who is master of the great Christian theological traditions; it is delivered moreover by one whose own theological work stems from a quite specific consciousness of his own calling and task within the Church. To read Balthasar's work is to be reminded again and again of the 'forgetfulness of being' of our age and of much contemporary theology. It is equally to be presented with a wealth of remarkable insights which are the fruit of his own labours to restore to theology its proper concern with the fundamental determinations of being: unity, truth, goodness and beauty. These essays are offered, in great respect and gratitude, as a contribution to that common theological task.

IN RETROSPECT

Hans Urs von Balthasar

1. The Salient Point

Twenty years ago an account of my literary work could be constructed on an objective and dogmatic foundation. In an earlier survey of my work, 'Kleiner Lageplan zu meinen Büchern', it was possible to begin theologically with Christ and the Church before addressing the position of the Church in the world and the practical tasks that lay before her. The subsequent changes in Church and Christendom require us to reverse this order and to set out now from what in the earlier piece was placed at the end as challenge and goal: the driving entelechy of the task that is given us. The latter had been at work, long before the author ever took up pen, and at the time of his first publications (*Veröffentlichungen*), it remained undisclosed (*unveröffentlicht*) even to him. His entire literary output will ultimately have been but a means to a strange *Meaning*, who, with his coming, is free to discard as past everything that was merely 'way'.

The last twenty years — inspiring both joy and alarm — have seen the real decision ineluctably set free from its preliminary forms. We were a beautiful group, resolute and exposed, and it was clear to us from the beginning that the bastions of anxiety which the Church had contrived to protect herself from the world would have to be demolished; the Church had to be freed and open to the whole and undivided world for its mission. For the meaning of Christ's coming is to save the *world* and to open for the whole of it the way to the Father; the Church is only a means, a radiance that through preaching, example, and discipleship spreads out from the God-man into every sphere. This pathos rallied us young theologians (Fessard, Bouillard, Daniélou and many others) around our older friend and master Henri de Lubac, whose *Catholicisme* I soon translated into German. From de Lubac we gained an understanding of the Greek Fathers, the philosophical mysticism of Asia, and the phenomenon of modern atheism; to him my patristic studies owe their initial spark. For patristics meant to us a Christendom which still carried its thoughts into the limitless space of the nations and still trusted in the world's salvation. At that time, I conceived the plan of a closely woven trilogy on the writings of Origen, Gregory of Nyssa, and Maximus the Confessor, of which unfortunately only fragments were completed: *Parole et Mystère chez Origène* (1957), *Présence et Pensée. Essai sur la Philosophie Religieuse de Grégoire de Nysse* (1942), and *Kosmische Liturgie. Höhe und Krise des griechischen Weltbilds bei Maximus Confessor* (1941). The latter work did not receive the title 'Cosmic Liturgy' without serious premeditation, and out of contemplation of the cosmic Christ grew the hymns entitled *Heart of the World* (German edition, 1945) as well as the book of aphorisms called *Das Weizenkorn* (1944: The Grain of Wheat). During my semester vacations — which I spent mostly in Munich at the offices of *Stimmen der Zeit*, where I also spent a further two years on completion of my studies — I worked on the three-volume *Apokalypse der deutschen Seele* (1937-39: Apocalypse of the German Soul), in which the eschatological thinking of German writers was depicted in the light of Christ. The encounter with Erich Przywara and later with Karl Barth — whose universalist doctrine of predestination confirmed what I had long been looking for — the collaboration with Karl Rahner on the sketch of a new dogmatics, the renewed theologising with Hugo Rahner in the patristic area: all this strengthened my determination to render the Christian message in its unsurpassable greatness (*id quo majus cogitari nequit*), because it is God's human word for the world, God's most humble service eminently fulfilling every human striving, God's deepest love in the splendour of his dying so that all might live beyond themselves for him.

In such a spirit I undertook at Basel in 1940 the direction of a series of publications designed to provide, at the end of Nazism, the corner stones for a spiritual Europe in which an open Christian attitude could take seriously all that is affirmative in Western culture. Also at that time came my programmatic piece entitled *Schleifung der Bastionen* (1952: Razing the Ramparts), which blew the last, impatient trumpet blast calling for a Church no longer barricaded against the world, a trumpet blast that did not die away unheard, but which has subsequently forced the trumpeter himself to pause and reflect.

Indeed, it was not as though we were unaware that with an opening to the world, an *aggiornamento*, a broadening of the horizons, a translation of the Christian message into a language understandable by the modern world, only half is done. The other half — of at least equal importance — is a reflection on the specifically Christian element itself, a purification, a deepening, a centring of its idea, which alone renders us capable of representing it, radiating it, translating it believably in the world. We knew this, for almost all of us were formed by the *Spiritual Exercises*, the great school of Christian contemplation, of attention to the pure and personal word contained in the Gospel, of lifelong commitment to the attempt at following and imitation ('choice of a state of life'), which for Ignatius is above all a decision regarding the form that a Christian may lend in his own life to the Lord's attitude of total and loving renunciation ('evangelical counsels'). For the so-called 'counsels' of Christ are nothing but the form of his redeeming love and apply to every believer, whether layman or religious. I translated the *Exercises* into German and had the opportunity of conducting them some hundred times: here, if anywhere, is Christian joy. Here, if anywhere, is what it means to be a Christian in its 'primordial' sense: effective hearing of the Word that calls and growth in freedom for the expected response. It is here too that we came closest to the sense and inspiration of the Reformation, from Luther to Karl Barth.

The last twenty years have shown inexorably that the most dynamic programme of openness to the world remains one-sided (and hence becomes exceedingly dangerous) if it does not cultivate with growing awareness its own distinctive counterpoise and balance: whoever desires greater action needs better contemplation; whoever wants to play a more formative role must pray and obey more profoundly; whoever wants to achieve additional goals must grasp the uselessness and futility, the uncalculating and incalculable (hence 'unprofitable') nature of the eternal love in Christ, as well as of every love along the path of Christian discipleship. Whoever wants to command must have learned to follow in a Christlike manner; whoever wants to administer the goods of the world must first have freed himself from all desire for possession; whoever wants to show the world Christian love must have practised himself in the love of Christ (even in marriage) to the point of pure selflessness. We knew all this and have always said it. Every programme of mission to the world must at all times contain what Guardini called 'the ability to distinguish the Christian element'.

And yet it appears today that the many no longer really know this. What has happened to them? A slight, perhaps only tactically meant displacement in the beginning — yet the effects are incalculable. For the beginnings are always decisive; the sequence of almost invisible proto-decisions forms history, as philosophy shows in its domain: Plato's Idea, Thomas's *De ente et essentia*, Descartes's *cogito*, Hegel's *Begriff*... The formulation of the question, I said, was clear to us: the world is the goal of the redemption wrought by Christ; the Church (as means) is sent to bring the salvation of Christ to the world. How then are these two things to meet? Must not the correct conclusion follow from the two premises: must not the means be judged and measured in the light of the goal? Since 'Adam' (that is, since the beginning of creation) and all the more since Christ, the world stands in the light of grace, nature as a whole is intrinsically finalised to supernature, whether it wants it or not, knows it or not. Natural knowledge of God, natural religious ethics stand under this secret sign, whose manifest character the Church proclaims and in a mysterious fashion is. Is this not the meaning of the old patristic doctrine of the *logos spermatikos*?

Were we to put this thinking into practice, the chief directions of contemporary intellectual life, the great impulses of modern times could also find a home in Christianity. 'The religious element in mankind' stands as a whole unconsciously in the light of grace and redemption; on every religious road man can find the God of grace. This is the christening of the Enlightenment and of liberal theology from Herbert of Cherbury down to the present day. Further: man as spirit in the world is finalised to the absolute spirit-being, and this transcendental dynamism is again supernaturally finalised through the self-opening of the inner love of God himself, so that whoever strives constantly can be called an 'anonymous Christian'. This is the christening of German idealism, into whose transcendental key even the metaphysical thinking of St Thomas can be transposed. Again: the cosmos, biologically considered, is in evolution up to man and beyond him; at a critical moment, the Incarnation of God immerses itself in the world-process as its supernatural motive force and brings it to the final maturity of *theosis*, which the Greek Fathers already saw as the point Omega; this is to make a home for Darwin, the monists, and Nietzsche's idea and ethics of the superman. And again: the categories of human existence are only to be defined dialectically; there is no reason why the existential process of following Christ (as, for instance, the *Exercises* express it) cannot lend itself to expression in Hegel's categories. Further: why shouldn't a Christian truth be hidden even in the Marxist total-labour process as the return of mankind from its self-alienation and as the transformation of the world and of man by means of technology? And if Marxism demands the self-immolation of the individual to the collective and to its ideal of the future, why can't this process, this sacrifice, this anonymity and poverty of the individual be understood more profoundly and transfigured by the light of the salvific order in a Christian 'theology of work', according to the principle of hope in an eschatological kingdom into which, in any case, the collective effort of mankind must flow? And again: is it not only through fellow-feeling that man truly becomes man? Is it not precisely here that the absolute and the divine shine forth and become understandable to him, as (following Fichte's profound speculation) Feuerbach and the modern personalists Scheler, Ebner, Buber, and Jaspers emphasise? One can almost discern the Sermon on the Mount lying behind all this. Doesn't the Parable of the Good Samaritan (where it is the 'heretic' who does the right thing and is put forward as the example) express precisely this 'one thing necessary'? Doesn't the Parable of Judgement Day (Mt 25) say precisely that even the just are astounded at the judgement ('Lord, when did we see you hungry, thirsty, naked, in exile, sick, and in prison?') and hence that the just too, even when they are actually Christians, are 'anonymous Christians' as genuine fellow men? Here, at last, the true humanism is begotten. And finally (to keep this series to a reasonable length): isn't Heidegger correct when he defines man as openness to being, whose ethical nature does not reside in his being a servant of laws and commandments, but in his ability to heed the call of being as a whole in the momentary situation? And since the Holy Spirit of God and of Christ holds sway in the All, why shouldn't this essentially mysterious call blowing hither out of the absolute be inspired in its depths by the command of the personal God of love — anonymously, of course — so that the waters of Baptism can be poured out even over Heidegger's thought?

If we survey all this and comprehend it as a unified whole, does there not lie in the many ramifications of this single doctrine the great release for Christians of our time? It rescues us, does it not, from the narrow ecclesiasticism which has become incomprehensible in its positive legalism and re-establishes our solidarity with all men in such a way, indeed, that the real law, under which everyone stands, is known by the Christians, who are permitted to announce to the others what they truly are: beloved children of the Father in Jesus Christ. No wonder that this wholesale method of supernaturalising what is worldly (in so far as it is not sinful) today achieves such colossal success, and that everyone now speaks of 'theologies' (of work, of evolution, of the earthly realities, of the ethical situation, etc.) where in the first instance simply a 'philosophy' might have been expected. No wonder, too, that everyone shows up, closes ranks, and marches along: it is plainly the path worn smooth by the vast crowd of travellers, which, even phenomenologically, must be designated 'the broad way'. The breadth of the cosmic outlook native to the Greek Fathers and even to Thomas Aquinas appears to have been recaptured on a higher plane. The connection with the culture of the time, after a period of 'inner emigration', seems to have been rediscovered. And everything ecclesiastical and positive appears transparent to the universal laws of man and cosmos — and thereby justified. The 'worldly office of the Christian' seems assured; the realm of the laity at last established as the Christian realm *par excellence*. Dark shadows, however, fall on those previously enclosed and 'cloistered': much of this was flight from the world, not to say outright fear and condemnation of it, even Manichaeism. Even the 'structures of the Church' (not only its outer 'bastions') appear in their instrumentality and relativity; and finally, after a centuries-old ice-age, confessional differences miraculously dissolve, awakening hopes where scarcely any existed before. Christians and Christians, Christians and Jews, Christians and non-Christians, Christians and anti-Christians: all commune at last in the great realm of God's creation, which as a whole is endowed with a dimension of grace. Grandiose. But it has a snag. When everything goes so well with anonymity, it is hard to see why a person should still be a name-bearing Christian. And it certainly seems that on the basis of this new theological vogue, the many (with the best conscience) are already prepared — perhaps out of solidarity with the Russians and Chinese and in order to become an unacknowledged leaven from within — to renounce the troublesome formality of the name.

To my misfortune, however, I had read Kierkegaard in my youth (Guardini had expounded him to us in Berlin), and there I learned that the apostle of Christ is one who lets himself be killed for Christ. And who today does not lay claim to the title of 'apostle'? In the same way Paul bears the stigmata of the historical Jesus in his body and desires to live and die only for him who loved him and gave himself up for him. If this is our model, then there is no such thing as an anonymous Christian, no matter how many other men — hopefully all! — attain salvation through the grace of Christ. But the grace for all depends on the form of life of him who through the shame of his poverty, his obedience, and his bodily 'castratedness' (Mt 19.12) embodied God's grace and desired at every stage (Mary; the Apostles; the women in Bethany, at the Cross, at the tomb) that others also partake of this form. Far from being one among many equally important 'eschatological signs' for the general public, as is said today in a pacifying tone of voice, this form of life is rather the archetype of all Christian existence, which as such is grounded in the process of dying with Christ for the old world (Rom 6). This form of life is the 'salt' of the earth that must not become insipid, and only this form can penetrate the profane world as 'leaven', since it means standing in the last place in foolishness, weakness, and contempt, as the 'manure heap of the world', the 'latrine for all' (1 Cor 4.10-13).

For this reason, lest everything in the Church become superficial and insipid, the true, undiminished programme for the Church today must read: the greatest possible radiance in the world by virtue of the closest possible following of Christ. At the point where the tension between being a Christian and being a man like other men is at its strongest, indeed so strong that it must appear to the natural man as lacerating and 'psychologically' unbearable by every standard of closed and harmonious humanity, there is raised up not only the outer 'eschatological' (i.e., world-vanquishing) sign — a kind of stimulating irritant — but also the reality itself, either in its visibility or (as with everything weighty in Christianity) in its invisibility. Today this form of existence takes a new shape in the 'secular institutes'. For these constitute the link between the lay state and the life of the vows and show not only the existential unity of the Church, but also its perennial and most 'up-to-date' mission in the world.

About this nucleus my activities as author, editor, and publisher are gathered. My goal has been to order the treasures of revelation, of church theology and spirituality critically around this centre, bound as much to the past as to the future. This task involves, above all, the administration of the vast literary estate of Adrienne von Speyr, of which some thirty volumes have already been published, with the most important still awaiting publication. Related to this is a series of writings on the secular institutes, including the very early little work entitled *Der Laie und der Ordensstand* (1948: The Laity and the Religious State), as well as two short pieces on the theology of the secular institutes (1955) and 'A Theology of the Evangelical Counsels' (*Cross Currents*, 1966; German version, 1964). The express theological foundation of the institute was supplied first in the context of contemporary ecclesial thinking in *Who is a Christian?* (German edition, 1966) and, more profoundly, in the reconsideration of the problem of form in traditional theology as a whole in *Love Alone: The Way of Revelation* (German edition, 1963). This last synthesis of many earlier efforts to express the meaning and form of theology sought to serve both as an exposition of Christian revelation and as a guide to Christian proclamation and ethics, by displaying the Gospel reality before our era as directly and abruptly as possible. The simpler and clearer the fathomless depth of God's love becomes to us, indeed the more incomprehensible to us the thought becomes that, in the face of such a mystery, man could be capable of something like correspondence and following at all, the sooner will we be rid of the distorted and simplistic thinking which makes the Christian message so unbelievable today. By the same token ecumenical dialogue can bear fruit only if it seizes on what is most deeply Christian and, faithful to its utter seriousness, develops a sense for what is secondary and relative, for what therefore can be conceded on both sides.

2. Rays from the Centre

If what we have just written provides an initial description of the existential centre for the Christian, the real theological centre, from which the world of creation and of history receives its structures, is occupied not by the Christian but by Christ. *A Theology of History* (German edition, 1950, revised 1959) begins by pointing exclusively to Christ's form of existence at the centre of history, where the time of sin and reprobation is reintegrated into God's original time by virtue of Christ's loving obedience to the Father. This earthly obedience has as its terminus the Father's coming 'hour', which the Son awaits even while bending under the creaturely time common to all men, so that in this attitude he becomes the measure and norm of every temporal existence. Biblically and theologically it is not illegitimate — indeed, for the following of Christ it is important — to see the fundamental act of Christ's existence as the archetypal act of faith, in whose expanse the possibility of the Church's faith is first and foremost established (cf. 'Fides Christi', in *Sponsa Verbi*, 1960).

This nucleus of a theology of history was developed in its universal historical dimensions in *A Theological Anthropology* (German edition, 1963). Beginning with an Augustinian consideration of 'distancing' (*diastasis*) between a pure time of love and a time of sin, this

203

work treats the perfectability both of mortal man and of history as a whole, ending with a sketch of a christological reintegration of man's fragmentary and concrete 'stages of life' into their final eschatological form. The emphasis is on the latter; such a notion of integration is the basis for my mistrust of every simplistic, straight-line evolutionism in past and present, as discussed in my article on the spirituality of Teilhard de Chardin (1963).

What *A Theological Anthropology* treats as a whole is separated into its individual aspects in the first volume of my collected essays, *Verbum Caro* (1960) published in English in two volumes, *Word and Revelation* and *Word and Redemption*. The conditions which revelation presupposes for the above mentioned integration of man to God through Christ are portrayed in the sketch 'God Speaks as Man', where human nature in all its forms is understood as the essential language of the *Logos*. In like manner, 'Implications of the Word' argues the inescapability of human thinking and philosophising as a presupposition for God's speaking ('revelation') and being understood ('theology'). *Vis-à-vis* Karl Barth, who like no other Protestant was concerned with this tension between the Christ-centre and the universality of salvation, I argued that the Christian 'exclusivity' demands precisely the inclusion of all human thinking: as something judged (*gerichtetes*), it is 'broken', realigned, and reset (*ab- aus-, und eingerichtet*). 'A Sketch of Eschatology' draws the consequences from *A Theology of History*, when it relates the last 'things' to the last (i.e., ultimate) 'person' Jesus Christ as to the freely judging measure and norm: a first draft which, if God allows, will be followed by a detailed theology of Hell as a commentary to still unpublished works of Adrienne von Speyr on the theology of Holy Saturday.

One stage further back lies the dialogue with Barth. In *The Theology of Karl Barth* (German edition, 1951), the fundamental reconcilability of Catholic and Protestant theology is described at the point where each is most consistently itself. For Barth this means that, despite everything, the truly evangelical element in Protestantism lies beyond Luther (and all the more beyond Calvin) in Schleiermacher: in the opening of the concrete universal which is Christ to the world-embracing *Logos*. For the Catholic, it means that the concept of nature which Catholic theology is accustomed to presuppose undialectically can in reality only be grasped dialectically, much in accord with Henri de Lubac's renewed vision of patristic-high-scholastic theology. If unity is once achieved at this level, then in principle everything else is open for ecumenical discussion. Hans Küng continued this discussion, taking it on beyond fundamental theology into the sphere of dogmatics (the doctrine of justification) and here Barth indicated his agreement in principle.

3. A Church of Disciples

The next circle of themes necessarily extends beyond those treated above. The second volume of my collected essays, *Sponsa Verbi* (1960), extracts of which appeared in English as *Church and World*, asks explicitly: 'Who is the Church?' According to the answer given, the Church in its deepest reality is the unity of those who, gathered and formed by the immaculate, therefore limitless and (by grace) 'Christ-formative' assent of Mary, are prepared to let the saving will of God take place in themselves and for all their brothers. This primordial act is what is meant by 'hearing the Word'; it justifies and demands contemplative prayer (as described in *Prayer*, German edition 1955), not in the mere Greek sense of the word, but normatively in the biblical sense of the whole man's openness in faith to the ever greater meaning of the Word of God. It justifies, likewise, the preparatory opening up of Scripture to this act, as in my meditations on the Thessalonian and Pastoral Epistles (1955). It justifies, precisely for our time, a life of sacrificial surrender to God's Word, as contemplatives live it in service to God for the salvation of all the world. An example of the latter was given in *Thérèse of Lisieux. A Story of a Mission* (German edition, 1950), where the discussion turns on the little saint's understanding of Carmel as the highest bridal fruitfulness for the Church. In *Elisabeth of Dijon* (German edition, 1952), this is completed by the latter contemplative's interpretation of her existence according to the Pauline formula 'in praise of God'. Precisely Elizabeth, who understood the splendour for which she lived (*doxa, gloria*) as both the exclusivity of crucified love and the absolute inclusivity of universal salvation, reveals once again how the Protestantism of Barth agrees with the innermost mystery of Catholicism. The penetrating power of Thérèse and Charles de Foucauld (whose mission I also treated) shows, even in this era of anti-contemplative lay-ideologies, how right they and their kind really are.

Wherever and to whatever extent this fundamental act of hearing the word takes place (as faith, love, obedience, bridal fidelity), there is the spiritual Church. Wherever this is lacking, the Church becomes itself the 'whore Jerusalem', as discussed in the lengthy article 'Casta Meretrix' (in *Sponsa Verbi*, untranslated). Reception of the word by the whole man, body and soul, requires a unity of word and sacrament, as described in 'Schauen, Glauben, Essen' (Seeing, Believing, Partaking, *ibid.*, untranslated). The institutional aspects of the Church exist for the sake of this act and receive their intelligible form from it (cf. 'Office in the Church' in *Church and World* and the untranslated article 'Priesterliche Existenz' in *Sponsa Verbi*). It is at this point, too, that the dialogue between Church and Synagogue takes place: like Barth, Przywara, Journet and Fessard before me, I attempted to situate it for both parties in the Pauline radicality of Romans 9-11, in *Martin Buber and Christianity* (German edition, 1958) especially and, more generally, elsewhere. The notion of the Church as 'chaste whore' makes such a dialogue doubly confusing and humiliating for the Christian.

From the standpoint of Marian and ecclesial spirituality (which is one with loving and hoping faith), it is both legitimate and necessary to examine the interpretation of this fullness in the endless variety of specialised 'charisms', 'missions', or 'spiritualities' in the Church. The inseparable unity of 'Charis and Charisma' (in *Sponsa Verbi*, untranslated), i.e., of sanctifying grace and the task of sanctification, was asserted against the (only partially defensible) tradition to the contrary in an extensive commentary on St Thomas's tractate, *Summa Theologica II-II*, 171-182, on charismata (1954, untranslated). This commentary treats historically and critically the three theological *loci* of such phenomena: namely, Old and New Testament prophecy, the gifts of the Holy Spirit as supernatural and experiential perfection of the Christian virtues, and the interrelationship between contemplation and action. In addition, beginning with my translation into German of Augustine's treatise on prophecy and vision, I undertook numerous editorial and critical tasks intended to bring to the attention of our all-forgetting era the richness of the ancient Christian and medieval vistas, a task which far exceeds the power of a single editor or publisher. Among the figures treated either in translation or scholarly monograph were Irenaeus, Origen, Gregory of Nyssa, Denys the Aeropagite, Maximus the Confessor, Augustine, Anselm, William of St Thierry, the two Mechthilds, Julian of Norwich, The Cloud of Unknowing, Hilton, Jeanne d'Arc, Catherine of Siena, John of the Cross, Lallemant, Surin, Peter Faber, Ignatius, Angelus Silesius, Görres, and, from our day, Thérèse of Lisieux, Maurice Blondel, and Divo Barsotti.

An important place is occupied by my collection into one volume of the Rules of the great religious orders, *Die Großen Ordensregeln* (1947), because here the speakers are not merely individuals but founders of the great directions of Catholic spirituality. Here I provided an introduction treating of the religious state in general, as well as, in the section on the Rule of St Basil, a discussion of the original relationship between the Gospel and the group of those in the community who know themselves called to represent its genuine form.

If all these undertakings add up only to a paltry selection from the inexhaustible plenitude of holiness which the Holy Spirit continues to draw from the evangelical source, Adrienne von Speyr's remarkable book on the prayer life of the saints will fill this out immensely. In any event, this fullness will only appear richer and richer as time goes on. Yet what it always involves is a proportion between the archetype and the copy, which permits us to treat 'The Gospel as Critical Norm for Every Form of Spirituality in the Church' (1965) and, among other things, to win a superior criterion for judging the new forms of Christian spirituality which announce themselves in the radical changes of the present.

With this norm in view, a few chief ideas can be selected: the Christian lives from the strength of Christ's grace; his living faith is essentially 'infused virtue'; his mission, whether it succeed or miscarry, is answered for by Christ's word of commission. Thus the mission, not the psychology of the saints, must always have the last word, even with — indeed, precisely with — the famous 'subjectivists' (Augustine, Pascal, Kierkegaard, Dostoyevsky, etc.), as my article in the *Schweizer Rundschau* (1948), questioning the notion of the psychology of the saints, points out. In reality, these individuals live by virtue of what on a philosophical plane has been called 'objective interiority'. Augustine, in particular, was interpreted in this sense, while Thérèse's *Story of a Soul* was interpreted as *Story of a Mission* and the writers Georges Bernanos and Reinhold Schneider were treated likewise in a pair of extensive monographs as yet untranslated into English.

Bernanos, the deeply suffering Christian, who could often appear as an almost lawless *Pneumatiker*, in truth simply exposed himself in terrifying nakedness of soul to the evangelical fire, as to a brand which, for the poet, is applied only by the sacramental torches which the Church kindles. The torch of Baptism is treated in *One Night*; holy orders and the eucharist, confession and extreme unction in *The Star of Satan, Apostates, Joy*, and the *Diary of a Country*

Priest; the objective, quasi-sacramental power of the vows in *The Carmelites*. And if the poet lived in an abysmal anguish, he understood how to assimilate this anguish ultimately to the anguish of Gethsemane, far beyond the philosophical dread of Heidegger and the slightly neurotic anxiety of Kierkegaard; genuine Christian anguish is the putrefaction of sin at last transposed into consuming fire. In my little book on anxiety and the Christian, *Der Christ und die Angst* (1951) I had already attempted to relate an important symptom of modern existence to biblical categories, and here the 17th chapter of the Book of Wisdom appeared particularly illuminating. On two subsequent occasions, without regard to Bernanos, the Bible had brought me close to his world of feeling: once in preparing the text for a series of monotypes by Hans Fronius on *King David* (1955): these stories from the Book of Kings have their place alongside the old Greek sagas of Titans and heroes, and the German sagas of the *Nibelungen*. A second time in preparing the text for Hegenbarth's *Way of the Cross* (German edition, 1964), where, just as the painter freely and responsibly had renounced his brilliance in order to descend with the Lord into the *kenosis* of all beauty (an impenetrable mystery of Christian art), the words too had to be broken and rendered helpless, in order to approximate an objective form of anguish which might serve only the unique anguish of the wholly Other.

Reinhold Schneider, the tragic Aeolian harp which finally broke, lived in conscious opposition to his time, out of an anti-psychological ethos of service and of the representation of a divine-kingly order. Certainly, in Schneider's case, this was an order in the void, a construction erected against a background of chaos, and thus this island of Christian sensibility was continually threatened by the pounding surf of a Buddhism that owed much to Schopenhauer. Nonetheless, the tension between a Christian mission of self-renouncing holiness and a worldly mission involving the princely exercise of power is portrayed in his historical dramas, epics, novellas, and sonnets with such a devastating dialectic, that it pales by comparison the superficial chatter of the theologians about the modern Christian's supposed 'worldly mission'. Indeed, who else has so described, even formally, the intense tension, referred to above, which exists between Gospel and world? Who else has demanded so calmly the 'heroic' renunciation of the Christian as the one presupposition for effectiveness in the world? And yet he was unable to endure all this so that there was for me no escaping the task of venturing the same thing with other means, amidst other historical and theological omens than those attending this lonely, tragic wreckage of a man, who knew about the greatest missions and yet was not fully able to live his own without the secret self-righteousness of the overburdened Job? Surely this is a warning and a pointer to the inner form of the secular institutes. And later, when engaged on a renewed study of Greek, there grew the certainty, which Schneider imparted, that the decisive dialogue between antiquity and Christianity lay not so much in the centuries-old exchange between Plato and patristic-scholastic theology, as in that between the Greek tragedians and the Christian saints about the meaning of human existence. I have discussed this in my article on tragedy and Christian faith (1965, now in *Spiritus Creator*).

Mere renunciation of the world cannot be tragic, but only the struggle for the proper love of the world in God, for an affirmation that, intersected by the Cross, does not separate Creator and creature. In this regard, all else was soon drowned by the powerful organ peal of Paul Claudel. After translating *The Satin Slipper* in the thirties, I proceeded to render into German the many volumes of his collected poetry, a task that stretched over more than twenty-five years. The lyrical mountain chain of his poetry continued unbroken, even if next to the complete successes (*Five great Odes, Cantata for Three Voices, The Architect, St Theresa, Hymn to Dante, Introitus, Mass from Afar*, and many others) there were also some mediocre, forced efforts, although only rarely complete failures and never anything talentless. Like his hero Roderigo, like his nearest of kin Dante, the everywhere alien and homeless Claudel was able to breathe only in the entirety of the world and hence to live only in a love whose horizons are the world, embracing Hell and Purgatory and Paradise at once: in the spacious kingdom of Doña Musique, who can rule even beyond the tragic strife dividing the celestial and subterranean Muses, who is at once the simile of the world in its inherent (created and redeemed) goodness and the symbol of the West, whose Christian dome is erected once and for all on the foundations of antiquity — '*Santa Maria sopra Minerva*', as Karl Barth mockingly said and as Claudel would have repeated affirmatively from the bottom of his heart. With my translation of *Tidings Brought to Mary*, the limitations of the young Claudel, still heavily dependent on symbolism and *Jugendstil*, became clear; it gathered dust in a way that never happened with *The Satin Slipper*.

Next to Claudel and of almost equal rank with him is Péguy: still a Christian in the tension between Gospel and world, one who for the sake of brotherly love left the Church and for the sake of brotherly love returned to it again. His *Portal to the Mystery of Hope*, which I translated into German, is a basic Christian text no less than his other two *Mystères*. In the third volume of *The Glory of the Lord* Péguy has the task of providing a valid representation of twentieth century Catholicism: for he understood fully the face-to-face encounter between Greek tragedy and Christian martyrdom (in the *Note Conjointe*). With him, however, the sphere of the world is not so much *physis*, as with Claudel; rather it is the un-Christian or anti-Christian communist brother. Jeanne d'Arc, who begins in the most serious commitment for the world and ends in the flames of the Cross, is for Péguy the beloved embodiment of this ideal.

One more name cannot be left out here: that of the Catholic artist and pilgrim to Greece Richard Seewald, with whom years ago I collaborated on a collection of texts and illustrations for the Christian year, *Das Christliche Jahr* (1944). We have both travelled a long way since that time. My volume of scholarly portraits describing the seminal thinkers and artists of Western civilisation (*The Glory of the Lord, Vols. IV and V*) is of a piece with the Occident that he has portrayed in the halls of the Munich *Hofgarten*. We both know clearly that we have no resting place here and that our earthly tent, together with the beloved spiritual landscapes which surround it, will in the end be folded up.

The present is continually pressing forward, into the unknown, forcing new decisions: daily, yearly, the whole must be seen anew with fresh eyes. While the fullness of the Church's tradition has been my concern, it is only for the sake of preserving what is valuable for the future, since only the best has a chance to survive. On the other hand, it is probably more important to have served this 'best' than the obvious ephemera of the present day. Many of the great works of the past have already moved on beyond the questions which to our contemporaries seem completely modern and without precedent. Does it make sense to explain to this modern man what distinguishes his special religious situation from that of previous generations? To a certain degree perhaps. And I have attempted the task in *Science, Religion and Christianity* (German edition, 1956), but the results disappointed me. Instead the thought arose of presenting in a somewhat rounded-off form the aspect of Christianity that can no more be outgrown by today's man than it was by men of the past. Thus there grew the plan of a vast trilogy, comprising a *Theological Aesthetics*, a *Theo-dramatics* and finally a *Theo-logy*: a work which has assumed such dimensions that it has often seemed that it would never be completed. It must however be a sustained piece of work, in order to offer something more unified than the usual 'collected titbits' of a 'team' presented in the guise of a '*Festschrift*', 'Dogmatics', or 'Theological Lexicon'. For, unfortunately, a hundred run-ups still do not make a single jump, nor a hundred separate castings a single mould.

4. *The Glory of the Lord*

Why is the first part of this synthesis called *The Glory of the Lord* (*Herrlichkeit*)? Because it is concerned, first, with learning to see God's revelation and because God can be known only in his Lordliness and sublimity (*Herr-heit* and *Hehr-heit*), in what Israel called *Kabod* and the New Testament *gloria*, something that can be recognised despite all the incognitos of human nature and the Cross. This means that God does not come primarily as a teacher for us ('true'), as a useful 'redeemer' for us ('good'), but for *himself*, to display and to radiate the splendour of his eternal triune love in that 'disinterestedness' which true love has in common with true beauty. For the glory of God the world was created; through it and for its sake the world is also redeemed. And only the person who is touched by a ray of this glory and has an incipient sensibility for what disinterested love is, can learn to see the presence of divine life in Jesus Christ. *Aisthesis*, the act of perception, and *Aistheton*, the particular thing perceived (radiant love), together inform the object of theology. The 'glorious' corresponds on the theological plane to what the transcendental 'beautiful' is on the philosophical plane. But for the great thinkers of the West (from Homer and Plato via Augustine and Thomas down to Goethe and Hölderlin, Schelling and Heidegger), beauty is the last comprehensive attribute of all-embracing being as such, its last, mysterious radiance, which makes it loved as a whole despite the terrifying reality it may hide for the individual existent. Through the splendour of being, from within its primal depths, the strange signs of the biblical events (whose very contrariness to all human expectations reveals their supraworldly origin) shine out with that glory of God whose praise and recognition fills the Scriptures, the Church's liturgy, and the mottoes of the saintly founders of religious orders.

The first volume, *Seeing the Form*, describes man's encounter with this most divine aspect of God. Starting with aesthetics may seem unusual or arbitrary; nonetheless, as is shown in *Love Alone*, it is

213

ultimately the only appropriate stance. Only such a stance can perceive the divine as such, without obscuring it beforehand by a theological relationship to the cosmos (which, imperfect, calls for divine completion) or to man (who, still more imperfect and lost in sin, requires a saviour). The first desideratum for seeing objectively is the 'letting be' of God's self-revelation, even if the latter is also 'his eternal love for me'. This first step is not to master the materials of perception by imposing our own categories on them, but an attitude of service to the object. Theologically this means that the unspeakable mystery of God's love opens itself to reverence and adoration on the part of the subject (*timor filialis*). This means, too, that God's splendour (surpassing the transcendentality of 'philosophical' beauty) reveals and authenticates itself precisely in its own apparent antithesis (in the *kenosis* of the descent into hell) as love selflessly serving out of love. Thus *The Glory of the Lord* points not only to the proper centre of theology, but also to the heart of the individual's existential situation, which we sought from the beginning and discussed in Section 1 of this retrospective. It can also be said that in *The Glory of the Lord* the Ignatian *ad majorem Dei gloriam* — as the last great motto of religious life since Benedict — is opened up to the Johannine interpretation of the total biblical unity *kabod-doxa-gloria* and thus to the final form of revelation's own self-interpretation.

The next two volumes, *Studies in Theological Style*, provide the evidence for the fact that truly epochal theology is illuminated by the glory of God, is touched in its depths by it, and in a mysterious fashion takes something from it and gives it out again. But if a transcendental attribute of being cannot be defined in a categorical-conceptual way, how much less the *proprium* of the living God: the form and content of great theologies will always attest the one miracle in new and different ways and, even in eternity, will not together form a surveyable system. Thus the selection of the twelve representatives of Christian thought discussed in this volume has something arbitrary about it: together they form but a constellation. Irenaeus, Augustine, Denys, Anselm, and Bonaventure are luminaries of the first magnitude (Origen had to be omitted, and I had already written fully on Maximus), but in the neo-scholasticism of the clerical figures after Thomas (who receives his due in the fourth volume), there is no longer such a direct radiance; hence laymen and religious come to the fore: Dante, John of the Cross, Pascal, Hamann and Soloviev (the watchmen at the dawn and dusk of German idealism), Hopkins (who represents the mystical tradition of England and Ignatius himself), and Péguy (the representative of the contemporary Church in dialogue with the world).

The emphasis in these two volumes is uniformly distributed. The reader will find that the unplatonic Irenaeus shines out especially brightly, that Denys appears indispensable to us because of his view of the Church as transparent to the sacred cosmos, that Anselm's prayerful thinking shines forth as a pure standard, that Dante's daring act of taking before the throne of God the earthly love between man and woman and of purifying Eros so as to make of it something akin to *Agape* is a theological event of the first order, that John's annihilation of every created thing before the presence of God's glory is as necessary for us today as is Pascal's synthesis of mathematical and charismatic thinking, that Hamann is the only one of his century able to read the divine beauty out of its *kenosis*, that Soloviev knew how to embed the depths of German idealism in the dimensions of his ecumenical thinking better than today's evolutionists. It would be much, indeed, if the nature of theological 'style' were to be thought out anew: it is something quite different from the theological shop-talk and journalism of our time!

The fourth and fifth volumes, *The Realm of Metaphysics*, have a contrasting task: in the preceding two volumes the radiance of Christian thinking proceeded kerygmatically from the (still invisible) sun of biblical revelation. Now the Christian element must be immersed as deeply as possible in the thinking of humanity. The splendour of the divine in the world was (in Homer) the first formed experience of the West; and it becomes evident that art is begotten and itself begets only so long as it is created out of a *mythos* lived and experienced. Philosophy (in the pre-Socratics and indeed in a Plato still steeped in the light of myth) replaces it, posing the ambiguous question of the fundamental meaning of transcendence: man's power and autonomy or God's revelation? Vergil and Plotinus provide the grand finale for antiquity with the same question. What will Christianity do with the '*kalon*' of antiquity? Forge from it a 'monstrance' for the bread of 'glory'? Boethius, Erigena, the Victorines, Thomas, Nicholas of Cusa: what precisely happens here? Is this *Eros* a raiment of *Agape*? What place has the Cross? The catastrophe of nominalism robs creation of every light of God; night falls. Which ways remain? For the time being, three: the Christian theology of self-abandonment (forming a single spiritual family from Eckhart via the mystical women to Ignatius and the *Grand Siècle*): but what is now the status of the world? Secondly, the renewed anchoring of a now unsupported theology in the foundations of antiquity (a strain that runs from Nicholas of Cusa through the Renaissance, the Baroque, and the Enlightenment to Goethe and Heidegger): but then where is the distinctiveness of the Christian element? Finally, the philosophy of spirit (again from Eckhart and Nicholas of Cusa to Descartes, Leibniz, Spinoza, and the Idealists): but if the (human) spirit masters all being conceptually, the splendour of being is extinguished and is detached from the 'sublimity' of the thinker (Kant, Schiller), which with Hegel once again becomes entrapped in the past; what then remains is only grim materialistic fatality. The problem of the relation of metaphysics and theology allows no violent solution. And not because modern man thinks 'thus' must the Christian proclamation, adapting itself, also think 'thus'. How can someone who is blind to being be other than blind to God? Ought one not rather to say that the Christian, as proclaimer of God's glory today, in consequence takes upon himself — whether he wants to or not — the burden of metaphysics?

The final volumes (VI and VII) are 'dogmatic'. They treat *gloria* first biblically, in the Old and New Testaments, culminating in the two final interpretations of what God's glory is; Paul (2 Cor 3) and John. Glory is eternal love descending into the uttermost darkness. The liturgy is a mirror for this. Then a quick passage through dogmatics. *Gloria* is (1) epiphany, nearness, being-with-us. Brotherly love is drawn into the eternal domain from which the light radiates. *Gloria* is (2) justification, incomprehensible *poiesis* of God. Here we need to engage in a dialogue with Luther: there is no other place than theological aesthetics where his ultimate meaning is seen in so positive a light; the 'juridical' only obscures it. *Gloria* is (3) *charis*, with the entire double meaning of the ancient concept (Pindar) operative on a higher plane. Here it is necessary to enter into dialogue with the Eastern Church and its self-understanding, which is entirely determined by the concept of glory. Only in a derivative way is the problem of Christian art to be treated: is it possible and, indeed, how is it possible for divine 'splendour' to be expressed by means of worldly 'beauty'?

Aesthetics remains on the plane of light, image, vision. That is only *one* dimension of theology. The next involves deed, event, drama (Schelling says: positive philosophy). God acts for man; man responds through decision and deed. The history of the world and of man is itself a great 'theatre of the world'; here must be related to each other the philosophy of the deed (Fichte, Blondel), the art of the deed (Shakespeare, Calderon), and the theology of the deed (Karl Barth), to name just the catchwords. The Christian meaning of role and representation will have to be explained, and the Church's tradition must appear under this aspect: what an immense risk is the very act of handing on in death the task of discipleship to the next (faithful?) generation. Moses, Jesus and Paul experienced it most intensely. Is not the entire existence of the Church, as well as that of the individuals inside and outside it, pure deed and risk? And is not the same true of theology? Everything 'good' stands and falls with freedom.

Only when these two parts have been finished can a theological *logic* be sketched. What, according to the Bible, is truth? What philosophical form does it have? For an approach, compare my book on the phenomenology of truth (*Wahrheit*, 1947), whose first volume on the truth of the world points in turn to a second, unfinished volume on the truth of revelation)? How does this philosophical form open itself to the incarnate form of Christ's truth? Then, too, how can human word and life witness credibly to this truth of God? Here again a vigorous discussion with Hegel and perhaps also with Origen would be required. But others will have to conduct it. In the short space that remains to a sixty-year-old neither images nor concepts are any longer decisive; only the deed. For its sake, even the activity of writing books will have to be buried: God grant that then not only paper rot, but that at least one grain of wheat achieve the grace of the Resurrection! All paper belongs to the broad way. It is not important that the patient record of our thoughts be printed (*bedruckt*), but rather that the impatient flesh be squeezed and compressed (*bedrückt und gepresst*), so that from it perhaps a few fruitful drops might flow forth. Compressed it must be, in order not to miss the narrow way, the strait gate, perhaps even the microscopic needle's eye that, invisible to the eye of men, leads into the kingdom.

5. A Word of Thanks

All charisms of Christians are inextricably interwoven; everyone owes himself, not only to God, but to the whole Church; everyone is borne by invisible prayers and sacrifices, has been nourished by countless gifts of love, is continually strengthened and preserved by the affection of others. 'All men are cannibals' (Baader). Who is able to say thanks? To repay the immeasurable realm of deceased and surviving individuals with the homage they deserve for the graces they have mediated? Where is the wonderful being known as Homer, that he might be thanked; where the chaste Vergil and the God-filled heart of Plotinus? Love and honour must suffice for them.

And where would a man end, if he wanted to begin thanking those of his fellow men who accompanied him on his way, formed him, protected him, made everything possible? Left and right the greetings would have to go: to the nameable and the nameless. A mother is there, who during the course of a long fatal illness dragged herself to Church each morning to pray for her children. Other close relatives, of whom (to what ends God knows) fearful sufferings were demanded. Only in the light of God will one really know what he has to be thankful for.

A few names must be acknowledged, however, because without them obviously nothing of what has been sketched out here would have been possible. To the student in Vienna, the friendship with Rudolf Allers, doctor, psychiatrist, philosopher, and theologian (he translated Thomas and the entire corpus of Anselm's works) was an almost inexhaustible source of stimulation. An opponent of Freud and a disciple of Alfred Adler, he possessed and imparted the feeling for interhuman love as the objective medium of human existence; it was in this turning from the 'I' to the reality of a complete 'thou' that he found philosophical truth and his psychotherapeutic method. Later, in Munich, Peter Lippert became a consoler of the young man languishing in the desert of neo-scholasticism, and Erich Przywara, an unforgettable guide and master. Never since have I encountered such a combination of depth and fullness of analytic clarity and all-embracing synoptic vision. The publication of three volumes of his works in my house is intended as an external sign of thanks; but none of my own books should hide what it owes to him. In Lyons during my theological studies, it was the encounter with Henri de Lubac that decided the direction of my studies. Because exegesis was weak the Fathers easily won the upper hand. Origen (who was for me, as once for Erasmus, more important than Augustine) became the key to the entire Greek patristics, the early Middle Ages, and indeed even to Hegel and Karl Barth.

In Basel, the mission of Adrienne von Speyr (which, in view of her books, can no longer remain incomprehensible to a Christian public) was decisive. What Ignatius had intended in his time meant henceforth for me 'secular institute'; the hard sacrifice which the transition demanded was accompanied by the certainty of serving the same idea more exactly. It was Adrienne von Speyr who showed the way in which Ignatius is fulfilled by John, and therewith laid the basis for most of what I have published since 1940. Her work and mine are neither psychologically nor philologically to be separated: two halves of a single whole, which has as its centre a unique foundation.

It is almost unnecessary to set out how much I owe to Karl Barth: the vision of a comprehensive biblical theology, combined with the urgent invitation to engage in a dogmatically serious ecumenical dialogue, without which the entire movement would lack foundation. He joyfully greeted and endorsed my book about him, followed my subsequent works with some suspicion, but perhaps never noticed how much a little book like *Love Alone* sought to be fair to him and represents perhaps the closest approach to his position from the Catholic side.

Albert Béguin, whom I had the joy of baptising, the great solitary whose heart beat in unison with all who suffered injustice in the world, with every humiliated and insulted individual, the one who in the years of distress united the spiritual forces of the resistance in his *Cahiers du Rhône*, who as soon as the borders were opened immediately travelled to Auschwitz *pour nous bien placer dans l'axe de détresse* (Péguy), who then as Mounier's successor took over *Esprit*: this man was to me an example of what the spiritual courage of a

Christian is — something that can rest on nothing other than the absoluteness of his mission. Péguy, Bernanos, Bloy were his kindred spirits; he made them accessible to many, including myself, and indeed made them indispensable to me beyond every fashion of the day.

The many friends whose names I now omit will certainly not fault me if I mention only one more name: Gustav Siewerth, the man with the brain of a lion and the heart of a child, fearful in his philosophical anger against those who had forgotten being, and thereby the freer to speak happily and tenderly of the innermost mystery of reality: of the God of love, of the heart as the centre of man, of the pain of existence, of the Cross borne by the Father's child. Without him the fourth and fifth volumes of *The Glory of the Lord* would not have received their present form.

Adapted from *Rechenschaft 1965* by Kenneth Batinovich, N.S.M.

ANOTHER TEN YEARS - 1975

As everybody knows, at the age of seventy a man has attained, according to the Bible, the apex of his life, so this should also be the right point, the final point, at which once more to draw up a balance-sheet. Personally, I thought I had presented this retrospective review to my contemporaries ten years ago — since for oneself there must be self-questioning every day — and owed nothing more of substance, from this point of view, to the world at large. At that time I published *In Retrospect*, an account of the fundamental motives for the great decisions of my life (that, by the grace of God, can be considered definitive), the most fruitful encounters with contemporary personalities, the choice of literary themes in so far as such a choice has been free and not conditioned, as is often the case in small works, by external stimuli. These exterior stimuli, with the passing of the years, have become ever more numerous, so that the literary legacy of the last ten years derives almost exclusively from responses to a wide variety of requests and petitions — so much so that I have just been left with finding free moments for developing what was considered the fundamental project, the goal of my life, what I had declared, a little presumptuously and rashly, to be the plan of a theological trilogy, on the outcome of which I will speak later.

Before doing so, I would like to mention two other points.

First, one is so taken with a fixed idea that it is present (as in the *Symphonie fantastique* of Berlioz) even in works that are not so-called masterpieces. This idea also permeates secondary works — to their advantage or disadvantage — and becomes a kind of signature, a style that keeps the most disparate themes united. From this one can also deduce whether this formative idea is at a sufficiently 'catholic' distance to embrace questions that are very remote from one another, apparently contradictory. At this point the connection between style and truth becomes visible, and the writer must submit himself to the judgement of his own ideas. In this judgement one will also have to decide whether this idea is 'actual' in a more profound sense, that it is not the fashion of the day. Themes can encounter history and then in some way run parallel to it. By ignoring his historical present, a writer might in fact pursue such a theme and claim it as one of his 'timeless certainties'.

But one must also be on the look-out for the other eventuality, where this fundamental theme, which initially did not seem particularly 'actual', reveals itself in the course of the years to be more and more actual in the historical sense and in this way receives a definite kind of confirmation, even though it is not of course the ultimate confirmation that will be given by the judgement of God. However, a judgement of this kind cannot come from the writer himself (anyone, in fact, who wants to have an influence on his time considers himself actual); no, it comes from his contemporaries or from posterity. Such a judgement, if it is worth the trouble, ought to refer to the *Kleiner Lageplan*, published twenty years ago, for once something has been offered to the public, one has neither the right nor the possibility of taking it away from their attention.

The second premiss is the simple repetition of the confession made ten years ago: the activity of being a writer remains and will always remain, in the working-out of my life, a secondary function, something *faute de mieux*. At its centre there is a completely different interest: the task of renewing the Church through the formation of new communities which unite the radical Christian life of conformity to the evangelical counsels of Jesus with existence in the midst of the world, whether by practising secular professions, or through the ministerial priesthood to give new life to living communities. All my activity as a writer is subordinated to this task; if authorship had to give way before the urgency of the task of which I have

223

spoken, to me it would not seem as if anything had been lost; no, much would have been gained. This is fundamentally obvious to one who lives in service of the cause of Jesus, the cause that concretely is the Church.

However, granted that here one can and must speak solely of the writer and not of his work in the Church, this can be done from the two following points of view: from the point of view, first, of the fundamental disposition described further on, and then from the point of view of the spreading out of that disposition and style of thinking in the multiplicity of responses to the demands of the present.

1. In the mean while the *Theological Aesthetics* has been completed (the advertised concluding volume on ecumenism will very probably not be published). In the preface to the first volume it was expressly introduced as the first panel of a triptych, and only as such is it justified in the economy of a Christian theology. And so to call the *Theological Aesthetics* the masterpiece, the work of my life (very often only the introductory volume has been read, and on the basis of that all the rest is presupposed), for which the author is famed as a 'theological aesthete', to do this is to misunderstand my fundamental intention. It is difficult to see how such a definition could occur to anyone who has read at least the two concluding volumes on the Old and New Covenants. What is involved is primarily not 'beauty' in the modern or even in the philosophical (transcendental) sense, but the surpassing of beauty in 'glory' in the sense of the splendour of the divinity of God himself as manifested in the life, death, and resurrection of Jesus and reflected, according to Paul, in Christians who look upon their Lord.

But the manifestation of God, theophany, is only the prelude to the central event: the encounter, in creation and in history, between infinite divine freedom and finite human freedom. This central issue is dealt with in the *Theo-dramatics*, the first volume of which,

Prolegomena, was published in 1973. God does not want to be just 'contemplated' and 'perceived' by us, like a solitary actor by his public; no, from the beginning he has provided for a play in which we must all share. This has already been clearly demonstrated in the *Aesthetics*, above all in the concluding volumes, which focus on the Bible. But such a play must now be dealt with directly, thematically, especially since the lack in our time of an explicit 'theodramatics' appears more and more glaring and painful, with the principal tendencies in modern theology — all more or less detached from the 'epic' of scholastic thought — seeming to converge on such a dramatics, yet without attaining it. In the introduction to the first volume the following tendencies were enumerated: the theology of event, historicism, orthopraxy, the concern with dialogue, the theology of hope and of the future, functionalism (structuralism), the sociology and psychology of roles, the preoccupation with the problems of freedom and of evil in the world. All these tendencies are aiming, like arrows, for a central point at which a theological dramatics, which has not yet been elaborated, ought to be found; only there can the individual tendencies meet, integrate and be fruitful.

It seems to me that instead of suddenly rushing into the construction of such a theology, one should first elaborate a 'dramatic instrumentation' of the literary and lived theatre, and thus of life itself, in order to prepare images and concepts with which one can then work (with an adequate transposition). This would be an occasion, with many possibilities, for speaking, among other things, of drama as the clarification of existence, of that strange trio — the author, the actor, the producer — and also of public performance and the horizon of comprehension. Then there is the question of the purpose of the dramatic action — of situation, freedom, destiny, death, the struggle for 'good' and for 'right' fought out in the dramatic action, of tragedy, comedy, tragicomedy. But the best approach to Christian theology is in terms of the problematic of

225

roles, so widely discussed today: who am I? (someone, an *unicum*, or, in the final analysis, no one?). What is the task that justifies, fulfils, forms my existence? And this question applies at both the individual and social levels.

Only when God appears on the world stage (and at the same time remains behind the scenes) can one work out what *the persons of the drama* stand for, what 'laws' this dramatic action follows, a dramatic action ultimately without parallel, because it constitutes the ultimate drama. All this is what every Christian knows in a spontaneous and unselfconscious way and what he strives to live out. What I am trying to do is to express this in a form in which all the dimensions and tensions of life remain present instead of being sublimated in the abstractions of a 'systematic' theology.

If such an enterprise is to be brought to completion, despite age, there must follow, as a third and final part, 'Theo-logy', at which so many people nowadays labour intensely. This 'Theo-logy' involves reflection on the way in which the dramatic event can be transposed into human words and concepts for the purposes of comprehension, proclamation and contemplation. It should therefore be a methodical, *a posteriori* reflection on what has been done in the first and second parts. This can happen because God has essentially and definitively pronounced His Word in time, and 'Theo-logy' certainly has something to do with the Logos.

In the course of expounding the dramatic Christian event, one is bound to confront already existing forms of thought and theological exposition, the modern attempts already mentioned, but also, and above all, the great contemporary non-Christian attempts at a synthetic interpretation of existence. The most important of these are oriental (pagan) religiosity (with its primarily contemplative constitution) and the (Judaic) Marxism that has arisen in the West (with its tendency towards activity and innovation). These two interpretations, with every possible seduction, woo the Christian soul tired of its Christian inheritance.

There is much talk of the 'de-Mediterraneanisation' of the Church. I can only believe in this conditionally. Let us not forget that Palestine too (with its relations with the East) is on the Mediterranean, and it was in Palestine that very diverse passages of the writings of the New Testament were formed. But the Christian proclamation can never be de-Biblicised; in other words, you can never take away its dramatic character, representing, as it does, the struggle between Heaven and earth, a struggle that goes on, moreover, in the personal dimension as well as in the social. And so the personal is brought back to itself by the social and *vice versa*, the contemplative by the active and *vice versa*, so that the Christian dramatic shows itself to be, as it were by its very nature, at the centre between, and raised above, the two fundamental attempts to give meaning to the world and to existence, attempts that are possible when you start with the world itself.

2. And so we reach the second aspect: the breaking up of the fundamental purpose into the multiplicity of what is 'actual'. Reviews and journals, for the most part, ask the theologian for contributions and standpoints on burning questions of the day. In such an undertaking I am very far from the creative imagination and power of composition of a Karl Rahner and only dare to move gropingly in such a field. Nonetheless, the last decade has reinforced this fundamental conviction of mine: you do good apologetics, if you do good, central theology; if you expound theology effectively, you have done the best kind of apologetics. The Word of God (which is also and always the activity of God) is self-authenticating proof of its own truth and fecundity — and it is precisely in this way that the Church and the believer are inserted into one another. The man who wants this Word to be heard in what he has to say, starting with himself, does not need to resort to another discipline (called Fundamental Theology) to gain a hearing for it. All the other promises prove to be insufficient in themselves and give way before the Word of God by the very fact that this Word presents

itself to men and to humanity together with its promises. Only the Word of God makes a personal impact on man of such force that he feels himself touched by it in the centre of his heart, and it is just no longer enough for him to sink into an impersonal identity in the manner of the Far East or to wear himself out through a transformation of humanity (for him as a person, unattainable) in the manner of the Marxist West. What these two human contributions, which confront one another as opposite poles, can never attain is offered only 'by the final stone sent from the vault of heaven on high' (Claudel), namely, by the Word of the Father, who became man to bring to completion, together with his Church, the ever perfectible edifice of the world and of history. And the Church has always remained that unity which to Jews and pagans seemed impossible.

In the last few years this theme has frequently been expounded in a variety of forms, for example in 'Three Faces of Hope' (1972, in *Die Wahrheit ist symphonisch*), more extensively in 'The Claim to Catholicity' (1974, in *Pneuma und Institution*), finally in rapid and almost sloganistic fashion, in my last little book, *Katholisch* (1975). And so an ancient, almost atrophied principle of apologetics has been revitalised: it is right to see beyond positions that elsewhere seem isolated, absolutised. The notorious Catholic 'And' — in contrast to all unilateral, heretical positions — is not in fact a lukewarm compromise or syncretism but rather the power to unite, once again in 'dramatic' fashion, what to men seems desperately fragmentary. Jesus Christ is, in this sense, the Catholic One: God and man, he who descended into Hell and ascended into Heaven, he himself explores the personal and social dimensions of human existence and re-establishes them out of his own experience.

Of course, there is no question here of a Catholic presumption, in the face of all the other Christian and non-Christian positions, trying to deliver itself from them by calling them partial. For the position of God and Jesus Christ can never be the position of an individual Christian, and non-Catholic positions serve, nearly always, to remind the Catholic (often very drastically) of all that he has lost sight of, whether culpably or by forgetfulness; they remind him how far he is still from his own centre.

Authentic Catholicity is so urgent for the Catholic that he must acquire it before he can afford to engage in dialogue with other confessions or visions of the world. Otherwise he runs the risk of his Catholicism being considered as one 'confession' among others and then of attempting, together with these other confessions, a higher synthesis — this is the delusion with which 'ecumenical dialogue' is often encumbered today. Precisely because this dialogue is nowadays not only important but indispensable, the Catholic must first of all be prepared for it. He cannot enter and take part in it with a purely empirical and theologically dilettante awareness of what Catholicity and the Catholic Church in general are.

My efforts in these last few years have been deliberately concerned with this premiss for ecumenical dialogue and for the dialogues with all the non-Christian visions of the world. In this context my efforts are chiefly a discourse *ad intra*, within the Church. We need above all to arouse a new sensitivity to the multiplicity and polyphony of divine truth, in conscious opposition to the vociferous stance taken up about ecclesiastical and ecumenical 'pluralism'. One can formulate the following obvious, basic affirmation: the more an organism becomes differentiated and alive in its individual organs and functions, the more it must possess a more profound internal unity. Individual aspects of this basic affirmation have been developed in the collection *Die Wahrheit ist symphonisch* (1972: Truth is symphonic); in the second part of this book particularly striking and relevant examples are expounded. This problem becomes especially intense when confronted with the dichotomy that threatens all of modern cultural life (with its technicalisation, cybernetics, etc.), the dichotomy that in the Christian/ecclesiastical consciousness is translated into the dualism of 'pneuma' and 'institution'. Precisely what in Christ and in the Church, the living organism in which a spiritual soul manifests itself (and *must* manifest itself corporeally in order to be itself), is and must remain united at all costs, is wrenched apart. The spiritual movements that are so numerous today (whether they be orientated towards the East or towards the Pentecost event) very often (though not always) take up a defensive position, voluntary or involuntary, in confrontation with a Church seen and understood as institution — and obviously the post-conciliar troubles inside the Church serve to reinforce this misunderstanding in a decisive way. In *Spiritus Creator* (1967), more directly in *Pneuma und Institution* (1974) and *Der antirömische Affekt* (1974: The Anti-Roman Animus), I tried to resist this disastrous resentment, which misrepresents the living, organic 'form', by equating it with a structure constructed with reason alone. In *Der antirömische Affekt* it was not at all a question of a pure defence of the isolated principle of the Papacy, as if this were an individual element which could be added in its own right to the rest, or from which one could abstract. It was instead a question of demonstrating in general terms the organic unity of the revelation of God in Jesus Christ, of investigating the different aspects and stratifications of this unity, and only after that of integrating the Petrine factor of unity with the other wider factors. Back in 1969 my little book, *Convergences*, had pushed in a similar direction; in it I wanted to show that there can be no theology without spirituality, that the multiplicity of theological disciplines can exist only thanks to the unity of theological science, that the numerous Biblical theologies are only partial aspects of a unity of divine truth existing in the Spirit in the Church but never systematisable. They are then brought into conscious convergence by the fact that the multiplicity of dogmas is only the mediation of the unique 'dogma', Jesus Christ, by all the parts. It is clear that the Christian art of integration (into Catholicity) is something completely different from what people nowadays like to call 'integralism'. Integralism is the debilitating, mechanical attempt to hold together a disparate collection of individual truths and traditions; integration, in contrast, is the spontaneous art of aiming always at the Whole through the fragments of truth discussed and lived. The Whole, then, is always greater than us and our powers of expression, but precisely as greater it animates our Christian life.

3. A concluding word is necessary in order to remove the impression that in the books that I have mentioned, and in others, I have simply expounded my own convictions. The greater part of so much I have written is a translation of what is present in more immediate, less technical fashion in the powerful work of Adrienne von Speyr, only part of which has been published. In the last ten years work on the patrimony bequeathed by this exceptional woman has been almost completed. Frau Barbara Albrecht has taken on the task of extracting from the complete works an anthology of representative texts and of writing a volume of commentary for it. Jaca Books of Milan has had the courage to publish this selection of texts in Italian with an introduction by me (*Mistica Oggettiva*, 1968). French and American editions of the same anthology are also in preparation (the Germans have little interest in the work, the Swiss none at all). The richness contained there will only be recognised in more mature times. Then it will be seen how strongly the intuition of this woman has influenced my books — *Heart of the World, Science, Religion and Christianity, Mysterium Paschale* (1969) — and various other works, which essentially are only a theological transcription of so much learned directly from her. This is an assertion that can only be verified at a later date.

On the other hand, what can be proved here and now is that the works of both of us are fundamentally opposed to the separation, common nowadays but lethal for the *Catholica*, of spirit and institution. While Adrienne von Speyr demonstrates the inseparability of the two aspects, beginning above all with John, to the same end I have made use chiefly of the Pauline epistles (2 Cor), the ecclesiological relevance of which is conspicuous enough. Wherever the convergence of the two aspects is visible — for example, in the *Communione e Liberazione* movement (to which in 1971 I dedicated my programmatic book *Engagement with God*), — there is hope for the comprehension of Catholicity. The Incarnation of the Logos, his nuptial relation with the Church (and through the Church with the world), involves the organic character of the Church. The more the Church has to keep herself Catholic, open to all, dialogal, dramatic, in the modern world, the more profoundly she must comprehend and live her intimate essence as Body and Bride of Christ.

Having said that, we can go a stage further. The works of Adrienne von Speyr, almost all of which were dictated to me, represent about a third of the books written with my own hand; a second, weak third is made up of the books published under my own name; a more full-bodied third, finally, is made up of books translated by me for my publishing house. And if now I search my heart, there are in this last category many books that are dearer and more important to me than my own books. There are the works of my friends, such as Henri de Lubac and Louis Bouyer, of the great poets, such as Claudel, Péguy, Bernanos, without speaking of Maurice Blondel or of Ignatius, Calderon and John of the Cross, to whom also I have dared to draw near. Then again there are works of less well-known authors whose voices, so it seems to me, ought not to be missing from the contemporary concert. For a great number of authors whom I have edited I have each time written a preface in order to situate them more correctly, with their specific tonality, in the orchestra. In this way, my publishing, which takes up much of my time, is more important to me than the completion of my own works. It offers a condensation of what I understand by contemporary Catholic spirituality (in theology, philosophy and literature). In a concert one instrument must no longer sound like just *one* instrument — the ensemble is involved, the whole orchestra. Were I to be asked which volumes of *The Glory of the Lord*, I love most, I would reply: the two volumes on 'Styles', in which I have tried to expound twelve great theologians, beginning with Irenaeus and ending with Soloviev; in their integrity they let the sound of what I have wanted to make heard ring out. Were I to be asked which of my own books gives me greatest joy, which I still take up from time to time, the answer would be: without doubt my Origen anthology, *Spirit and Fire*, for in Origen I discovered that brilliant sense of what is Catholic, which I myself would like to attain; but also my translations of the poems of Claudel — among which, it seems to me, there are some of incomparable beauty — which breathe the same spirit of Catholicity. Both of these authors lived the Church above all as a *Communio Sanctorum.*

And since we have met with that word 'communion', we must, finally, mention our review, *Communio*, of which I am a 'co-founder', together with other members of the International Theological Commission, and which almost every year comes out in a new language. It is not a question of a uniform review, mechanically translated into several languages, but of a living association of reviews that choose and discuss their themes in the same spirit of Catholicity; according to need, they exchange articles and so realise, across nations, cultures and continents, what I have tried to do at a more restricted level. Those who collaborate on the review in the spirit of a living Church are all much younger than me, so there is hope: when before long the old trunk, by now sterile, is chopped down, a living tree will be able to continue to grow unharmed; it may even, perhaps, spread out its branches more quickly.

Translated by John Saward.

SELECTED BIBLIOGRAPHY

Hans Urs von Balthasar. Works, with English translations, in order of publication.

1937

Apokalypse der deutschen Seele. Studien zu einer Lehre von letzten Haltungen. Bd. I: *Der deutsche Idealismus*, Salzburg.

1938

Origenes, Geist und Feuer. Ein Aufbau aus seinen Werken, Salzburg.
English: *Origen: Spirit and Fire. A Thematic Anthology of his Writings*, Washington D.C., 1984.

1939

Apokalypse der deutschen Seele. Bd. 2: *Im Zeichen Nietzsches*, Salzburg.
Bd. 3: *Die Vergöttlichung des Todes*, Salzburg.

1941

Kosmische Liturgie. Höhe und Krise des griechischen Weltbilds bei Maximus Confessor, Freiburg.

1942

Présence et Pensée. Essai sur la Philosophie Religieuse de Grégoire de Nysse, Paris.

1944

Das christliche Jahr. Text zu den Bildern von Richard Seewald, Lucerne.
Das Weizenkorn. Aphorismen, Lucerne.

1945

Das Herz der Welt, Zurich.
English: *Heart of the World*, San Francisco, 1979.

1947

Wahrheit. Bd. I: *Wahrheit der Welt*, Einsiedeln.
Die Großen Ordensregeln, Einsiedeln.

1948

Der Laie und der Ordensstand, Einsiedeln.

1950

Therese von Lisieux. Geschichte einer Sendung, Cologne/Olten.
English: *Thérèse of Lisieux: A Story of a Mission*, London, 1953.
Theologie der Geschichte, Einsiedeln.

1951

Karl Barth. Darstellung und Deutung seiner Theologie, Cologne/Olten.
English: *The Theology of Karl Barth*, New York, 1971.
Der Christ und die Angst, Einsiedeln.

1952

Elisabeth von Dijon und ihre geistliche Sendung, Cologne/Olten.
English: *Elisabeth of Dijon*, London, 1956.
Schleifung der Bastionen. Von der Kirche in dieser Zeit, Einsiedeln.

1953

Reinhold Schneider. Sein Weg und sein Werk, Cologne/Olten.

1954

Thomas von Aquin. Besondere Gnadengaben und die zwei Wege menschlichen Lebens,
Heidelberg and Graz-Vienna-Salzburg.
Bernanos, Cologne/Olten.

1955

Das betrachtende Gebet, Einsiedeln.
English: *Prayer*, London, 1961.
König David. Text zu den Bildern von Hans Fronius, Einsiedeln.
Thessalonicher- und Pastoralbriefe für das betrachtende Gebet erschlossen, Einsiedeln.
'Kleiner Lageplan zu meinen Büchern', *Schweizer Rundschau* 55, 212-225.

1956

Die Gottesfrage des heutigen Menschen, Vienna.
English: *Science, Religion and Christianity*, London, 1958.

1957

Parole et Mystère chez Origène, Paris.

1958

Einsame Zwiesprache. Martin Buber und das Christentum, Cologne/Olten.
English: *Martin Buber and Christianity*, London, 1961.

1959

Theologie der Geschichte, Einsiedeln.
English: *A Theology of History*, New York and London, 1963.

1960

Verbum Caro. Skizzen zur Theologie I, Einsiedeln.
English: *Essays in Theology I. Word and Revelation*, New York, 1964.
Essays in Theology II. Word and Redemption, New York, 1965.
Sponsa Verbi. Skizzen zur Theologie II, Einsiedeln.
English: *Church and World* (Selection), New York, 1967.

1961

Herrlichkeit. Eine theologische Ästhetik. Bd. I: Schau der Gestalt, Einsiedeln.
English: *The Glory of the Lord. Vol. I: Seeing the Form*, Edinburgh, 1982.

1962

Herrlichkeit. Eine theologische Ästhetik. Bd. II: Fächer der Stile, Einsiedeln.

English: *The Glory of the Lord. Vol. II: Studies in Theological Style: Clerical Styles*, Edinburgh, 1984; *Vol. III: Studies in Theological Style: Lay Styles*, Edinburgh, 1986.

1963

Das Ganze im Fragment. Aspekte der Geschichtstheologie, Einsiedeln.

English: *A Theological Anthropology*, New York, 1967.

Glaubhaft ist nur Liebe, Einsiedeln.

English: *Love Alone: The Way of Revelation*, London, 1968.

1964

Der Kreuzweg der St.-Hedwigs-Kathedrale in Berlin, Mainz.

English: *The Way of the Cross*, London and New York, 1969.

'Evangelische Räte in der katholischen Kirche von Heute', *Reformatio* 13, 289–297.

English: 'A Theology of the Evangelical Counsels', *Crosscurrents* 1966.

1965

Herrlichkeit. Eine theologische Ästhetik. Bd. III/I: Im Raum der Metaphysik, Einsiedeln.

Wer ist ein Christ?, Einsiedeln.

English: *Who is a Christian?*, London, 1968.

'Das Evangelium als kritische Norm für jede Form kirchlicher Spiritualität', *Concilium* Vol. 1, pp. 715–722.

1966

Cordula oder der Ernstfall, Einsiedeln.

English: *The Moment of Christian Witness*, New York, 1968.

Herrlichkeit. Eine theologische Ästhetik. Bd. III/2, 1. Teil: Alter Bund, Einsiedeln.

1967

Spiritus Creator. Skizzen zur Theologie III, Einsiedeln.

1968

Erster Blick auf Adrienne von Speyr, Einsiedeln.

English: *First Glance at Adrienne von Speyr*, San Francisco, 1981.

1969

Theologie der drei Tage, Einsiedeln. Subsequent edition as 'Mysterium Paschale' in *Mysterium Salutis III/2. Grundriß heilsgeschichtlicher Dogmatik*, ed. J. Feiner and M. Loehrer, Einsiedeln/Cologne, 1969, pp. 133–326.

Herrlichkeit. Eine theologische Ästhetik. Bd. III/2, 2. Teil: Neuer Bund, Einsiedeln.

Einfaltungen. Auf Wegen christlicher Einigung, Munich.

English: *Convergences: To the Source of the Christian Mystery*, San Francisco, 1984.

1970

Romano Guardini. Reform aus dem Ursprung, Munich.

1971

Klarstellungen. Zur Prüfung der Geister, Freiburg.
English: *Elucidations*, London, 1975.
In Gottes Einsatz leben, Einsiedeln.
English: *Engagement with God*, London, 1975.

1972

Die Wahrheit ist symphonisch. Aspekte des christlichen Pluralismus, Einsiedeln.

1973

Theodramatik. Bd. I: Prolegomena, Einsiedeln.

1974

Der antirömische Affekt. Wie läßt sich das Papsttum in der Gesamtkirche integrieren? Freiburg.
Pneuma und Institution. Skizzen zur Theologie IV, Einsiedeln.

1975

Katholisch, Einsiedeln.

1976

Henri de Lubac. Sein organisches Lebenswerk, Einsiedeln.
Theodramatik. Bd. II: Die Personen des Spiels. 1. Teil: Der Mensch in Gott, Einsiedeln.

1977

Christlicher Stand, Einsiedeln.
English: *The Christian State of Life*, San Francisco, 1984.
Der dreifacher Kranz. Das Heil der Welt im Mariengebet, Einsiedeln.
English: *The Three-fold Garland: The World's Salvation in Mary's Prayer*, San Francisco, 1982.

1978

Theodramatik. Bd. II: Die Personen des Spiels. 2. Teil: Die Personen in Christus, Einsiedeln.

1979

Neue Klarstellungen, Einsiedeln.

1980

Fibel für verunsicherte Laien, Einsiedeln.
English: *A Short Primer for Unsettled Laymen*, San Francisco, 1985
Kennt uns Jesus — Kennen wir ihn?, Freiburg.
English: *Does Jesus know us — Do we know him?*, San Francisco, 1984.
Theodramatik. Bd. III: Die Handlung, Einsiedeln.

1982

Du krönst das Jahr mit deiner Huld, Einsiedeln.

1983

Christen sind einfältig, Einsiedeln.
Theodramatik. Bd. IV: Endspiel, Einsiedeln.

1984
Christlich meditieren, Freiburg.
Leben aus dem Tod. Betrachtungen zum Ostermysterium, Freiburg.
English: *Life Out of Death: Meditations on the Easter Mystery*, Philadelphia, 1985.
Unser Auftrag, Einsiedeln.
1985
Theologik. Bd. I: Wahrheit der Welt, Einsiedeln.
Theologik. Bd. II: Wahrheit Gottes, Einsiedeln.

NOTES ON CONTRIBUTORS

Andrew Louth is Head of Religious Studies at Goldsmith's College, London.

Donald MacKinnon was formerly Norris-Hulse Professor of Divinity in the University of Cambridge.

Brian McNeil C.R.V. is an Augustinian Canon who has taught theology at the University of Vienna and presently works in a parish outside Rome.

Noel O'Donaghue is Lecturer in Systematic Theology at New College, Edinburgh.

John Riches is Lecturer in Biblical Studies at the University of Glasgow.

John Saward teaches theology at Ushaw College, Durham.

Martin Simon teaches for the British Council.

Ulrich Simon was formerly Professor of Christian Literature at King's College, London.

Rowan Williams is Dean of Clare College, Cambridge and Professor elect of Theology at the University of Oxford.